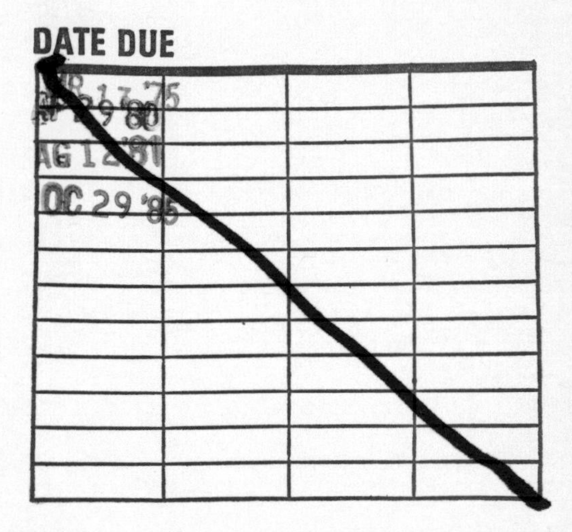

The Managed Economy

The Managed Economy

MICHAEL D. REAGAN

OXFORD UNIVERSITY PRESS

LONDON OXFORD NEW YORK

OXFORD UNIVERSITY PRESS

Oxford London New York
Glasgow Toronto Melbourne Wellington
Cape Town Salisbury Ibadan Nairobi Lusaka Addis Ababa
Bombay Calcutta Madras Karachi Lahore Dacca
Kuala Lumpur Hong Kong Tokyo

Library of Congress Catalogue Card Number: 63-19946
First published by Oxford University Press, New York, 1963
First issued as an Oxford University Press paperback, 1967
This reprint, 1970
Printed in the United States of America

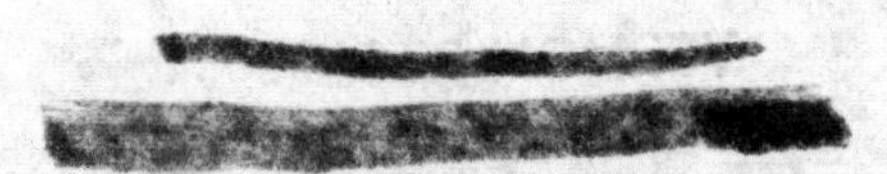

To Vera
who made this book possible

Preface

This book elaborates a theme that flows from a fact and a political belief. The fact is that the American economy no longer functions in accord with Adam Smith's concept of the invisible hand but is increasingly administered by corporate executives and government officials. The belief is in economic and political democracy and the ability of responsible government to apply democratic controls to economic behavior. The theme is that more — and more effective — public control over the economy is essential, both to achieve such economic goals as full employment and a higher growth rate and, more importantly, to retain our self-respect as masters of our fate.

The intelligent citizen is the primary audience for whom these pages have been written. It is not a research monograph and it does not avoid value judgments. Rather, it is an attempt to bring together a series of developments, each of which is separately a subject of scholarly specialization, and show their combined effect on the system of political-economic relationships in the United States. The primary tool of analysis is neither statistics nor the computer; it is thought.

The thought expressed owes a great deal to a great many people, including academic colleagues, the authors of many books and articles which I have enjoyed and profited from, and my students at Williams College, Princeton University, and the Maxwell Graduate School of Syracuse University. I am happy to acknowledge my debt to these people; however, responsibility for the views expressed in the pages following is my own.

I am grateful, too, for financial support extended at various stages by Williams College (in the form of a grant from the Ford Public Affairs Research Fund), Princeton University, and, especially, the Louis M. Rabinowitz Foundation, whose willingness to back one's individual approach to public problems is perhaps unique in today's world of organized technical research.

I would like to say a word about the point of view from which I have written this book. Today most social scientists emphasize collection of empirical data and the construction of theoretical models. We do need fuller, more accurate explanations of social phenomena, yet I believe there are other tasks of equal validity for the social scientist. One of these is to be an analyst of public policy; another, a critic of society. These roles, which are too little attended to today, are the ones that have provided my orientation in this book. They involve a particular view of the relationship between facts and values, empirical investigation and normative judgments.

My view of that relationship emphasizes interdependence. To me, it would be nonsense to say that the social scientist has nothing to contribute, professionally, to discussion of public policy. The ultimate choice of economic and social goals is, of course, for the citizenry to decide, but the academic person can enrich public discussion in a variety of ways. He can analyze the probable consequences of alternative courses of action. He is, or should be, especially perceptive regarding logical inconsistencies in an argument or a policy proposition. He may be committed to a particular set of social values, but at least he usually does not have any group interest to defend. He is accustomed to thinking of social patterns as an integrated system and to considering the long-run relevance of short-run actions. In short, he has a greater opportunity than most men have to achieve perspective on the passing scene. Therefore, he has an obligation to contribute to the public good by applying his perspective to the problems of his time.

Few other men are as well placed as is the academic social scientist to ensure that the fire of democracy is kept alight by the spark of informed, independent criticism. We are, I hope, as committed to the values of democratic government as to the values of academic inquiry. This book represents one man's way of expressing his commitment to democracy.

Syracuse, New York M. D. R.
April 1963

Contents

The Managed Economy

1 | Introduction: Reality in Search of Recognition

The myth of a self-regulating, individually operated free enterprise system was exploded by the Crash of 1929. It was formally buried by the Employment Act of 1946, by which it became the explicit responsibility of the national government to promote maximum production, employment, and purchasing power. Yet the myth lives on.

The oil industry balances supply and demand through the inappropriately titled Texas Railroad Commission, an interstate compact, market projections of the national Bureau of Mines, and mandatory import quotas established by the Secretary of the Interior. This industry nevertheless has published institutional advertisements praising free, individual competition as the basis of all industrial progress. American Telephone and Telegraph advertises its own economy and efficiency as an "only in America" result of the "free enterprise system." Yet A.T.&T. is the nation's largest monopoly and its operations are supervised by state regulatory commissions and by the Federal Communications Commission. The president of one of twenty-nine electrical equipment firms convicted of price rigging in the biggest antitrust case of recent years was quoted as saying that no one involved was so stupid that he did not know he was violating the law. "But," continued this executive, "it is the only way a business can be run. It is free enterprise."

If price fixing and regulated monopoly constitute free enterprise, then perhaps the persistence of the phrase can be explained. But the phrase becomes meaningless. Worse than that, it encourages an avoidance of the fundamental change that has taken place in our economic system during this century: from a market-regulated economy we have shifted to one directed by the personal, visible hands of governmental and corporate managers.

Laissez faire was always more a prescriptive than a descriptive slogan. The vaunted separation of business from government never was, nor could be, complete. At the very minimum, government had to provide a legal framework (e.g., laws of contract, of bankruptcy) and a monetary system for even the freest of free enterprise systems to operate. And American government always in fact intervened beyond this minimum to promote business and to act negatively, through the courts, against challenges to laissez faire from labor unions and humanitarian reformers.

Given these qualifications, however, until the Great Depression there was a definable content to the term free enterprise; a listing of its major features will serve to illustrate just how far we have moved from this concept.

First, the word "free" once meant the freedom of the individual entrepreneur to compete against other businessmen without being subject to monopolistic restraints: freedom to meet the market price, to bargain for resources, to enter a profitable field — and to go out of business.

Second, the entrepreneur was free from governmental restraints. Treating human labor as essentially just another commodity, the courts interpreted attempts at protective legislation (e.g., child labor laws, hours and wages regulation) as interference with the entrepreneur's property. Even a right to cheat the consumer was defended as a prerogative of property ownership under the hallowed doctrine of *caveat emptor* — let the buyer beware.

Third, free enterprise meant independent enterprise — independent of government support for a producer's markets. The tariff was a logical inconsistency from the start, for its protection clearly contradicted the assumption that every business must stand on its own feet and take on all comers. But this exception was permitted and easily enough glossed over, probably because it "only" discriminated against foreigners.

All of these are characteristics of free enterprise from the producer's viewpoint. From the public side, the outstanding traditional feature of a free enterprise system was its automaticity. A free enterprise economy meant an unmanaged economy. Overall, the system was assumed to be self-adjusting, one that just naturally produced the right products, the right number of jobs, and the right distribution of income to keep people and resources fully employed. Say's Law, one of the economists' less successful laws, held that producers' expenditures for materials and labor would always put just the right amount of income into the hands of consumers to ensure that the goods produced would be bought. It ignored the possibility, now accepted by economists, that some of the income generated by the productive process might be saved rather than spent, hence interrupting the system's neat balance. The cycle of boom and bust could not be ignored, but it was asserted to be self-correcting and in any case beyond human control. Only laziness was recognized as a reason for joblessness until 20 per cent of the labor force was jobless in the Great Depression and no one could seriously argue that several million men had developed a sudden preference for the bread line over the assembly line.

At the level of the individual firm, protection against abuses of economic power was thought to be automatic, too. As our leading critic of conventional wisdom, John Kenneth Galbraith, has written, "Given [classical economic thought's] prescription of competition, there was very little scope for the exercise of private economic power and none for its misuse." Prices, the rate of innovation, the rate of national investment, and the tastes of consumers—all these were independent factors: they could not be managed or controlled by the individual entrepreneur. In fact, according to the gospel of Adam Smith, the individual businessman served society more effectively by pursuing his own interest than when he really intended to promote the public interest. In so pursuing his own interest, he was guided by "an invisible hand to promote an end which was no part of his intention."

It takes no foundation-sponsored investigation to demonstrate that free enterprise as the name for a system possessing these qualities cannot be applied to the American economy of the 'sixties.

The individual entrepreneur has disappeared from all but marginal areas of enterprise. No one — except possibly J. Paul Getty of Texas — is economically free to enter into competition with the dominant giants of American manufacturing. What the classic concept of freedom of entry means today is a merger in which a giant enterprise buys a smaller one operating in a field the giant has not previously touched. A private collective — the corporation — has replaced the individual as the organizational base of the system. We can speak of *corporate* freedom to compete, but not of an individual's competitive freedom. While small businesses are still permitted to die of natural causes, if a giant enterprise were threatened with collapse, government would step in to revive it, for the economy depends on the giants.

Within the corporation, freedom of business decision-making now means liberty within guidelines set by statutorily established public policy: wages and hours, safety, child labor, union recognition, advertising practices, and securities flotation are all areas of regulation. Whether government intervenes too much or too little in managerial discretion is hotly debated; that it intervenes considerably is beyond question.

At one time it would have been a simple matter to list the industries that were dependent on government support, such as the railroads with land grants. Today it would be only a slight exaggeration to say that the list of industries independent of government support is the shorter list. Quite apart from the tariff, free enterprise has been transformed into safe enterprise by such things as the depletion allowance for oil and many other extractive products, including sand and gravel; airline and shipbuilding subsidies; postal subsidies for magazines and advertising circulars; stockpile purchasing of "strategic" metals and minerals; rapid amortization certificates; vocational schooling; defense procurement; and a great number of risk-assumption props for housing, banking, railroads, etc.

While some promotional aid does go to small business, thanks to the solicitude of Congressional committees, the vast bulk of government support goes to corporate giants because defense procurement is the biggest source of public financial support. Twenty-two billion dollars worth of military prime contracts were awarded in the fiscal year 1959. One hundred companies and their subsidiaries received 74 per cent of that total. Walter Millis's description of the aviation industry serves to characterize the impact of cold-war finance upon the economic system:

> Almost wholly dependent on Government military orders, concentrated in the hands of no more than a dozen big corporations, operating within a system of "administered"

> prices, wages and raw material allocations, and directed by an essentially self-perpetuating managerial elite far removed from the theoretical owners of the enterprises, [the aviation industry] presents a picture surely not much different from that of the state-owned trusts and subcontractors who have produced the triumphs of Soviet military-industrial technology.

Finally, in this résumé of a quiet revolution, the only thing automatic about the new economy is the reflex tendency of all economic groups — business, labor, and farm — to run to Capitol Hill or the White House with their problems. In the age of intervention, the aim of industry is not to keep politics out of business but to control the direction of public policy by getting business into politics.

At the level of the individual firm, the pattern is one of oligopoly: a very few firms, of large size, account for the bulk of production in industry after industry: automobiles, plate glass, steel, aluminum, television receivers, cigarettes, meat packing, cellulose plastics, human antibiotics, aircraft, etc. According to the Senate Antitrust Subcommittee's 1957 report, between 1947 and 1954 the share of total value added in manufacturing enterprises accounted for by the 100 largest firms rose from 23 to 30 per cent. Although economists dispute among themselves over the degree of concentration today as compared with that in 1890, 1900, or 1918, the power of industrial giants incontestably extends beyond the assets they own. Suppliers to and dealers for the giants appear in census statistics as independent enterprises; but ask an automobile dealer or gas station "owner" how independent he is. Just as this chapter was first being drafted, the Federal Trade Commission filed a complaint against certain tire manufacturers for paying bonuses to major gasoline companies that promoted particular lines of tires through their dealers. Although the

FTC's major concern appeared to be with the competitive impact upon other tire manufacturers lacking such arrangements, the most interesting thing is the revelation that to earn their bonuses the gasoline firms compelled their dealers to handle these lines of tires. The selling job is the dealers'; the bonus is received by the giants. This is but one minor example of the way in which the giants administer the economic affairs of their formally autonomous satellites. In the economy of giants, little is left to chance or to the market. Bargaining between equals has, to a significant degree, been replaced by administration from above; persuasion has been replaced by command.

Closer still to the heart of the emerging system of corporate administration of resources stands the phenomenon known generally among economists as "market power" but labelled "administered pricing" by Gardiner C. Means in 1934 and popularized under that name since 1957 by Senator Estes Kefauver. Prices of a wide range of industrial goods, instead of being determined by the intersection of supply and demand curves at one specific point, are determined as a matter of managerial policy within a considerable range of discretion created by the indeterminateness of market forces. That is, the sale of steel beams will be about the same whether the price is x, $x - 2$, or $x + 2$, so the producer can make it his policy to set the price at $x + 2$. The limitation on managerial discretion is that, even for products with the most inflexible demand, there is some point above which a price rise will cause a loss of sales. We may continue to purchase the same amount of bread whether the price is 30 cents or 38 cents a loaf, but if it goes to 75 cents we are likely to shift our consumption to some other product and buy less bread.

Yet deviations from the pattern of automatic, impersonal forces determining the prices, products, and survival chances of individual firms in a free-enterprise economy are not signs of economic pathology. Industrialization requires some stability in prices to permit planned production in large quantities for distribution over a large area and over a considerable time span. The economist Edwin G. Nourse told the Kefauver committee in 1957: "The economic institutions and business practices described as 'administered pricing' grow naturally and properly out of the conditions of modern industrialism." But they do break down our received understanding of the functioning of the economic system. Failure to recognize the reality that corporations manage resources and manipulate markets is a sign of political pathology. For, as this book will show, the quite natural development of a managerial economy raises questions of power and purpose that we cannot ignore if we would retain democratic mastery over our fate.

The price decisions of particular firms with regard to particular products are not the only elements of the economy that are now managed rather than left to the directions of the market. Achievement of goals pertaining to the whole economy — full employment, economic growth, stability of purchasing power — has also become a matter for policy and planning, for conscious human direction. The Employment Act of 1946 constitutes our recognition of the miseries to which an undirected industrial economy is prone. To the great rights against government control embodied in the first eight amendments to the Constitution, the Employment Act added a right of the citizen to receive aid from his government in maintaining the economic security upon which political freedom has always depended. Seen in this light, the commitment of government to be the gyroscope that is otherwise lacking in a market economy takes on constitutional significance in fact though not in form. The invisible hand cannot do the job. The visible hand of the national government is needed.

But the matter is more complex. In addition to the full employment problem, we have the conflict between corporate and public planning. What is good for a particular business (especially in the short run) is *not* always good for the country (especially in the long run). Resale price maintenance laws may help the small family store to withstand the competition of the national chains, but they work against the consumer's interest in low prices. In periods of falling demand, the interest of a firm may lie in restricting production and curtailing employment, though the combined effect of every firm doing so would be to make the spiral descend even faster. Business investment tends to slacken off exactly when it is most needed to maintain employment. To these long-existing conflicts between business needs and national needs has recently been added the international gold problem. At precisely the point of maximum concern for the outflow of United States gold in 1960, the Ford Motor Company announced that it was exporting $200,000,000 to purchase total control of a British subsidiary. This may have been good for Ford, but it was certainly not good for the nation.

Just as the idea that full employment requires government action is gaining public acceptance—a generation after the economists had described the reality—we are being faced with new and equally important goals for national economic behavior that cannot be achieved by the automatic interplay of the market. One of these is an acceptable rate of economic growth. Another is a proper balance between the production of goods and services for private use and public needs—e.g., between private use of rotary lawn mowers and the inadequate care we give to our public parks; between pocket-size transistor radios and the provision of adequate educational facilities for developing the scientists who will dream up the new marvels of the 1980's.

To fulfill the needs and ever-increasing expectations of our own expanding population and to contribute toward a viable world economy requires constant expansion of our productive capacity and constant improvement in productivity per man-hour. The perennial argument of business spokesmen that federal tax laws constitute a major obstacle to such expansion may not be valid, but it does constitute an inadvertent admission that government policies are inevitably intertwined with "private" business performance. Thus again, the question cannot be whether government should act but what kind of action is appropriate.

Similarly, when a quarter of the national income circulates through government coffers, it is utterly unrealistic to describe the process by which we decide for what products and what needs our scarce resources will be used as one of market decisions made by individual consumers. As the range of governmental services and functions broadens, there inevitably arises the question of how and by whom the priorities among proposed programs for expenditure are to be determined. And there is the even more basic question of determining politically what proportion of national income should be devoted to what the individual can purchase or desires to purchase for himself, ranging from food and shelter to gidgets and widgets, and what proportion should be devoted to collective, that is, governmental, purchase of what the individual wants but cannot buy except in association with his fellow citizens, such as defense, education, roads, parks, public health.

In sum, free enterprise has become not only a meaningless phrase, but a dangerous one, for it obscures reality. Like the French generals who failed to recognize the reality of air power and so prepared the Maginot line to fight in the manner of the previous generation, we may lose the struggle for mastery of our economy if we continue to apply the slogans of yesterday to the struggles of tomorrow.

Fortunately, some pieces of reality are becoming evident. Some American economists now recognize that the gap is increasing between their analytical model of frictionless, automatic competition and the real world of oligopolistic power, corporate planning, and a rising need for publicly provided services. Reality will be reached when we fit the pieces together and acknowledge that the system has changed; that it is not just a matter of more vigorous enforcement of the antitrust laws; and, finally, that the very size of the public sector today makes government the most important single factor in the economy, whether we will it or not.

"Free enterprise" has been a shorthand way of referring to an economy of individually and privately owned, competitve firms whose "decisions" were made by impersonal market forces. It now becomes clear that, while one can still find marginal sectors that show these characteristics, the dominant and dynamic part of our economy is "free enterprise" only in that firms are privately owned. This is the only rational meaning that can be given to the phrase as used in the institutional ads of the oil industry, American Telephone and Telegraph, and large corporations generally. But private ownership is no longer a crucially important factor since it does not necessarily connote private control.

The British Laborites discovered, when in power after World War II, that socialism in the sense of public ownership solved few problems so long as the effective control of enterprises remained in the hands of the same types of people as before, even though they were now operating as nationalized boards. We in the United States are slowly learning the same lesson in reverse. As industrialists now point out to us (though generally without realizing themselves the implications of their statements), the "rights of property" are no longer the same. Employees, consumers, and investors have rights, too, and governments have been called in to protect them by cutting into the scope of discretion accorded to business decision-makers, without any notable increase in the "socialization" of basic American industries. It is possible today that business institutions that remain formally private in their ownership can be as effectively under public control as they could if they were directly nationalized, or at least under as much public control as a democratic society would wish to impose.

It is often said that labels are unimportant. It is true that they do not prove anything, but they are significant because they serve to organize our thoughts. When the label used is irrelevant or outmoded, it impedes rational discussion. Since "free enterprise" does just that, we need a new descriptive phrase that points to the essential elements in the present situation. Probably the most frequently employed substitute labels are "mixed economy" and "mixed enterprise." These have the merit of focusing attention on the fact that government has become an integral part of the economic system. But they tell nothing of the qualities characterizing the mixture; they do not give us the essentials of the relationship.

One of the few economists to focus his attention on the characteristics of the whole system is Gardiner C. Means, co-author with Adolf A. Berle, Jr., of the 1932 classic, *The Modern Corporation and Private Property*. Means has written that the modern corporation "has undermined the preconceptions of classical economic theory as effectively as the quantum undermined classical physics at the beginning of the twentieth century." He suggests the phrase "collective capitalism" to emphasize the dominant role of the giant corporation in the system. With hundreds of thousands of stockholders, many thousands of workers, and billions of dollars of capital aggregated under a single management, the corporation replaces the individually-owned firm as the leading actor on our economic stage. Like Berle, Means sees the system as capitalism without the capitalist; that is, ownership is private, production is for profit, but the number of owners in the prototype firm is so great that individually they have no power and are reduced to dividend receivers. The extreme instance is American Telephone and Telegraph: having over 2,000,000 shareholders, no one of whom holds more than one-half of one per cent of the stock, this corporation is a managerially directed collectivity of vast human and material resources.

The market system assumes that the separate economic activities of a vast number of individuals operating independently need only be co-ordinated by self-interest operating through the price system. Manhattan families want to eat eggs and New Jersey farmers want to sell eggs. Without any need for overhead direction, an exchange takes place. Means argues that co-ordination in a system of collective capitalism is only in part achieved in this manner, that it also, and more significantly, results from administrative direction of one power center over many participants in the economic process. Thus an automobile producer may own a steel mill and even an iron ore mine, in which case the auto firm does not bargain through the market for these supplies but determines by direction the price to be paid. American Telephone and Telegraph includes both the operating telephone companies of the Bell System and Western Electric, which manufactures the equipment used by the operating firms. It is thus possible for the parent company to raise the prices paid by the operating companies and include the equipment expense in its rate base, so that it can then claim higher telephone rates. To the extent that a supplier or distributor may be dependent upon a larger manufacturer, as in the relationship of a small clothing manufacturer to Sears, Roebuck or of an automobile dealer to the Ford Motor Company, the phenomenon of administrative co-ordination extends far beyond the scope of resources owned outright by the large firms. Because in an economy characterized by a few giant firms those firms will control prices as much as be controlled by them, Means believes that we need a kind of "economic planning without compulsion" if we are to use our resources effectively "and avoid the pressure for government direction." Thus the concept of collective capitalism emphasizes the new shape of the private economy, yet refrains from recognizing any correspondingly large shift in the economic role of government.

Closely related to this conception, though more narrowly conceived, are the descriptions by business spokesmen of corporate social responsibility in the modern economy. Richard Eells, formerly of General Electric, has written most interestingly, for example, of what he calls the metrocorporation, a multipurpose firm whose tasks are to balance the interests of employees, suppliers, customers, stockholders, and the general public by means of a set of managers who are not controlled by any of these groups or by market forces. An economy in which businessmen have the power to balance other people's interests is obviously not the classical competitive system. In this respect, the creed of social responsibility does point to a real change; but it is deficient as a description of the whole system because it centers exclusively on decision-making within the firm.

Then there is the idea of a "laboristic economy" advanced by the late Sumner Slichter and the concept of a "laboristic capitalism" put forth by Edwin G. Nourse. Nourse describes this as "a system in which decisions covering the character and direction of the productive process and determining the nature and proportioning of the distributive process are not arrived at unilaterally by the owners or representatives of capital but bilaterally by these executives vis-à-vis the workers and, typically, in joint negotiation with the latter's representatives." Granting that national labor unions share with corporate managements the administration of resources in the modern economy, it is yet something of an overstatement to treat this fact as the central one. In the first place, union power is largely derivative from corporate power. "Corporate capitalism" would be a more apt label. Secondly, the latter phrase, like the former, ignores the governmental role.

If one focuses on the governmental side, one of the possible tags is "state capitalism." As used, for example, by Paul K. Crosser, it refers to the government subsidies enjoyed by economic groups and to the fact that much of public policy is directed toward the promotion of private group goals. Capitalism, understood as profit-seeking production, does enjoy a high degree of governmental protection today, yet this is only one part of the system. Furthermore, the term "capitalism" has become almost as ambiguous as "free enterprise."

Another, broader conception of a growing alliance between government and the private economy is advanced by economist Alvin H. Hansen under the name the "dual economy." Says Hansen: "The Government is much more than a driver at the wheel. It is furnishing a growing share of the motive power that keeps the economy moving." The widening of the public sector of the economy, which is primarily the result of an urban society's need for community services, he sees as no transitory phenomenon. Rather, a "structural rebuilding" of Western societies is taking place. Hansen's stress on government's role in managing resources toward the goal of sustained growth contrasts with (and supplies a corrective for) the private sector orientation of those views which emphasize the corporate role to the neglect of the political one. Yet it, too, is incomplete.

Each of these attempts at characterizing the modern economic system contains part of the truth. What emerges as a common theme, though only implicitly in some instances, is the notion that conscious human management is replacing the market as the basic allocator of resources, distributor of income, and stabilizer of employment and production. John Maurice Clark, dean of political economists, has summed up the situation of indeterminacy that pervades our economy: "We still need all we can get of automatic adjustments; but there are growingly strategic areas in which the power of organized groups is such that, if sound terms of settlement are to be reached, people must consciously intend to reach them." The automatic economy is dead. "The managed economy" is the phrase that applies to both the public and the private sectors, and it also indicates the specific quality of the mixed economy: that both elements are managed.

Once we begin to look at our system as one that is consciously planned rather than impersonally directed by market forces, some essentially political questions come to the fore. Who will do the managing? For whose benefit? What will be the goals? Who will set them? How? Are the institutional arrangements of our society, designed as they were for a quite different situation, adequate to the managerial tasks? If not, what needs to be changed? Are the lines of power and accountability clear? Do they fit the needs of our situation?

These are political questions in the best sense because they are concerned with power and purpose, that is, with policy. E. H. Carr argues that "you cannot in these days plan for inequality," and therefore planning must be directed toward equality. But this is a prescription, not a description: the ends toward which the economy will be directed will depend upon the balance of social power that lies behind the planning. Thus the rise of the managed economy reunites politics and economics into a truly political economy, not just because government intervention has increased, but because even the important decisions of the private sector are now human decisions embodying personal values. The analysis of economic behavior and evaluation of economic performance therefore require consideration of power and values, not just of supply and demand.

Most discussions of the national economy cover public policies and economic processes without mentioning the problems of power they raise, except for ritualistic obeisance to the antitrust laws. We know of the Employment Act commitment and of the current stress on economic growth. Thanks to Galbraith, we have become aware of the problem of social balance. But we do not know what kind of government-business relationship is implied by these policy developments. This book is concerned with analyzing the problems of power raised by their existence, and with arguing the necessity for national economic planning — public, not corporate — as the free society's way of directing economic forces toward human ends.

Part I reviews the literature of American political thought dealing with the relationship of property distribution to power and personal freedom, and it suggests the extent to which theory needs to be reformulated to meet a changed situation. The reader who is impatient with doctrinal analysis and prefers to begin immediately with a description of today's concrete situation, may wish to defer reading this part until after Parts II and III, in which the power and functions of corporations and government, respectively, are analyzed. Part IV sets forth recommendations for institutional reforms that would aid in revitalizing democratic control of economic power.

I | Property, Power, and American Political Thought

2 | The Jeffersonian Dream Versus Industrial Reality

All men are created equal. From this powerful and hallowed premise flows a basic theme of American political democracy: one man, one vote. This fundamental expression of human dignity, the vote, had been reserved, in all earlier societies, to noblemen, landowners, clergymen, or other notables. But in America titles of nobility were constitutionally proscribed from 1789 onward, and property qualifications for the franchise were swept away in the decade 1820–30 as the equalitarian logic of Jefferson's Declaration of Independence forced revision of one state constitution after another.

The principle of universal suffrage thus acknowledged was not immediately put into law; it took two revolutions — the Civil War and the Nineteenth Amendment — before this could be achieved. And even today the Justice Department and the Commission on Civil Rights are engaged in turning principle into practice, particularly in regard to Negro suffrage. Yet the United States was the first nation to commit itself to the proposition that a voice in political decisions was a right due to every man because he was a man, not just to some men because they had a financial stake in government.

At first glance it might seem that the doctrine of political equality implies denial of the close relationship that had existed historically between the distribution of property and the distribution of political power. Indeed, it was Charles Beard's theme in *The Economic Basis of Politics* that this was so, that there was "an inherent antagonism between our generally accepted political doctrines, and the actual facts of political life." The "actual facts" to which he referred were the continued importance, down to the present day, of economic group interests in determining men's political opinions and the outcome of legislative battles. The doctrine of one man, one vote does not, however, require that differences in economic status be ignored as a basis of political behavior, and indeed recent voting behavior studies show a close correlation between income levels and party affiliation. What the doctrine does require is that political opinions, from whatever source derived, be given equal weight. Nor does the doctrine of political equality deny that, in fact, political power is not always equally distributed. Political equality is — and always will be — the aspiration of democracy: something to be approached if never entirely realized. It is thus prescriptive, not descriptive, and the appropriate question is not whether the objective has been totally attained, but how it can be approached more closely than it has been so far.

That politics could not be divorced from economics was well understood by American political leaders of the constitutional period. James Madison, the Father of the Constitution, wrote in *The Federalist* No. 10 what remains the classic American expression of the view that politics is essentially about economics:

> The most common and durable source of factions has been the various and unequal distribution of property. Those who hold and those who are without property have ever formed distinct interests in society. Those who are creditors and those who are debtors fall under a like dis-

> tinction. A landed interest, a manufacturing interest, a mercantile interest, with many lesser interests grow up of necessity in civilized nations and divide them into different classes actuated by different sentiments and views. The regulation of these various and interfering interests forms the principal task of modern legislation.

Building on this economic foundation, Madison went on to argue that the constitutional structure of the new nation must take the social diversities into account by giving to each "faction" a locus of access to power so that the factions could balance each other and thus prevent both the tyranny of the propertied few over the unpropertied many and the tyranny of the majority over the minority.

The relationships between property and political power and between property and individual freedom were thoroughly debated in the states in the 1820's when they were discussing removal of state property qualifications for voting. The range of opinion was wide. The conservative argument against universal suffrage was expressed by Chancellor James Kent of New York:

> there is a tendency in the poor to covet and to share the plunder of the rich; in the debtor to relax or avoid the obligation of contracts; in the majority to tyrannize over the minority. . . .

The moderate view was voiced by Chief Justice John Marshall:

> the generality of mankind, doubtless, desire to become owners of property; left free to reap the fruit of their labors, they will seek to acquire it honestly. It can never be their interest to overburthen, or render precarious, what they themselves desire to enjoy in peace. . . .

And the radically optimistic position was typified by Charles Morgan, a delegate to the Virginia Constitutional Convention of 1829–30:

> All free men ought to vote, because they are free men. Then they will act independently. Such men can never be purchased by the cash of candidates, or the power of demagogues.

Perhaps the most complete examination of the property-power-independence complex, however, came from Daniel Webster. Webster cited political theorists from Aristotle onward, but particularly James Harrington of the seventeenth century, in support of the proposition that "political power naturally and necessarily goes into the hands which hold the property." Harrington had written in 1656 in *Oceana* that, if one man were "sole landlord" in a society, that man would be the absolute ruler, but, if the whole people were landlords, then a commonwealth would prevail. Webster, following this line of reasoning exactly, argued that the laws of property distribution "fixed the future frame and form" of government. Popular government, then, rested on a broad distribution of property: political equality required economic equality. "Universal suffrage," said Webster, "could not long exist in a community where there was great inequality of property." Since he had no intention of subjecting existing property inequalities to radical leveling, he argued for continuance of property restrictions on voting.

This was in a sense deterministic reasoning anticipating Marx, yet there is another side to Webster's thought, too, which suggests, in reverse, that politics is the basis of economic relations. If property determines power, but property distribution and its relationship to the franchise are themselves defined by law, then the relationship is at least reciprocal and law in some respect becomes prior even to property as a determining factor. Further, Webster and other conservatives whose political goal lay in the protection of the propertied minority feared the vote as an independent power base. Chancellor

Kent expressed this fear; so did Webster, in arguing that where there was great economic inequality there would have to be a restriction on the suffrage lest the "right of suffrage would ere long divide the property." It is not easy to reconcile the view that power will necessarily follow property with the assertion that the unpropertied might, through the vote, have sufficient political power to overturn the property system. But the assertion that power will necessarily follow property should be taken as the expression of a tendency rather than a rigid law, and as an expression of a necessary equilibrium between related systems rather than a description of fact; then, the apparent inconsistency diminishes. What is important for our discussion is to recognize that there is a "normal" connection between economic and political power, and that universal suffrage might constitute an unprecedented factor causing exceptions to normal expectations.

Two additional points remain to be discussed. In what did the political power of property consist? How was property ownership translated into political power? In the parliaments of Europe the answer was simple: only those with property could vote; the few holders of large property were often given representation equal to that of the many holders of small property. But American opponents of free suffrage argued that, even if it did exist, men of property would obtain greater power because they would control the votes of those without property. The landowner would control the votes of his tenants and laborers; the operative in a factory would vote as the factory owner demanded. Few men of the early 1800's were willing to challenge the proposition that economic dependence would result in political dependence. Thomas Jefferson feared it was true, and this is one reason why he feared the rise of cities, with their centralization of economic power. His solution to the problem of political independence was a straightforward assertion that an agricultural economy of freeholders — every man an owner of his own self-sufficient plot of land, every man his own "boss" — was essential to democracy. Such a society of individual property holders would of course carry with it relative economic equality, since the family farm was limited in size.

With the exception of a few mavericks like Charles Morgan, the democratic spokesmen of the early 1800's thus did not envisage political equality as breaking the historic relationship between property and power. Rather they saw free suffrage as the appropriate accompaniment in politics to the broad diffusion of property that characterized the American economy at that time. The Jeffersonian dream was of a political economy, not a purely political system. Frank in their appreciation that economic divisions exist, that they have opposed interests, and that these will be reflected in politics, the leaders of American democratic thought hoped to minimize political inequality and its conflicts by mimizing the economic inequalities that constituted the bases of conflict.

Once the battle over suffrage had been won by the "radicals" in the state conventions, the defenders of property were hard pressed to devise a theory which would serve their ends yet not alienate the unpropertied masses who now had the political power of the vote. As Arthur Schlesinger, Jr., has shown in *The Age of Jackson,* the conservatives were equal to the challenge. Those who had earlier described the conflict between the propertied and the unpropertied in language worthy of a Marx, now proclaimed that every laborer was a capitalist, every capitalist a worker, and the interests of the two classes were not only harmonious but identical — a sort of nineteenth-century "people's capitalism."

At this point frankness left American politics — at least, American conservative politics. The Whigs tried to delude the people and eventually, suggests Schlesinger, succeeded in deceiving themselves. It is no longer the radical equalitarians who most strongly attempt to separate political equality from economic inequality, but conservatives who fear that popular thought may see a connection between the two spheres and begin to ask whether protective measures may not be needed to prevent concentrated property from undermining political democracy.

After the Civil War, industrialization's rapid growth foreclosed with utter finality any possibility of realizing the Jeffersonian dream. So long as businesses were individually owned, there was an inherent limit to the scope of economic control held by an individual or small group. But, once the legal device of incorporation had changed from a special privilege granted only for the public interest (e.g., for toll bridges and roads, inns, and railroads) into a universal right to be exercised for private purposes, there was no longer any obstacle to concentration. With liability limited to one's investment, the money available for investment could be gathered into a single large entity, rather than dispersed among individual entrepreneurships.

Underlying the changes in legal forms of ownership, moreover, was the logic of industrialization itself. When machine power began to supplant man power, a difference in the scale of production was necessary if the full benefits of mechanization were to be achieved. Industrial machinery was more complex than the simple tools of a handicraft economy and, hence, more expensive. The design of machines for specific tasks induced a more detailed division of labor, the logic of which called for many men to work together, each doing a part of the production job. Finally, the machine process changed into the assembly line, mass production system associated historically with Henry Ford's breakthrough; this required mass markets and replaced individual economic independence with collective dependence.

The Jeffersonian family farmer was, ideally, a man who, helped by his family, could produce on his own property the kind of shelter, food, and clothing his family needed. The modern American is not self-employed, let alone self-sufficient. Whether the president of General Motors or a floor-sweeper in a Chevrolet plant, the "worker" today is what Marx defined as a proletarian: a man who sells his labor to those who control the "tools of production," in exchange for which he receives a "wage" payment. No individual is wealthy enough to own personally the vast capital resources required for modern industrial production; hence, we all become employees, that is, economic dependents of organizations. The inexorable tendencies of technology and labor specialization are even moving the professions of law and medicine in this direction. Group medical practice is on the rise; the young holder of a law degree is likely to make his best start by joining a metropolitan "law factory." In the United States today only about 10 per cent of the working population is self-employed. Even those who are self-employed are not necessarily economically independent. The local franchised dealer for a national corporation may have his economic affairs as effectively administered by the manufacturer as though he were a direct employee.

In short, if political independence requires economic independence, the pattern of property ownership can no longer supply this requisite. If political equality requires the equal distribution of property ownership or of personal income, then our society does not have an appropriate base for the maintenance of political democracy. The Jeffersonian solution to the problem of property and power has been killed by industrialization. Since we would not, even if we could, forego the advantages of industrialism, we have to ask: Is there another solution? Except in the mind of the most inveterate cynic, the presumptive answer must be that there apparently is at least a partial alternative. For political independence is evident in America, and the power of property has not been so overwhelming as to foreclose all democratic measures. From the Granger movement, the Sherman Act, and the graduated income tax to TVA, the minimum wage, and federal medical care the ability of small property owners and the unpropertied population to obtain some legislation — inadequate though much of it is — that is oriented to their needs belies the existence of any automatic translation of economic differentials into political power. The fears of conservatives like Daniel Webster and Chancellor Kent have been at least in part realized: popular action *has* cut into the once nearly absolute rights of property.

The way this has been done vindicates early conservative fears, for the factor that has upset the pattern of power following property is universal suffrage. Under some circumstances and to some extent it is evident that vote-power can be separated from and act as a counterbalance to property-power. If this were not so, then industrialization would by its very existence destroy democracy, for there can be no industrialism without concentration of property. And although democracy may now be in a precarious state, it does exist.

We are thus faced with two contradictory tendencies, both representing developments that came after the period of constitutional development in America: industrialization, which concentrates power, and political democracy, which diffuses power. The problem of property and power that we face today differs in crucial ways from that faced by earlier ages. In all earlier societies, either the worker was an owner (the Jeffersonian ideal) or he had neither freedom nor property (as in slavery and feudalism). Only in the past century has there developed a kind of society in which men are personally and politically free yet economically dependent upon others who control the means of their livelihood. This unprecedented situation was named "the adventure of capitalism" by Goetz Briefs, when he wrote, in the 'thirties:

> It is the unique distinction of capitalism that it has broken up this historic alliance between property and freedom. The system it constructs rests upon a foundation of wage labor, the wage laborer enjoying the freedom of a citizen and, theoretically at least, equality with other citizens in the eyes of the law. . . . Personal freedom, equality before the law—both to be combined with permanent propertylessness on the part of the working class: this . . . constitutes the adventure of capitalism.

Shifting Briefs's focus slightly, we may characterize the present-day problem of political equality as the adventure of democracy in an industrial society.

3 | The Adventure of Democracy

Perhaps the most widespread assumption today about the relationship of property to power is that economic democracy has been achieved by a general rise in incomes which bestows middle-class status on nearly every family and by the specific redistributive mechanism of a progressive income tax system. A catch phrase, "people's capitalism," has gained vogue to express the belief that widespread ownership of shares of stock in American industry has brought economic power under popular control. Such assumptions and beliefs are consoling, for they enable us to continue to picture our society as Jeffersonian. It is the purpose of this chapter to subject such notions to critical analysis, that we may better face up to the realities of economic power in our time.

WHO OWNS WHAT PROPERTY?

In the simpler society of 1880 there was necessarily a close link between the distribution of wealth and income and the distribution of capital resources, for the latter typically consisted of personally owned and personally managed agricultural or mercantile property. Today the connection must be investigated rather than assumed, since the corporate form of organization raises the possibility of combining concentration of assets for production purposes with diffusion of ownership in the form of shareholding certificates. Furthermore, personal income can be high without the income receiver's holding legal title to any tools of production, as is the case with doctors, many business executives, baseball players, and movie stars. The distribution of wealth has to be considered from two viewpoints, that of personal income and that of effective ownership.

Because conservatives now fear to admit what they once loudly proclaimed — that political equality cannot exist in the face of substantial economic inequality — an attempt has been made in recent years to proclaim a myth of economic equality belying the evidence of our personal observation. The progressive federal income tax, we are told, is continually leveling personal incomes. Much is made of the fact that the "working man's Chevrolet" looks like the boss's Cadillac — and that sometimes it is the boss who drives the Chevrolet! Much is made of the inexpensive copies of Dior fashions that are available at Macy's and Ohrbach's, and of the ubiquity of nylon stockings. At another level, the emphasis is on "people's capitalism," a label intended to signify the broad popular ownership that lies behind the corporate concentration of productive facilities, and on "corporate democracy," which refers to diffused stockholder control over concentrated corporate management. Even major universities have co-operated with the Advertising Council in the sponsorship of roundtables devoted to people's capitalism.

The New York Stock Exchange, a major proponent of people's capitalism, investigated the distribution of stock ownership in 1956 and trumpeted forth the finding that 8,630,000 individuals were "capitalists" in this sense. More recently, the Exchange has reported that the number of shareholders had risen to 17,000,000 by 1962, 39.9 per cent of them having incomes below $7,500. Five of the 17 million are housewives. If one assumes what the phrase "people's capitalism" implies, then the hopeful conclusion is that 17 million people run American industry, not a few hundred corporate managers and members of boards of directors and a few dozen banks and investment houses. Even A. H. Raskin, the *New York Times* labor editorialist and a man unlikely to be easily swayed by business propaganda, has written of the annual stockholders' meetings of large corporations as an adaptation of the old New England town meeting and a method by which the corporation is made "accountable to the titmice, as well as the tycoons, in its family of proprietors."

The trouble with these assertions about diffused property and increasing income equality is that they give a false impression of the American power structure and lead to a false sense of complacency about it. First, in regard to the matter of personal income and wealth, the following are the basic facts:

Average family income has undergone a real increase in recent years, with the notable result that there are now more families with incomes in the $4,000-$7,000 range than in the below-$4,000 category. The income graph is now diamond-shaped rather than pyramidal.

But the pattern remains one in which inequality is the dominant characteristic. In 1958 the top fifth of consumer units received 45.5 per cent of the national income, while the bottom fifth received only 4.7 per cent. This is only a one per cent proportional improvement for the latter group since 1935. In 1959 there were still 7.5 million families and unattached individuals receiving incomes below $2,000. And half a million migratory farm families live on incomes below $1,000 per year.

The tax system does not change this picture by much. The bottom fifth's position improves by about one percentage point after taxes are taken into account; the wealthiest 5 per cent, who receive 20 per cent of before-tax income, retain 18 per cent after taxes. The equalizing effect of federal tax rates has been much eroded by income-tax exemptions and special privileges, such as depletion allowances and special treatment of dividend income. Although the rates run from 20 per cent to 91 per cent, the effective top rate is only 50 per cent, because those persons with very high incomes derive much of their income from sources that escape the full tax: capital gains on stocks, tax-exempt municipal bonds, etc. Economist Robert J. Lampman estimates that to restore the value of the personal exemption — which helps the lower income groups the most — to its 1929 value it would have to be $3,500 instead of the present $600, to compensate for the effect of inflation.

Reliance upon regressive taxes, those which take a higher proportion of low than of high incomes, has also played a large role in undermining the little redistribution that the federal personal income tax has provided. Some of the regressive taxes are also federal, such as excise taxes on transportation and the social security tax, under which only the first $4,800 of income are taxed, so the man with a $4,800 income is taxed as much as the man with $48,000. The most sizable of the regressive taxes, however, are state and local sales taxes and property taxes.

In summary, millions of American families continue in the 'sixties to have such low incomes that they must be classified as poverty-stricken, and our tax structure does little to diminish the vast inequalities that exist in before-tax income.

If we turn from current income to wealth distribution, a family's "assets," the picture remains much the same. Robert

Lampman's analysis shows that the share of personal wealth held by people in the top one per cent wealth bracket had indeed declined after 1929, for it was 36.3 per cent in that year and only 20.8 per cent in 1949. But his study also reports that since 1949 the same group's share has again been rising and was back up to 26 per cent by 1956, the last year for which he had data. Since 1949, the distribution of wealth has become less equal. This has occurred mainly through the rise in stock market values, because stock ownership is, despite the claims of people's capitalism, heavily concentrated in the hands of the already wealthy. While all incomes have risen some, the middle groups have gained most of what the top has lost, the bottom group has gained little, and the relative inequality between income groups has remained almost constant. The Sixteenth Amendment, in short, has not recreated the Jeffersonian social situation, and there is no sign that it ever will.

Since Lampman's figures seem to contradict the New York Stock Exchange's contention of broad diffusion of stock ownership, we should now take a closer look at that contention. The Exchange's statistics present the first problem; then there is the question of how these statistics are to be interpreted; finally, there is the necessity to discover other relevant factors which the Exchange does not mention.

Seventeen million shareholders seems to be a large number, and it does represent a considerable increase in the ranks of stockholders as compared with a generation ago, thanks in part to the use of profit-sharing plans and to the invention of the monthly stock-purchase plan that puts investment on the installment basis. The profit-sharing plans give to each of many employees of a firm a share or two of stock each year; it is estimated that one-third of General Electric's "owners" got their shares in this manner. But the population has been growing, too, and the latest figure of 17 million loses some of its initial force when one considers that it is but 9 per cent of the population. This is double a 1952 estimate of 4.2 per cent, but hardly justifies the connotations of the phrase "people's capitalism" when 91 per cent of the people own no shares.

The most telling weakness in the implication that a people's capitalism exists lies in the information not given: Who owns how much? A stockholder's dividend receipts and his voting strength in corporate meetings are directly dependent on the number of shares he owns. And in this respect it is utterly impossible to make any claim of democratic equality. A 1956 report showed that only 2.1 per cent of shareholders held over 1,000 shares, but that their combined holdings accounted for 58 per cent of total shares held. That means that over half the shares are in the hands of about 200,000 people! Lampman, in his report on wealth distribution, estimates that the 1.6 per cent of the adult population having gross estates worth more than $60,000 held 82.4 per cent of all publicly held shares in 1953.

As for stockholding as a device for popular control over concentrated corporate managements, the greater the diffusion of shareholding, the less the chance that individual shareholders can ever get together to form a solid front in opposing or presenting alternatives to management-sponsored propositions. Unlike political elections in which the voter is presented with alternative candidates, corporate elections normally offer only a "single party" slate and an opportunity for a write-in vote. The write-in is meaningless unless someone has the time, money, and degree of personal involvement required to organize a unified second "party."

POWER WITHOUT PROPERTY?

Thirty years ago Berle and Means first delineated the divorce of ownership from control. As the industrial corporation developed into an entity with thousands — even hundreds of thousands — of "owners," that is, stockholders, the fusion of ownership with control and management that had characterized the personal property of earlier ages disappeared. A bifurcation followed in which one group "owned," in the sense of having a claim on the earnings or on the proceeds from sale of assets if the corporation were dissolved, while quite another group controlled or managed the use of the firm's assets. The important element here is not the device of incorporation alone, but the increase in the number of shareholders as well. In a family corporation, ownership of all or a clear majority of the stock would provide control for the owner or the small, unified group of owners. In the large, publicly held firm, however, the individual owners hold only a fragmented voting power, which is useless as a device for control for the reasons noted in the previous section of this chapter.

Sometimes a united group holding less than a majority of shares, but holding a larger single block than any other individual or unified group — say, 20 to 40 per cent — exercises what is called minority control. In such instances, there still remains some connection between the ownership title and the effective control. But in the prototype case — and it is perhaps becoming typical — no single individual or group will hold a substantially greater block than any other; such is the case with A.T.&T. and probably with U. S. Steel. When this situation obtains, the "divorce" is complete and control of the corporate property rests not at all with the "owners" but with "management," meaning by this word both the directors and the top officers. Since the nominations made by existing boards of directors to fill vacancies among their ranks are normally unopposed (and normally unopposable), Berle has in recent years described those who exercise corporate control as a "self-perpetuating oligarchy." Thus, in Berle's view, those who own property (the stockholders) are separated from those (the managers) who exercise economic power by virtue of their use and direction of property. Does this constitute a reversal of the historical connection between property and power?

It would seem that Berle thinks it does, for one of his recent books is entitled *Power without Property*. In this, he points to a new development in the property situation: the rise of pension funds and the concentration of control of the assets of these funds in the hands of a few dozen giant banks and insurance companies. In one way, the pension funds reverse the direction pointed to by Berle and Means in 1932, for, as the pension fund trustees invest the monies they are managing (and out of which corporate employees will receive pension benefits), they tend to reconcentrate the voting power derived from stock certificates because they buy very heavily in the stock of a small list of blue-chip companies. Their purchases total thirty billion dollars already; within twenty years, they may reach seventy billion dollars. This appears to mean the reconcentration of ownership and its reunion with control—which could hardly be called "power without property." But Berle maintains that property has undergone fission to such an extent that we can now separate voting rights (i.e., the power element) of corporate ownership from the beneficiary rights (i.e., the passive receipt of income), and, reserving the word property for the latter element, he then says that property has been diffused while power has been concentrated. Thus the pension fund trustees would hold the power while the employee-beneficiaries hold the property.

Following the same line of thought, but differing in terminology, is Father Paul P. Harbrecht, S.J., who ends an analysis of *Pension Funds and Economic Power* with the assertion that ours is rapidly becoming a "paraproprietal society." By this he means that "our society has passed from a property system to a power system," one in which "ownership itself as an operating reality is diminishing." The basis of his assertion, like that of Berle's, is the intangibility and divisibility of property rights. Where one individual or group (a pension fund beneficiary) has a right to receive the income from property, another (the trustee bank's officer) the right to vote the stock from which the income is derived, and yet another (the board of directors) actually manages the tangible assets, which are "owned" by the corporation (as a legal person) which is in turn "owned" by shareholders — where this fragmentation of formerly unified property ownership occurs, says Harbrecht, we no longer have a property system at all in any economically meaningful sense. But while property ownership is now an "inert concept," property control is very much alive. Instead of control being derived from ownership, however, it derives from a man's institutional position — from, essentially, his rank in the corporate hierarchy. Thus Harbrecht, unlike Berle, does not contend that there is power without property, but only that power follows the control of property rather than the ownership of property, once the two have been separated. One property-power tie has been broken, but another has become stronger in its place.

What Berle and Harbrecht have in common is their insistence that ownership has become unimportant; the difference between them is that only Berle takes this to mean that power has been divorced from property. In either case, however, the situation seems less novel if we think of property ownership in a sociological rather than a legal sense. Our notion of ownership, after all, derives from a situation in which the man who owned was the man who controlled. And from this situation we derived the notion that to own something means to use, enjoy, and dispose of it — to be free to do with it what one pleases. If we apply this notion rather than a legal definition of ownership to the corporate economy today, we reach the same type of conclusion that Milovan Djilas reached concerning the system of property in a communist state: that he who does use, enjoy, and dispose of the property is, effectively, the owner. In our case this means that for all practical purposes the owners of corporate assets — and hence, with some exaggeration, of the American economy — are those who control and manage these assets: boards of directors, top officers, and bank and insurance-company trustees of pension funds. The ordinary stockholder, it is true, does retain a vestigial hold on ownership to the extent that he has a claim on profits. But this has in reality little more to do with ownership than the claim of a creditor. What the stockholder owns, as David T. Bazelon has perceived, is the share of stock; it is only this that he can use, enjoy, and dispose of at will, not the assets of the issuing corporation.

The importance of managerial ownership as a crucial fact in the power structure of the American political economy will be considered further in Part II. What we are concerned with here are, first of all, the conclusion that the dispossessed "owner," the small stockholder, is powerless, and, second, the invalidity of Berle's thesis that the power of directors and trustees is a power unrelated to property. The power of corporate managers does derive, as Harbrecht says, from their institutional position rather than from their personal wealth: their positions give them ownership, meaning use and disposition, of industrial property in a very real sense. The difficulties and confusions of our thinking reflect changes in the economic locus of ownership that have not yet been assimilated by legal terminology. The proceeds of the corporate system may be indirectly diffused via pensions, savings-bank dividends, and so forth; but effective ownership is as tightly concentrated as ever — even more so, if Berle's misgivings concerning pension-fund trustees turn out to be correct. Reality diverges ever further from the Jeffersonian dream.

HAVE POLITICAL AND ECONOMICAL POWER BEEN SEPARATED?

If wealth and economic power were fairly evenly distributed among the population, the achievement of political equality would not require an attempt to disengage political from economic power. But, as has just been seen, the distribution is decidedly uneven. Now we must turn to another complacent contention: that an effective separation of the political and economic spheres has been achieved.

We have already noted Charles Beard's flat assertion that economic and political power cannot be separated. An equally strong assertion to the contrary has been made by E. E. Schattschneider: "American democracy was an early attempt to split the political power from the economic power. This is the great American experiment. . . . The divorce of the two power systems is perhaps the greatest American political achievement." The picture Schattschneider presents is of continuing tension between two power systems: the equalitarian, democratic system of politics, in which numbers are important, and the concentrated, unequal system of business, in which wealth is the important factor. The function of democracy, it follows, is to counterbalance the undemocratic force of industry. As Schattschneider sees it, we do not want the government-business conflict resolved; we want it perpetuated because "liberty is a by-product of competing power systems." Thus, it is not a case of the political force (voting strength) having become dominant over economic power, but of an equilibrium of two power systems. How, then, is the equilibrium to be maintained? Schattschneider suggests that alternation of the parties in power will do the trick. However, if one of the parties, as he says, "tends to be more greatly interested in the maintenance of the power and freedom of business," where is the competitive force to come from when that party is in power?

While socialists have generally inclined toward the inseparability of economic and political power, one of the most prominent of living socialists, Britain's John Strachey, takes a position very similar to Schattschneider's. In a discussion of the economic consequences of democracy, Strachey contends that the Marxist view, which sees political developments as always the result of economic developments, is "enormously oversimplified." The interaction, he says, has been reciprocal, with the extension of the franchise, plus labor-union organization, having accomplished some diffusion of political power, while at the same time economic power has been undergoing increasing concentration in oligopolistic industry. Thus the tension he poses is the same as Schattschneider's. But Strachey does not see a permanent equilibrium. "Such contradictory trends," he writes, "can hardly co-exist indefinitely. One must overcome and absorb the other." His view recalls that of Daniel Webster, quoted earlier.

One other difference between these two views is that Strachey sees two kinds of democratic force: one is the voting franchise, the other is labor organization. To the former he attributes the ability of American wage earners to improve their standard of living before labor unions achieved the legal support of the Wagner Act (1935); to the latter he attributes the political-economic successes of British labor before the Labor party had achieved voter-based power. This would appear to suggest that democracy could have either a political base or an economic one comprised of the unions. Yet the political base may be the more essential one, for, as Strachey himself notes, "it seldom proves possible for wage earners to develop their industrial power in trade unions, till they have acquired a measure of political power by enfranchisement."

Still another observer of political-economic power relations, Alpheus T. Mason, characterizes the pattern of American politics as "economic power vis-à-vis political power, interests versus numbers, property against persons." Arguing not only that the two power systems can be separated, but that they have been, Mason has written that Franklin D. Roosevelt disproved the dogma that political power is always the slave of the dominant economic power. Mason believes that, despite conservative attempts to walk backward, "the dominant trend of our history has nevertheless been, in the long run, democratic." And, unlike Schattschneider, Mason asserts that political dominance, not political-economic equilibrium, is the key to liberty under law, "To escape anarchy politics must be dominant over economics." The New Deal constitutes his proof that the victory of popular power has been in fact achieved. About why and how economic power was dethroned, however, he has little to say; his apparent judgment that the problem of property and power has been solved amounts to little more than an act of faith. (This is also true of Schattschneider's equilibrium, though not of Strachey's analysis, for the latter contains an intensive examination of political and economic structures.)

Among the most dogmatic of all modern commentators in his insistence that economic power does not control politics is the legal theorist Hans Kelsen, who says that "it simply is not true that within a democratic state economic power can ever override political power." He bases this proposition on a chain of reasoning that might be summed up as "the political basis of economics." Given a "formal" democracy, i.e., free political expression and competitive parties, Kelsen says economic power can only achieve what the electorate is willing to give it. So long as no monopoly of capitalist propaganda can be established, political movements cannot be completely controlled by wealth. Further, economic power rests on a legal base of property and contract legislation, and this base can be altered by those who have political rights. The openness of the political system is thus Kelsen's guarantee against the dominance of economic power. He is, of course, legally correct. Like Strachey, he properly stresses the reciprocal nature of political-economic interaction. But his sanguine view ignores the whole problem of mass propaganda. Formal guarantees of free expression may not have much practical effect when the instruments of communication are concentrated in the hands of one interest and access to the media depends primarily upon wealth.

The contention that politics can be or has been effectively liberated from economic power is not universally accepted. One approach that questions the separation might be termed that of the technological imperative. Assuming the importance of economic affairs to the functioning of any society, it is argued that those upon whom the society relies for the production of goods and services will possess a strong — some would say irresistible — claim to general social power. The claim, at least, is currently illustrated by the insistence of business spokesmen that the rest of the society must be shaped to fit the goal of a "better business climate." The assertion that power will necessarily gravitate toward the managers of the productive system is forcefully articulated in James Burnham's brilliant polemic, *The Managerial Revolution.* Stressing the crucial requirement of technical skills in organizing and co-ordinating the productive process, the loss of a purposeful role on the part of owners who do not manage, and increased government ownership and control necessitated by the failure of a profit-oriented economy to maintain full-employment, Burnham argues that production by government will continue to increase until the private sector disappears. At that time, he contends, since there will be no more capitalists and the workers will lack the administrative and technical skills to take over industrial production, the managers will have unchallenged control. The thesis is essentially one of technocratic determinism.

While it would not be fair to characterize Burnham's analysis as one that assumes its conclusion on the basis of an unexamined premise, it is less than complete because it ignores totally what Kelsen emphasized totally: the openness of the political process, the reciprocal impact of politically determined allocations of power upon the economic system. As David Spitz has pointed out, industrial managers under Stalin and capitalists under Hitler were not politically dominant despite their functional importance to the productive system. And, we can add, in the United States the political fortunes of propertied individuals and business associations have waned as well as waxed, even when corporate growth was bringing a steady increase in the concentration of economic power. At the least it seems safe to say that the variable of labor organization for political purposes would have to be taken into account as a countervailing tendency: since industrialization produces a laboring as well as a managing group — and the former is much the larger in potential voting strength — an open political system would not automatically be dominated by the latter group. Yet Burnham's argument is only modified, not destroyed, by these missing factors. The scale of modern industry and the obvious necessity that someone be in a position to co-ordinate the separate elements of a complex division of labor do constitute strong reasons for believing that those who perform this task will command high status.

Less dogmatic than Burnham, but notably pessimistic nevertheless in their estimates of democracy's chances vis-à-vis economic power, are American critics of business like Robert A. Brady, Robert S. Lynd, and the late C. Wright Mills. While they differ in detail and in the factors they emphasize, they agree on the proposition that property ownership in the modern form of corporate management threatens to destroy political equality and political freedom.

Brady's focus was on business trade associations, particularly the broadest associations such as the National Association of Manufacturers, and their tendency to fight attempts at democratic control of business power. Examining the rise of large business associations in dictatorial Germany, Italy, and Japan, as well as in democratic England and the United States, Brady described with a great wealth of documentation the process by which these associations concentrated economic power. Writing at the beginning of World War II, he saw the choice before business as being either to shake off "all popular restraints" on its power and to assert itself as economic policy determiner for the society — a path which he saw as having led to fascism — or to "force the growth of a sense of responsibility to democratic institutions . . . by steadily widening the latitude for direct public participation in the formulation of economic policies affecting the public interests."

Describing the policies of business associations, Brady characterized their economic goals as monopoly, protection, and privilege; their social policies as status, trusteeship, and harmony; and their political aims as bureaucracy, hierarchy, and totalitarianism. The notions of trusteeship and harmony are of particular relevance, I think, because they continue to be explicitly and openly avowed today in the propaganda of the corporate conscience and the "better business climate." Their undemocratic character lies in their similarity to the concept of the benevolent despot.

Thus Brady sees organized economic power as an undemocratic force, but he has no faith in an easy separation of political power from economic. To obtain and protect monopoly privilege, argues Brady, business associations seek control over government, one important means being representation of the business interest in the policy-forming agencies of the state. His fear is that political power will not be a democratic counterbalance to business, that instead government will become a tool of business power. He offers no solution, although by implication he does suggest that our goal must be to democratize industry by some form of public participation in the important economic decisions, to make industrial structure compatible with a democratic political system.

Robert Lynd, whose Middletown books are classic studies of the unity of economic and political power at a community level, has been writing about power for many years. In his foreword to Brady's book, he states his central theme that "the attempted harmonious marriage of democracy to capitalism doomed genuinely popular control from the start." "Capitalist economic power," he continues, "constitutes a direct, continuous, and fundamental threat to the whole structure of democratic authority everywhere and always," and he poses the question: "Will democratic political power absorb and use economic resources, bigness and all, to serve its ends, or will big economic power take over state power?"

This sounds as though Lynd believes the two power systems can be separated, a thought implied also by his references elsewhere to "the new power of numbers which the extension of the suffrage was to put formally within the reach of the masses" and to "the enormous potential of democratic power."

Yet Lynd also feels that business propaganda has blinded us to the possibility of using democratic power to achieve social ends, that our class structure, based on capitalism, contradicts democracy, and that business control is being extended to "education, media of communication, freedom of speech, and politics."

This emphasis upon the informal dynamics of opinion formation is, in effect, a pessimistic rejoinder to Kelsen's optimistic reliance upon the formal structure of democracy. The openness of the political system, Lynd is saying, will mean little if propertied interests so dominate the media of communications and opinion formation that the electorate's consent can be engineered and manipulated at will.

That this dismal prospect may at present be in process of developing is one of the themes in C. Wright Mills's *The Power Elite*. "Authority," he wrote, "*formally* resides 'in the people,' but the power of initiation is in fact held by small circles of men." The small circles are comprised, in Mills's view, of the institutional power-holders in government, the military, and the corporations.

While this concept of the power structure includes bases of power other than economic, Mills assigns great weight to the industrial corporation and the "corporate rich." The trend of our time he sees as the fusion of economic and political power, exemplified by the dominance of "corporate chieftains" in the "permanent-war economy." Yet he does not adopt the position that these two power systems are inherently inseparable, for his view of the New Deal is one of "competing centers of power that challenged those of the corporate directors." This period he describes as the one time in American history when there existed an effective pluralism:

> In the decade of the 'thirties, a set of shifting balances involving newly instituted farm measures and newly or-

> ganized labor unions—along with big business—made up the political and administrative drama of power. . . . These groups pressured, and in pressuring against one another and against the governmental and party system, they helped to shape it. But it could not be said that any of them for any considerable length of time used that government unilaterally as their instrument. That is why the 'thirties was a *political* decade: the power of business was not replaced, but it was contested and supplemented: it became one major power within a structure of power that was chiefly run by political men, and not by economic or military men turned political.

But this is the only period, out of five into which Mills divides American history, in which he does not see economic power as ascendant over politics. If economic dominance is not an assumption to Mills, it is at the least a very powerful tendency.

While his concept of the power elite has become the most widely known of Mills's many provocative writings, his special contribution to the doctrines of property and power being examined here is in the consideration of property as a base for personal political independence. On this, Mills articulates vigorously the fear that the Daniel Websters of the 1820's may have been right: that without property ownership men cannot be politically free, or, conversely, that the man who controls the property will also control the politics of his employees, thus translating his economic power into political currency.

The foundation stone of Mills's book on the social psychology of the new middle class is a distinction between two types of property:

> The individual who owns democratic property has power over his work; he can manage his self and his working day. The individual who owns class property has power over those who do not own, but who must work for him; the owner manages the working life of the non-owner. *Democratic property* means that man stands isolated from

> economic authority; *class property* means that, in order to live, man must submit to the authority which property lends it owner.

The concentration of ownership and productive facilities constitutes class property. The consequence of this type of property, writes Mills, is that:

> For the employees, freedom and security, both political and economic, can no longer rest upon individual independence in the old sense. To be free and to be secure is to have an effective control over that upon which one is dependent: the job within the centralized enterprise.
>
> The broad linkage of enterprise and property, the cradle-condition of classic democracy, no longer exists in America.

For the political system as a whole, the result is to upset a tension that has characterized much of U. S. political history — the tension between small and large property. Potential conflict between property and numbers was, until very recently, "distracted" by this conflict between properties. Now that small property has atrophied in economic and social power, Mills's conception is of two large power-blocs, business and labor, organized to contest for control of government, with the amorphous and heterogeneous new middle classes constituting a political "rearguard." Rather than becoming a power-group in its own right, the propertyless middle class, in Mills's view, is most likely to follow the winner among the organized blocs. The middle class, he writes, is "up for sale."

The next logical step — and the final one — in this debunking of the Jeffersonian dream has been taken by the young political scientist, Andrew Hacker. Contending that the conservative argument of 1800 remains valid today, that "the man without property is powerless and defenseless," he argues that the dependent middle-class corporate employee is a man without a political interest of his own. "The political wants of these people — a sound dollar, peace with honor, social position — are too vague to be treated as interests." Thus a vacuum is created in the political system — but not for long: "impersonal corporate interests are replacing personal interests . . . as the participation of individual members of the middle class declines, the participation of the corporations for which these people work increases."

The middle class is no longer up for sale; it has been sold to the corporation. Even when the corporate employee of the middle and upper ranks does think and act "for himself," we might add, "his" ideas turn out to be overwhelmingly identical with those of his corporation. In popular mythology, the "labor vote" is often spoken of as a deplorable departure from the American norm of the independent voter. Yet union precincts show no more monolithic a voting pattern than those of the high-executive suburbs. And now that some of the largest corporations are adding political representation of the firm to their executive job descriptions there will be even less opportunity for political deviation than there was when the corporations discouraged their managers from participating in politics.

The logic of industrialization, the loss of personal ownership of the productive resources with which one earns a living, and the rise of "political consciousness" in that legal "person," the industrial corporation, unmistakably make democracy in an industrial society a true adventure, a risk. But an adventure becomes unalloyed tragedy if the challenge is clearly insurmountable. Is that the case here? Does corporate political activity threaten to swamp political equality? Or can some way — or ways — be found by which a new base for personal independence and popular power can be created? To that quest we can now turn our attention.

4 | New Bases for Personal Freedom and Popular Power

We can identify three possible bases for political independence, to replace individually owned productive property: new kinds of "property," the franchise, and public allocation of resources.

EMPLOYEE PROPERTY

The pictures in our heads about property generally reveal a case of cultural lag. We tend still to think of property as a tangible thing — something like farm land that one can touch and see — even though we know, upon reflection, that property is a socially defined, and socially changeable, bundle of rights regarding someone's use of something. Because our stereotype focuses on the thing rather than a person's relationship to the thing, we tend also to consider property rights to be indivisible and individual, just as the thing owned — a washing machine, for example — is indivisible. We do not think that others share in our personal property or have some rights regarding our property. In short, our understanding of property continues to reflect the meaning of property current in 1800, although today the socially important forms of property are producer goods, collectively owned (in that private collective, the corporation), with the rights of use and disposition held predominantly by a single management group that, formally at any rate, is exercising powers delegated by the "owners."

The lag between these modern facts and the received doctrine is best exemplified by the concept of the "prerogatives of ownership." By applying this unthinkingly and without qualification to the industrial corporation as it developed in the nineteenth century, we created a situation in which men who were in fact not the owners but the hired managers of property that was in fact not individually but collectively owned exercised rights of use and disposition that in fact affected not just the property holders but also the employees, the consuming public, and the community in which the firm was located.

When the unsocial consequences of such unrestricted and unshared rights became apparent, collective bargaining and protective legislation began to develop as a way of enforcing what have come to be the shared rights of non-owners in the ownership of industrial property. Today, the interdependence of an industrial, urban society requires a lengthening list of community-protecting limitations on the uses of "private" property, even in the area of personal ownership of consumer goods. The obvious example is traffic rules: a "piece" of my right to use my car as I wish has been sliced off and handed to my fellow motorists, who have thus gained legally enforceable rights of their own regarding the operation of "my" car, to ensure that their rights to enjoy their property are not destroyed by mine in my property.

Industrially, the once unified right to use the productive machinery of a corporation has been fragmented despite the vigorous and continuing protests of managers and owners.

Employees, through unions, have secured job rights: seniority, skill differentials in pay, grievance procedures, and so on. Through government, employees have obtained additional rights vis-à-vis the property holders who employ them: minimum wages and maximum hours, unemployment and retirement benefits, the right to organize, and so on.

Consumers, through government, have acquired a right to honesty in advertising, a right to expect competition among sellers, a right against fraudulent investment schemes, and, generally, a shift from "let the buyer beware" to "let the seller beware." Distributors and dealers have begun to acquire legal and informal rights vis-à-vis the manufacturers whose products they handle. Rhode Island, for example, has legislated a grievance procedure for auto dealers whose franchises are cancelled. And, since stock ownership and corporate control have been divorced and an identity of interest between the two cannot always be assumed, the rights of the nominal owners, the shareholders, have been accorded explicit, if largely ineffective, separate recognition by the Securities Exchange Commission against the rights of the *de facto* owners, the directors and managing officers.

Whether minimum wage, the application of seniority in layoffs, or a dealer's opportunity to appeal a franchise cancellation are called property rights and treated as such in the legal textbooks, or whether some other rubric is applied to them, the fact remains that the rights of ownership are being divided up. New rights are being recognized by judicial interpretation or created by legislative action. And these rights in the job, to single out now the area most pertinent to our concerns here, may be looked upon as a developing substitute for the lost base of individual property ownership.

This significant shift in the source of economic security was pointed out by Goetz Briefs in the 1930's in his discussion of exactly this question:

> Having a job to work at, with good prospect of finding another on occasion, is the economic and social equivalent of having a piece of property. . . . If the time is to come when the anchorage a man needs is no longer provided for him by property, it follows that his place in industry must take on the attributes that belong to property. His right thereto must be secured by an exclusive title. . . . It is entirely conceivable that the job, which is really a functional form of property, might usurp the place of material property.

Though he failed to develop the point, C. Wright Mills was saying the same thing when he wrote that "to be free and so be secure is to have an effective control over that upon which one is dependent: the job within the centralized enterprise."

As we have already noted, bargaining through workers' organizations has been the source of improvements in job security. In fact, many economists argue that the major social gain from unionization is not higher wages but the injection of "due process" into the hiring, assignment, and firing of workers. Neil Chamberlain, for example, writes that "the unions' chief contribution to their members' welfare has been to free them from the tyranny of arbitrary decision or discriminatory action in the work place." Recent developments suggest that further extension of economic security gains — and thus, to some extent, independence — is both possible and probable. Some unions have been able to obtain clauses requiring that management consult with, and even obtain the approval of, labor representatives when contemplating removal of a plant from one community to another. And on the West Coast, the Pacific Maritime Association and Harry Bridges's Longshoremen's Union agreed in 1960 upon an employer-financed fund to protect workers against technological unemployment, in return for which the union agreed to eliminate all work rules tending to retard the introduction of labor-saving machinery. William Gomberg's evaluation of this agreement is of interest:

> Hitherto, it has been taken for granted that a liquidating enterprise had only two responsibilities: for its liabilities to its bondholders, and for its equities to the stockholders. Now a new property interest is established: the enterprise also becomes responsible for the property loss of its workers. In other words, a basis for assessing the property value of a job begins to emerge when we think in terms of capitalizing the earning power of the job of which its holder is deprived.

Promising as this line of development seems, it is a long way from fulfillment. In the first place, only about half of industrial wage earners are organized for collective bargaining. Then, the scope of decisions that affect workers but are made unilaterally by management under the sole prerogative doctrine remains large. In Frank Marquart's words:

> A sole prerogative clause is contained in almost all union contracts, sometimes spelled out, sometimes implied. In plain words, this clause means that the employer has the sole right to determine what is to be produced, how it is to be produced, how much is to be produced, what plants are to be built and where, how much capital is to be invested, what kinds of machinery are to be installed, when workers are to be hired and when they are to be laid off, and how production operations are to be rationalized.

Finally, the white-collar middle class — from file clerks to executives — stands almost entirely outside the protections accorded blue-collar workers by unionization. The constitutionalization of decision-making affecting the jobs of white-collar employees has hardly begun. In fact, the very notion of industrial corporations as "private governments" has yet to permeate our consciousness in depth, despite all the public relations stress on "corporate citizenship."

Akin to the notion of jobs as property is that of skills as property: possession of wanted skills may give one job security. Modern production requires a high level of technical and managerial skills, which cannot be learned easily or quickly on the job. Because these call for lengthy formal education and many of them are in scarce supply, the person who possesses them comes to have a leverage with his employer, even in the absence of collective bargaining. Hence the functional meaning of property shifts from useful things to useful intangibles.

All of the measures considered thus far are directed toward protecting the security of a job against arbitrary personal or political infringements. But they cannot safeguard the job that does not exist, nor protect against the loss of income that results from a general rise in unemployment. If the economy as a whole underwent a prolonged depression, no single firm could hope to guarantee jobs or continue to provide jobless income when its own income was inadequate. To the protections accorded by individual skills and collective bargaining thus must be added public protection of income. Unemployment, disability, and retirement insurance are now accepted; within the decade we may expect that social insurance against catastrophic illness will be added to this list. These types of insurance are still incomplete in coverage and deficient in level of benefits, but the basic principles are now solidly embedded in the social fabric of the nation. These "welfare state" measures — plus public education and public and subsidized housing — have been characterized by John Strachey as the equivalent of the old propertied-class notion of a "stake in the society."

Underlying all of these is one other income-protecting public policy: the commitment to full employment of men and resources. All other welfare measures stand on the economy's ability to generate a level of national income that will enable us to pay the bills. Not only is full employment a financial necessity in this sense, it is essential to the successful exercise of collective bargaining and to the worker's sense of independence. When the unemployment rate is high, employer resistance to employee demands is heightened, too. And when the worker who feels pressured by the foreman, or who wants to get away from a particular employer's political propaganda in the employee newspaper, sees others being laid off and the "help wanted" signs coming down, he fears to take a chance on quitting and seeking new employment.

On grounds of the harmful economic and social effects of inflation, many people argue against "too full" employment. The problem of inflation cannot be denied, of course, but it is doubtful whether the evils of inflation (gradual rather than galloping, at any rate) are as great as those of unemployment. While inflation cuts a man's income, unemployment may destroy his self-respect and his income. Unemployment is too high a price to pay for price stability. Exactly because having a job, or the opportunity to find another, is the modern equivalent of property ownership, it is essential that full employment be given high priority in public economic policy.

ORGANIZING TO USE THE FRANCHISE

In the nightmares of spokesmen of the NAM, political dominance by labor is an unfortunately automatic consequence of its great voting strength, unless businessmen make extreme efforts to "educate" voters and organize their own ideological allies. Yet political victory is not a simple function of numbers, despite formal political equality. "The jump from numerical growth . . . to increased political power requires, at a minimum, political awareness and political organization," wrote C. Wright Mills in pointing out that white-collar men have little of either. With occasional exceptions (as in Michigan where the United Auto Workers union has developed truly professional competence in precinct politics), labor is not well enough organized, nor are workers sufficiently conscious of their political interests, to translate numbers into political success. Despite Hacker's comments on the apolitical quality of corporation executives, their proportion of political participation is a good deal higher than that of the lower middle class or blue-collar workers.

Nor is electoral organization the only problem. Given the American political system's heterogeneous, undisciplined parties and its still-powerful legislature, victory at the polls is no warranty of control of public policy. The contrast between the liberal victories in the 1958 Congressional election and the passage of the Landrum-Griffin Labor Act in the following year is sufficient evidence on this point.

The fact remains, however, that the franchise does offer the most open route to power. Given some degree of organization, minimal funds, and skilled leadership, the system of formal political equality indeed constitutes an alternative to property as a basis for popular power, even though its full potential has never been realized. Sometimes popular power takes the initiative, as it did in the Progressive movement and the New Deal period, and sometimes its major role is as a defensive bulwark to restrain wealth-oriented political forces, as it does when demands arise from business groups for less welfare spending. But even when the defensive function is uppermost, the gains for democracy are great.

In the long view of American history, perhaps the greatest

single victory of the franchise was the so-called constitutional revolution of 1937: by the size of Roosevelt's unprecedented 1936 mandate, the Supreme Court was put on notice that the myths of laissez faire individualism would no longer be accepted as an excuse for governmental inaction in the face of severe social distress. As has been said many times, Roosevelt lost the battle to increase the size of the court — his so-called court-packing plan — but won the war, when Justice Owen D. Roberts switched his position so that what had been a 5-4 lineup against socio-economic reform legislation became 5-4 in favor. The Court had been property's dike against the tides of popular power for sixty years, but finally popular power broke through, temporarily and unevenly, just as Webster had predicted more than a century before.

If the equally weighted vote expresses each individual's economic interest as derived, in Madisonian terms, from his social position as debtor or creditor, wage earner or stock-option executive, floor sweeper, lawyer, mechanic, accountant, or whatever, then political equality becomes not an attempt to override the economic basis of politics but the perfect vehicle for expressing that basis democratically. When Beard wrote that labor union exemption from the antitrust laws was not the work of "the people" but of persistent activity by the American Federation of Labor, he was not using a true dichotomy. The A.F. of L.'s political strength derived primarily from its organized numbers, not from its wealth, and thus it constitutes an illustration of franchise power more than of economic power. To the extent that voting is a reflection of economic interests of individual voters, it is itself a fusion of economic and political power.

There are of course certain qualifications to the broad picture limned in the paragraphs above. For one thing, those who most depend on vote-based power — the poor, the unorganized lower white-collar groups, farm workers, those with little formal education or political skill — are the groups that make least use of the ballot: the tendency to vote correlates closely with income, high-status occupation, and education. And those who today need to use political power most desperately as a base for gaining economic leverage, the migratory farm workers, are effectively disfranchised by the residency requirements of most states.

It is also true that some workers support parties and candidates oriented toward the demands of business and wealth. The desire to be "middle class" and share the "respectability" of persons in high-status occupations leads many low-status people to vote as the higher-status people do, thus throwing away, in effect, the countervailing power that universal suffrage has placed in their hands. Similar results flow from the continued belief in the adequacy of individual action in an age of organized power, in the supposed evils of an enlarged governmental control of the economy, and, generally, in those myths of American political ideology which teach us to fear popular power by equating majoritarian action with mob rule.

Although the spirit of the American community has become vastly more democratic than was the spirit of the aristocratic Federalists whom we revere as the Founding Fathers, conservatives continue to play on our patriotic sentimentality by referring back to the constitution-makers' fear of majorities and to Madison's dicta regarding separation of powers. We have failed to develop, as Robert Lynd has noted, a theory of the positive use of democratic power to achieve popular ends. We have failed to perceive that our real protection against tyranny lies in social diversity, not in formal provisions of the Constitution. As Robert A. Dahl has written:

> The Madisonian argument underestimates the importance of the inherent social checks and balances existing in

> every pluralistic society. Without these social checks and balances, it is doubtful that the intragovernmental checks on officials would in fact operate to prevent tyranny; with them, it is doubtful that all of the intragovernmental checks of the Madisonian system as it operates in the United States are necessary to prevent tyranny.

And, finally, we have forgotten Madison's own order of priorities. In framing a government, he said, "you must first enable the government to control the governed; and in the next place oblige it to control itself." Our exclusive emphasis on controlling governmental power, while neglecting to control the private centers of concentrated power produced by industrialism, has left the way open for wealth to seize power unchecked. If popular power is to use its potential to protect democracy from concentrated economic power, it must do so by a frank and open use of the government; for Schattschneider is right about the tension between democratic government and the undemocratic force of business property, even if he is recklessly optimistic about the maintenance of a balance.

Galbraith's attack on the "conventional wisdom" and his argument for an increased public sector of the economy for the sake of achieving social balance are illustrative of the kind of thinking we need. Because so many of the ingredients of good living—schools, playgrounds, housing, medical care—can only be distributed widely enough if supplied by the government acting as the instrument of popular demand, the logic of democracy, as a form of government that fulfills the needs of all the people by actions subject to the people's approval leads inexorably to a position favorable to increased governmental provision of goods and services.

It is probable that the important but negative function of the franchise—staving off attempts of the propertied class to whittle away at what democracy has achieved — can perhaps be served at present by the simple weight of numbers at the polls. To take the initiative, to achieve new gains for democracy and popular control of economic power, requires sustained, well-organized action at the legislative level as well as periodic action at the polls. Can or do existing voluntary organizations — interest groups, we usually call them — provide the substitute base in this regard? Replying to the contention that industrialization has destroyed the only source of political independence and participation, William Kornhauser argues:

> The trouble with this argument is that it is based on too narrow a conception of the bases of social participation and social power. It may be granted that the property basis of social power and participation is weakened by the shift from an entrepreneurial to an employee society. But at the same time new forms of organization, such as professional associations and civic groups, have been developing to take its place. As a result, members of the new middle class have high rates of participation in voluntary associations, political affairs, and community life.

Kornhauser has something here. Consider, for instance, the gains made by Negroes in recent years. Initially through the judicial politics of the National Association for the Advancement of Colored People, and more recently through the direct-action politics of the sit-in movement (with CORE, the Congress of Racial Equality, providing much of the organizational support), the most unpropertied and "proletarian" — in the sense that they are in the society but not of it — group in America has at last begun to acquire some social and political rights. Even the inadequate civil rights acts of 1957 and 1960 testify to the powerful potential of the franchise as a device for social change.

Labor unions, with all their organizational weaknesses and

narrowness of interest, are the working-class equivalent to middle-class civic groups. In the political struggle for national medical insurance and federal aid to education, the unions provide the major locus of counterpressure against the intransigent stands of the American Medical Association and the national Chamber of Commerce. In a January 1960 "Memo to Congress" the AFL-CIO listed twelve legislative goals. Bread-and-butter issues like extension of the minimum wage, protection of labor standards, and improved unemployment insurance were of course on the list, all of aid to nonunion labor as well as to union members, and the list also included civil rights, aid to education, housing, protection of unorganized farm workers, and health care for the aged. If the unions support general welfare measures as vigorously as they do union-protecting measures, it can mean a more democratic society.

Mention must also be made of general welfare pressure groups whose membership is largely middle-class but who work for social reform and a more equal distribution of good living standards. The National Advisory Committee on Farm Labor, the Friends Committee on National Legislation, the National Consumers' League, the National Council of the Churches of Christ, and equivalent Catholic and Jewish welfare organizations — these are but a few. One by one, they have little power; together they can make an impact, and it is usually on the side of democracy. Co-ordinated legislative activity by labor, Negro, religious, and consumer groups is one substantial means by which the potential of numbers can be turned into the power of democracy.

The other crucial element, in addition to the efforts of interest-group organizations composed of or favorable to democratic interests, is the political party system. Strachey points out that in Britain even the Conservative party serves egalitarian ends to some degree, because to win elections it must garner a sizable minority of working-class votes. Similarly, in the United States the Republican party, while not notably in the vanguard, accepts — and under Eisenhower even increased — the social legislation that universal suffrage has produced. So long as parties have to compete for every man's vote and not just for the votes of the propertied, possession of the franchise will remain an independent source of political power. In this respect Kelsen is quite correct in asserting the fundamental importance of an open political system. But while the suffrage is essential, the question remains whether it is sufficient. If men's ideas and their conception of their own interests and of the good society are formed through a free market place of ideas, then formal democracy will be real democracy. If the distribution of power in the society — what might be called the social constitution — is badly unbalanced, that is, if instead of pluralism there is single-interest dominance of social institutions and communications media, then formal democracy will not be enough.

At this point a connection between the franchise and the new forms of property becomes apparent. As in the conundrum of the chicken and the egg, it matters less which came first than that each is essential to the other. In the absence of some kind of economic security and independence, those who control jobs are likely to control votes. They will not usually control votes through physical coercion, but through the fear of the economically dependent that any demonstration of political independence will jeopardize their jobs, and through manipulation of the climate of opinion. Equally, in the absence of the voting right and formal political equality, no degree of economic security could make the powerless powerful. Each is necessary but insufficient of itself; together, economic security and universal suffrage can constitute a substitute for individual ownership of producer goods as a basis for political independence.

PUBLIC ALLOCATION OF RESOURCES

While political democracy creates an opening for the exercise of popular power, it does not of itself bring about that exercise. The formal power of democracy was as great in 1880 as in 1936; the difference in effective power was tremendous. One way of expressing the reason behind the difference is to say that government had not yet, in the earlier period, taken on the function ascribed to it by Schattschneider: it had not yet used its power to countervail the economic power of business.

The nightwatchman, non-interventionist state left to economic power the decisions that shaped society. But this did not have to be, and, beginning with the Sherman Anitrust Act, the creation of the Interstate Commerce Commission, and the passage of the income tax amendment, there has been a sporadic, yet cumulative, development of the national government, and especially the Presidency, as the people's decision-maker. The limitations of market forces as a system of social control having become apparent, some decisions formerly left to the holders of economic power have been wrested away and placed in the hands of people accountable to the public. Slow and incomplete as this transfer of decisional power from the economic to the political arena has been, it has progressed far enough to make the size and scope of the public sector of economic control a leading issue of our time. The direct social power of property diminishes in direct ratio to the extent that this transfer takes place. As Daniel Bell has written, "In a managed economy, politics, not dollars, will determine what is to be produced, [and] the intervention of the government will not only sharpen pressure group identifications, but also force each to adopt an ideology which can justify its claims, and which can square with some concept of 'national interest.'" Within this framework, the outstanding political development of our time may have been the emergence in the 'thirties of a liberal-labor counter-ideology that provides continuing support for governmental action in the interests of the majority.

In the article just quoted, Bell speaks of the shift in decision-making from the market to politics as constituting a "basic and fundamental shift in the relations of economic power to political power." This is the kind of shift that socialist doctrine has long envisaged, yet Bell is not writing about a process of nationalization — that is, the government's taking legal title to factories — but of a process of public allocation of resources within an economy still having a private ownership framework. Although some British Laborites have blamed the failure of the postwar nationalization program to produce any basic change in social power on an insufficient amount of nationalization, Bell's analysis suggests that nationalization may be unnecessary. A combination of progressive taxes and public control over major investment and allocation decisions, might serve to strip private ownership of its social power just as effectively as compensated nationalization could ever do.

Because nationalization as such is so obviously anathema to the American ideology, while the exercise of popular political power is not, it is fortunate for American democracy that public allocation of "privately owned" resources can serve the same social ends. Let the self-appointed guardians of the free-enterprise way of life keep the familiar forms; that will simply make easier the task of infusing them with a new substantive meaning! The Employment Act of 1946 is a case in point: its avowal that government must keep the economy going constitutes a basic rejection of capitalist ideology's premise of automaticity. Yet, because it did not affect the legal bases of property ownership, it was assimilated into most businessmen's expectations without great difficulty. The same will be true with the next major step: the transfer from private to public hands of decisions that determine the rate of economic growth.

If we add public allocation of resources to the other elements discussed above, we can then say that democracy's power to overcome property-based power rests on a tripod of which one leg is universal suffrage, the second is economic security obtained through collective bargaining and public policy, and the third is the developing transfer of economic decisions affecting the whole society from business to government control. Property itself may not be eliminated, but its social power can be circumscribed.

Thus, we have seen that property has not become unrelated to power — not by any means. But it is not the only variable in the equation of social power. Its inequalitarian tendency is forced to compete with the equalitarian thrust of political democracy, and the latter is not necessarily the weaker force in the long run. Laments for the Jeffersonian economic structure of the early 1800's are unnecessary and irrelevant. New forms of economic security are being and can be achieved, and the system is open to the demands of democracy. Our efforts should go less toward protesting against the inevitable and more toward creating an effective institutional base for democratic action to strengthen and concentrate popular power as the industrial corporation has done for property power.

II | The Public Role of the Private Corporation

5 | Business Power and Influence: Sources

A THEME AND AN OBJECTIVE

Most businessmen give little or no weight to the assessment of their position and power in American society made by "outsiders," and indeed they usually deny that they possess power in any marked degree. Yet in this chapter we will be concerned with the breadth and depth of business power and influence, and so it is only fitting that we have a statement about this power from one of their own number. James C. Worthy, vice-president of Sears, Roebuck, has the proper credentials: he is an insider and in high position in a major American corporation. His assessment is this:

> Business in America occupies a place of unique prestige and power. Collectively, businessmen represent one of the leadership groups of our society. Here there is no landed gentry, ancient nobility, or party elite to compete with, and high social position itself is usually based on means and status acquired in business pursuits. Businessmen enjoy wealth above average levels and with it the respect accorded wealth. They have a remarkable record of philanthropy . . . and they benefit from the prestige which philanthropy confers. Their control of economic resources

> vests them with great power, in the use of which they are permitted wide discretion.
>
> Nor is their power confined to economic affairs. They are consulted on all matters involving the welfare of the community, and their advice carries weight. Businessmen sit on the boards of universities, are active in church affairs, and provide leadership in a broad variety of civic causes. They are appointed, and sometimes elected, to important government [positions].
>
> . . . .
>
> The business system itself is one of the key institutions of American society. Business occupies in the American scheme of things a place it occupies nowhere else in the world. The position of business in the American institutional framework is one of major significance.

As a generalized statement of the scope of business power, this statement can stand without change. But specific examples will be necessary in order to give the generalization meaning and to lay a foundation for questions of legitimacy and democratic accountability. Several questions come immediately to mind: What are the bases of business power? How, where, and with what consequences are business power and influence exercised?

Since power and influence are concepts of social analysis which are impossible to measure with precision, it is first necessary to define them in general terms and then determine exactly what we can hope to "prove" about them. By "power" I mean the ability to make decisions having effects upon a substantial portion of the community, or a considerable impact upon a smaller public. "Influence" will be used to mean a weaker cousin of power: the ability to affect in some way a social decision which is made by others.

One cannot measure the power or influence of corporations or business associations on a numerical scale as one can take a reading of temperature and humidity or estimate the gross national product. Nor can one compare business strength with that of other social groups — say, unions — in the same way that one can compare the tensile strength of a copper wire with that of a steel wire. But, even granting all the difficulties of power measurement, it seems to me useful and even essential to the cause of democratic mastery of our national life to combine such hard facts as do exist with reasoned extrapolations, to produce at least an informed "guess-timate" of social power structure. Conservative analysts always place the burden of proof on those who would challenge the accepted academic image (itself more assumption than demonstrated fact) of a completely fluid, pluralistic power structure comprised of "veto groups" and "countervailing powers." Yet we can show that opportunities exist for the exercise of corporate power and influence, that great effort is made to utilize them, and that these opportunities are greater for business than for other groups. The onus then shifts to those who would deny that business has a generally superior position in the American power structure.

BASES OF BUSINESS POWER

It will come as no surprise to the reader of Part I that I suggest wealth and property control as the first items in a listing of the sources of business power. The corporation is, after all, legally a collectivity of funds, severally owned but singly directed. These two economic components, wealth and property control, are related but distinguishable. To the economist, concentration of productive property, with a consequent possession of market power (i.e., power over prices paid for purchases and prices charged for goods), is the important factor. To the social analyst, the funds generated by this market power also have an importance of their own as they are expended toward the purchase of corporate influence in nonmarket areas, such as the media of communications, the political arena, and the shaping of educational and cultural patterns.

In the matter of concentration of productive property, the basic fact is the less price competition, the greater the economic power of the firm. "The chief virtue of a competitive market in practice is not necessarily that it leads to economic efficiency but that it constrains private economic power," observes Galbraith. The prime requisite of competition is a large enough group of sellers and buyers so that the individual producer has to adapt himself to price changes, rather than have them within his control. The economy of modern America, with most industries dominated by just three or four firms, does not meet this condition. The concentration of production (i.e., the extent to which a very few firms produce all or most of a given product) is either increasing or remaining fairly stable; no one seems to claim that it is declining. In any case, the present extent of oligopoly (dominance of a few firms) already means the existence of a quite sizable degree of market power, that is, power to determine how many of what kind of product will be made available at what price.

The possession of market power means that within very broad limits a firm can manage its prices and therefore its profits, too. Witness the recently burgeoning phenomenon of profit "targets" in large corporations. No farmer or competitive dressmaker can set his prices to achieve a target profit—to him a target is only a dream. To the oligopolistic firm, however, it is a realistic goal which can be planned for, if not in a single year at least as an average over several years. The classic instance—as of so many corporate phenomena—is provided by General Motors. Its target rate of return is 15–20 per cent. In the years 1948–55 it averaged in fact 25 per cent.

U.S. Steel showed how such a firm is relatively independent of market forces, for it successfully raised prices in a period of low and falling demand. However they may compete in styling, advertising, and conspicuous philanthropy, the prototype giants of American industry do not compete in price. By avoiding price competition, corporations are able to enjoy a relatively steady and substantial surplus of income over costs, and this enables them to purchase prestige, influence, and power through a variety of expenditures that firms close to the margin cannot afford.

Beyond concentration of productive assets in the traditional sense lie additional forms of concentration that further enhance the power and influence of some corporations compared to others and in relation to the economy as a whole. One of these is the existence of relationships which are essentially dependent in nature. It may be the dependence of the dealer upon his manufacturer, which received considerable attention in the automobile industry a few years ago; or it may be the dependence of a seller, especially a small one, upon a large buyer. While formally General Motors or Standard Oil of New Jersey and a prospective dealer or machine shop supplier engage in independent bargaining to arrive at a contract, the leverage is clearly in the hands of the large manufacturer. On occasion this leverage may even be used politically. It was rumored, for example, that Standard Oil used its economic power to persuade dealers in New Jersey not to support Representative Fred Hartley when he was contesting Clifford Case in the New Jersey senatorial primaries.

The concentration of economic power is also solidified by the development of conglomerate mergers and super-oligopolies. A conglomerate merger may be simply good business from the viewpoint of the firm that diversifies its operation by the addition of separate product lines. Charles-of-the-Ritz, a beauty-products firm, merged with Venus Pen and Pencil. General Dynamics Corporation includes an Astronautics Division, an Electronics Division, a Telecommunications Division, Convair, Liquid Carbonic Division, and Canadair Limited (the leading Canadian aircraft manufacturer). In addition, its subsidiaries include Stromberg-Carlson Credit Corporation (long-term financing for independent telephone companies), Northwestern Gravel Company, and a coal mining company. In this way the profits of one division can keep the corporation going while another is losing money, perhaps because of underpricing its product temporarily so as to kill off competitors. If the competitor has no other line to sustain him, he is at a serious disadvantage. Thus diversification may be good for the firm while bad for the competitive health of the economy as a whole. A super-oligopoly is defined by Morton S. Baratz as a firm that holds simultaneous positions of market power in a number of potentially competing industries. Examples are Alcoa, which produces magnesium as well as aluminum, and Koppers, which handles natural gas and bituminous coal in addition to the coke for which it is best known.

While the kind of bigness most often associated with market power consists of a large share of a given product market, the absolute size of a firm may also be an important source of power. Giants generally have advantages over midgets, even granting the occasional David-and-Goliath exception. Corwin Edwards, a close student of monopoly problems, has argued that, even in the absence of market control, large firms have power over smaller ones because they can spend larger sums of money in competition for resources, sites, and inventions, they can create their own components and thus possess a bargaining lever over potential suppliers that the smaller manufacturer cannot match, and they can transfer risks to dealers and suppliers.

Perhaps the power of absolute size boils down to the power of a larger exchequer. While the sheer amount of money at the disposal of corporate chieftains is indeed impressive, more striking and significant is the way the money is obtained. The business firm, alone among non-governmental institutions, generates its own wealth. Whereas a labor union, a taxpayers' association, a charitable institution, a neighborhood recreational club, or a political party receives the money it uses out of its members' pockets and consumes its assets in the course of performing the functions for which it was organized, the business enterprise obtains funds from outsiders in the process of performing its primary function of producing and distributing goods and services. The better a corporation performs, the more money it obtains; the better a voluntary association serves its members, the more money it is likely to spend and to require from its members.

This is a simple fact, but one of fundamental import. It means that business institutions have a security of financial base superior to that of other types of institutions. And it means that expenditures aimed at enlarging the firm or gaining public acceptance of the businessman's views are made with *other people's money*. Expenditures made on behalf of business, that is, are made possible by the assessment of consumers, without the people being aided — the managers — having to dig into their own pockets. The assessment of consumers is, in effect, a private tax representing that portion of the price one pays for a product which goes not for reimbursement to the factors of production but for plant expansion, institutional advertising, and contribution to educational or charitable institutions made by the firm. Not only do we as consumers make a hidden contribution to corporate efforts at influencing the market place of opinions, but we as taxpayers also subsidize corporate institutional strength in relation to non-business institutions by giving business tax privileges not enjoyed by individuals.

One simple example illustrates both forms of assessment. In a bid for the fealty of employees to their corporate benefactors, many firms have undertaken to service the "whole life" of their employees, not just their work-day environment. To this end, recreational facilities are often provided by the corporation — the same kinds of facilities that a membership club might build. But the corporation gets the money it uses to build a recreation center from the purchasers of its products, whose intent is to pay for the product, not for an employee recreation center. The managers who provide the facility will reap the reward of gratitude for generosity — generosity in the expenditure of consumers' dollars. In addition, our tax laws permit the deduction of the cost of the facility from the firm's taxable income as a "business expense." With the corporate income tax at 52 per cent, if the money is not spent, the government will get 52 per cent of it; if it is spent, the government gets none of it, and the taxpayers are, in effect, subsidizing more than half of the corporation's generosity. If the employees formed an independent voluntary association, however, to build the same facilities for themselves, the money would have to come out of their personal income, and each member would also have paid a federal tax on his payments to the club.

These peculiarities of business revenue and tax privileges are not inherent attributes of private economic activity; they are legal privileges, given by the public, if unwittingly, and recallable by the public. That is, the economic source of business financial power — its ability to generate income by performing its allotted role — is magnified by a political base.

This secure financial base and the very size of funds available to the larger corporations provide other sources of power. For the individual firm in a position of market power, the ability to set its desired rate of return enables management to finance expansion internally, whether it is plant construction or purchase of existing plants through mergers. The small firm in a competitive field generally cannot expand significantly without going to the capital market for funds. To obtain funds there, it must meet the test of that market: the independent appraisal of the company's prospects made by the potential investors. The firm with larger funds bypasses this test: management "judges" its own potential and invests accordingly the funds received from consumers.

For business as a whole, superior financial position means the ability to outbid other institutions for talent. In a society where income is the major measure of success, and the ingredients of good living are preponderantly obtainable only through individual purchase, he who offers the highest income will draw a more than random share of the best talents available. Power, prestige, and social purpose enable government and educational institutions to obtain at least some of the very best talent, and humanitarian impulses will draw others into financially unrewarding but socially important areas of service; but these are the exceptional cases. Superior ability to purchase skilled services must rate as another source of business power. Not only does the large business have this opportunity; it also has an influence on the ability of other institutions to compete for talent, because businessmen sit in large numbers on the boards of directors of colleges and service institutions and participate in shaping the salary policies of these organizations.

Industrialization itself is a source of business power, too. Because industrialization has brought about fewer and larger production units, operational direction of production has come to reside in fewer hands, each of them with a larger scope of authority. For example, there may now be a company of 10,000 employees under one president, where formerly there were ten companies of 1000 employees, each with its own president. We have already seen how the divorce of the workman from ownership creates a dependent salariat. In the absence of unions or other mechanisms of job security, members of the salariat will only rarely dare to challenge the actions or pattern of thinking of their employing institutions. When the directing executives of the firm propagandize their white-collar work force, there is little to oppose the influence exerted. This dependence is usually increased by the grant of retirement and other fringe benefits, which are dependent on continued employment with the same firm and which therefore make it more difficult for employees to quit.

In an industrialized national economy the individual parts are much more dependent on the whole than in an agricultural, locally organized system. This has the consequence of extending the scope of impact made by decisions of the larger business units. There may have been a greater frequency of monopolistic situations when a local manufacturer had to buy his steel from the only local producer, or the individual consumer had only one druggist, one grocer, one dry-goods store from which to make his purchases. But, while the rise of national firms and increased size of communities has given the consumer broader effective choice in many areas, the nationalization of the economy also means that where a firm has market power the impact of its decisions will be felt not just in one town but in hundreds. When a local mill shut down in the nineteenth century, the consequent economic distress was localized; when the auto manufacturers have an off-year now, the whole nation feels the pinch, not only because the three or four largest producers account directly for the employment of many hundreds of thousands of men, not just in Detroit but across the country, but also because the auto industry consumes a large share of the production of other national industries: glass, rubber, steel, paint, fabrics. Few firms or communities can isolate themselves from national economic tides today. Interdependence, plus the size of individual producers, give the latter power over the economic activity — employment, production, prices — of the entire nation. Thus, when corporate leaders say that this or that must be done or, more frequently, must not be done, because it will help or hinder their efforts to maintain a "sound" economy, their words carry great weight.

This weight that we give to what the businessman says is an intangible, but fundamental, source of business power. What it means is that we the public tend to accept the criteria presented by business in our efforts to evaluate business behavior and social needs. The definitions of the issues made by business are frequently the definitions we accept, and, as E. E. Schattschneider has written, "the definition of the alternatives is the supreme instrument of power."

As an example of the effect of the formulation of a problem, many of us would answer affirmatively when asked if the President of the United States should be granted sufficient power by Congress to enable him to act swiftly and decisively to protect the national security. But the answer might well be negative if we were asked whether Congress should surrender any of its constitutional authority to the President. Yet the substantive issue involved, the proper balance of executive-legislative roles in protecting the nation, is the same in both instances.

We are usually unaware that the way we think about a public issue is being determined for us by business-oriented definitions of the alternatives. Even businessmen themselves are frequently unaware that they are allowing their views as citizens to be determined by their positions in the business world.

In the early stages of drafting this chapter, I was talking one day with an executive of one of the larger corporations, and our discussion turned toward the domestic economic programs of the Kennedy Administration. When I expressed the opinion that improved unemployment compensation, health care for the aged, and depressed area aid were good for the country, he said that, as a businessman, he felt such programs might mean higher corporate taxes, and so he was opposed to them. But he went on to say that he supposed that if he were not a corporation executive, or if he thought about these matters from a viewpoint other than that of their impact on business profits, he might very well approve of them. The exceptional thing about this man was that he recognized that business welfare and public welfare may not be identical; he recognized a distinction between his views as businessman and his views as citizen. Regrettably few of his colleagues, or of the general public either, seem to be able to make this distinction.

Because the difference is not recognized, we are inclined to accept a definition of issues, even remotely involving business, that identifies the good of business with the good of all. Take, for example, the "better business climate" campaigns that have been introduced into a number of communities in recent years. These campaigns are focused on persuading wage-earners to restrain their pay demands and city governments to avoid increased services that would increase local taxes. The major exception is revealing of the criteria being used: greater local expenditure on education is sometimes supported because the more sophisticated businessmen now realize that the technical training they require of workers will in this way be provided at far lower cost to the firms in taxes — shared with the rest of the community — than if they had to provide the same training privately.

"Business climate" appeals rest on a simple, though unadmitted, premise: aid to business should receive top priority in any community's value pattern. On this premise, the major issue in any problem is: Will this help or hurt business? But phrasing more in keeping with the spirit of democratic pluralism would be: What is the best accommodation we can reach of business needs with non-business values? A more humanistic premise would be: That climate is best which is best for people — not just for business institutions. Healthy economic institutions are indeed a "good thing." The mistake of business rhetoric is to assume that they are always the chief good.

While the range of issues upon which business influence is felt is indeed great, the most immediate and central area in which business uses its power is on those issues which affect the corporations themselves. A close student of pressure politics, V. O. Key, has written that the "great political triumph of large-scale enterprise has been the manufacture of a public opinion favorably disposed toward, or at least tolerant of, gigantic corporations, in contrast with an earlier dominant sentiment savagely hostile to monopolies and trusts." The validity of this judgment is supported by comparing the electrical equipment price-fixing scandal, involving twenty-seven firms, with the McClellan investigation of the Teamsters Union. The evidence uncovered in the latter instance led to widespread denunciations of unions as generally racketeer-controlled. The evidence uncovered in the former instance led to some wrist-slapping comments and some self-righteous avowals by the men at the top (who personally escaped prosecution) that such things would not be allowed to happen again. The contention that business as such had clean hands, that it was only a small group of executives who had flouted the law, has apparently been accepted by the public, since there has been no cry for preventive action equivalent to that which led to passage of the Landrum-Griffin Act in the labor field.

American business has been immensely productive, and business spokesmen invariably stress productivity as the primary, often the only, criterion to be applied to business performance. What price productivity? is a question business itself ignores and would have us ignore. But the public needs to ask other questions: Are the pricing decisions of big industry made responsibly from the viewpoint of full employment needs? Is a saving in taxes really worth the ultimate cost in lowered community standards of education when services are reduced to fit budgetary criteria? Is the annual new-model push of the automobile industry worth the human cost to workers subjected to a speed-up for a few months and then laid off once the peak season has passed? Is high productivity worth, or does it require, commercial intrusion into family life through television appeals to the children to ask Mother to buy brand X? The infrequency with which such questions are asked provides some measure of our unthinking acceptance of the criteria business puts forth.

When we come to examine business's position in relation to government, the first fact that emerges is government's dependence on business. In the cold-war economy that prevails today, the national government is heavily dependent upon business co-operation in fulfilling the most basic of all government responsibilities: national survival. Not only are defense products manufactured privately rather than in government arsenals, but even the research for and design of new military devices is produced under contract to private industry. This procedure is not necessarily wrong, nor is there any doubt that this system is a flexible one. But the fact remains that government is thus made dependent upon business, and so defense producers are given leverage over government. If anyone doubts that such leverage will be used, let him review the record of defense conversion just before World War II, when manufacturers engaged in what has been called, accurately if unkindly, a "capital strike" until their conditions were fulfilled — the major condition being a virtual guarantee of profits. Let him consider that an antitrust suit in the oil industry was postponed "for the duration," in order that the co-operation of this vital industry would be forthcoming. And let him explore how dependent government was upon business for executive manpower to run the mobilization program.

The President's most notable domestic role is that of "manager of prosperity." By the provisions of the Employment Act of 1946 he has been made responsible for analyzing the economic state of the union and for devising a program to promote "maximum employment, production, and purchasing power." Whether these goals are realized, however, depends heavily on the behavior of business firms over whom the President has no authority. The dependence is both direct and indirect. Directly, prosperity depends upon private-sector decisions regarding such factors as the rate of business investment, the rate of product innovation, and the movement of prices. Indirectly, business influences, or indeed determines, the ability of the government to take appropriate steps to improve the nation's economic performance. That is, through lobbying in Congress in opposition to a President's anti-recession program, business organizations may impede the President's ability to compensate for the original inadequacies of private-sector decisions — as was the case with President Kennedy's 1961 program for full employment and a higher growth rate.

This mention of lobbying leads us into the second aspect of the government-business relationship that supports business power. Since the society largely believes in business and private enterprise, the primary political task of business has been the negative one of maintaining the status quo; that is, of preventing action rather than achieving action. It is increasingly doubtful whether even the direct needs of business are well served in the long run by inaction. But most businessmen do not yet realize this. While government itself has undergone a considerable degree of centralization in recent generations, political power remains much more diffused. This looseness of the American political system is well suited to the political needs of business and is indeed ardently supported by it, for it hinders majority action and enhances the ability of articulate and well-financed minorities to exercise a veto over legislation which they deem inimical to their interests. Thus the United States Chamber of Commerce was credited in the press with stopping federal aid to education in 1957 — helped, it must be said, by the National Education Association's ineptness in supporting the legislation. Oil producers have also been able to turn back all attempts to repeal the 27.5 per cent depletion-allowance tax benefit they receive. If the political system were more tightly integrated — if President and Congress responded to the same constituencies; if party discipline were stronger; if campaign money were a less vital factor in electoral chances — it would be possible to reduce appreciably the ability of groups, without a large membership but well financed, to exercise such vetos over legislation they do not favor. Since our system is not integrated, special groups can still thwart the apparent majority will with comparative ease, and one result is that business has greater political influence than it would otherwise have.

Finally, we note that the inherent economic advantages of business firms in the expensive lobbying process have recently received a little noticed but substantial governmental boost: the tax bill passed in October 1962 contains a provision overturning a long-established public policy that lobbying expenditures are not a tax-deductible business expense. Henceforth, the taxpayer as well as the consumer subsidizes the efforts of business firms to lobby their views through Congress and state legislatures. Because political activity by corporations has been increasing, it is worth our while to review the matter of deductions for political expenditure in some detail.

Ever since 1918, the regulations of the Internal Revenue Service have excluded from the category of deductible expenses for business any "sums of money expended for lobbying purposes, the promotion or defeat of legislation, the exploitation of propaganda, including advertising other than trade advertising, and contributions for campaign expenses." This clearly covered direct lobbying before a legislature but was ambiguous in its coverage of two other types of lobbying expenditure. One is in regard to initiative and referendum measures under consideration by a state electorate rather than by the legislature. Another is the phenomenon of institutional advertising designed to provide a climate of opinion favorable to business, for such advertising may have a close as well as a remote relationship to legislative issues.

The initiative and referendum question was considered by the Supreme Court in two decisions handed down in 1959. One case, Cammarano *v.* United States, concerned deductibility of a beer distributor's contributions to a trade association fund used to finance a publicity program directed against an initiative measure which would have placed retail beer and wine sales in the hands of state stores in Washington. The other, Strauss & Son, Inc., *v.* Commissioner of Internal Revenue, involved a wholesale liquor dealer's contributions to a propaganda campaign against an initiative measure calling for statewide prohibition in Arkansas.

Justice Harlan's opinion, which denied deductibility in both cases, confirmed that the tax regulations were applicable to publicity directed at the electorate as well as that directed at legislators, and that they applied to initiative and referendum measures as much as to action by a representative legislature. In rejecting a contention by the litigants that to deny them a deduction would be to violate their right to free speech under the First Amendment, the Justice said that Strauss and Cammarano are not being denied a right to speak, but "are simply being required to pay for those activities entirely out of their own pockets, as everyone else engaging in similar activities is required to do under the provisions of the Internal Revenue Code." Noticing that the policy of non-deductibility had stood for over forty years, Harlan said it appears to "express a determination by Congress that since purchased publicity can influence the fate of legislation which will affect, directly or indirectly, all in the community, everyone in the community should stand on the same footing as regards its purchase so far as the Treasury of the United States is concerned." In other words, they continue to have a right to speak out in defense of their business, but not to make the taxpayer at whom the publicity is directed pay for 52 per cent of that publicity.

The point was further elaborated in a concurring opinion by Justice Douglas. He stated explicitly that "a protest against government action that affects a business occupies as high a place" in the constitutional framework of the First Amendment as any other use of free speech. But he also pointed out that to say that free speech for business firms required tax deductions for their messages to the public would savor of the notion that First Amendment rights "are somehow not fully realized unless they are subsidized by the State." This conclusion the court would not accept, and properly so.

A second line of argument on behalf of deductibility, one which has a high degree of plausibility on first acquaintance, stresses the business-relatedness of many public policy decisions, rather than the free-speech issue. In the words of a Chamber of Commerce bulletin, "Today, with all forms of business activity affected by legislative actions — city, state, or national — the businessman should clearly have the right to treat his lawful expenses in connection with legislative issues on the same basis as any other necessary and proper business expense."

As a General Electric spokesman, Robert A. Burns, has said, "political determinations have become in large measure controlling factors of our economic life." Subsidies, tariffs, labor legislation, tax legislation, fiscal and monetary policies, regulatory activities, procurement policies — all these and many more areas of governmental activity affect the fortunes of industrial enterprises by establishing the "business climate." It is natural enough, then, that businessmen feel corporations have a right to "invest in a good political environment as well as in plants or raw material resources," as Leland Hazard of Pittsburgh has written.

In a political system based on the pluralist ideal that each interest will receive political expression in competition with every other interest, and that the best public policy will take into account the felt needs of every part of the society, there can be no quarrel with the argument that the interests of businessmen should be expressed, and that those interests today necessarily include a good many political questions. Since a business can be affected as much, or more, by an action of government as by market developments, there is a rationale for the position that expenses directed toward creation of a "better business climate" are as essential as any other business-related expenses.

If this were all there were to the matter, however, the regulation excluding lobbying expenditures from deductibility would not have existed for a single moment, let alone for forty-five years. The reason why the rule has existed, and why the question is not as simple as the Chamber of Commerce would make it, is that the political decisions that affect business performance also affect the kind of society we will have: they are matters of public interest as well as private interest, and the former is the more important. From a public-interest viewpoint, the consideration voiced in the Cammarano and Strauss cases comes to the fore and the issue changes from, "Does business have a legitimate interest in the shape of public policy?" (to which the answer is obviously "Yes") to, "In matters of public interest, should one of the competing viewpoints be given a tax advantage over all others?" To this the answer is clearly "No."

Individuals are not permitted to deduct political expenditures from their income taxes. Surely it cannot be maintained, when a corporation as an artificial person takes a stand on medical care for the aged or federal aid to education, that its interests are greater in these matters than those of the people of the United States in their capacity as citizens. Yet such a position would be logically contained in a demand that the corporation's views be tax-subsidized while the individual's are not. The fallacy in the jump from recognition of a legitimate business interest in public policy to the conclusion that expression of that interest should be tax-deductible is that this would tend toward a situation in which the climate for people was subordinated to the climate for business. In an individualist society, the ideal is the other way around: social institutions, whether industrial or governmental, exist to serve the people, and the needs of these organizations are to be subordinated to, and bounded by, the limits established to protect the people's ideal of the good society.

In 1959 the Internal Revenue Service attempted to clarify its rule regarding deductibility. It was acting partly in response to the Supreme Court decisions in Cammarano and Strauss, and partly in acknowledgment of the burgeoning of institutional advertisements devoted not to the advertiser's product but to views on national issues which have a partisan political tone, such as taxation, labor legislation, foreign aid, inflation, aid to education, medical care for the aged, and public power. The revised rule, adopted over the protests of both labor and business groups (the former because one provision would make non-deductible that portion of dues to a labor union that were used for legislative purposes), reads, in part, as follows:

> Expenditures for lobbying purposes, for the promotion or defeat of legislation, for political campaign purposes (including the support or opposition to any candidate for public office), or for carrying on propaganda (including advertising) related to any of the foregoing purposes are not deductible from gross income. For example, the cost of advertising to promote or defeat legislation or to influence the public with respect to the desirability or undesirability of proposed legislation is not deductible as a business expense, even though the legislation may directly affect the taxpayer's business. On the other hand, expenditures for institutional or "good will" advertising which keeps the taxpayer's name before the public are generally deductible as ordinary and necessary business expenses provided the expenditures are related to the patronage the taxpayer might reasonably expect in the

> future. For example, a deduction will ordinarily be allowed for the cost of advertising which keeps the taxpayer's name before the public in connection with encouraging contributions to such organizations as the Red Cross, the purchase of United States Savings Bonds, or participation in similar causes. In like fashion, expenditures for advertising which present views on economic, financial, social, or other subjects of a general nature but which do not involve any of the activities specified in the first sentence of this subparagraph are deductible if they otherwise meet the requirements of the regulations under section 162.

This expression of the rules seems to broaden the scope of non-deductibility by disallowing expenditures "for political campaign purposes," in place of the earlier wording which more narrowly forbade deduction of "contributions for campaign expenses." The revised phrasing takes account of a recent tendency of some corporations to engage themselves indirectly in the electoral process. They cannot legally make contributions to campaign funds in any case, but can — and some have done so — distribute voting records of candidates in a context which by implication suggests clearly which candidates are approved or disapproved. Such activity would not explicitly be covered by the earlier rule, but presumably is covered by the new rule.

The last sentence of the quoted paragraph, however, makes the clarification less than crystal clear. Permitting deduction of expenditures for presentation of economic, financial, and social views not related to lobbying, legislative promotion, or candidates' campaigns, it simply opens up a question of how close the connection may be before the two are said to be related in such a way as to void the deduction.

Former Commissioner of Internal Revenue Dana Latham said that "the distinction is tenuous and exceedingly difficult to draw." That the Internal Revenue Service will draw it at some point, however, is clear from a suit filed in 1961 by the Timken Roller Bearing Company to recover assessments which the Service disallowed on 1.3 million dollars of the firm's advertising for the years 1951 through 1954. The advertisements in question concerned inflation, communism, strikes, taxation, and federal aid. One of the anti-inflation advertisements focused on wage increases and expressed the view that "if the few powerful labor leaders who are more concerned over their own empires than they are for the welfare of our republic are not stopped in their drive for more and more inflation, our country could very well collapse from the weight of a worthless currency." This, the company contends, was not political. Another set of advertisements was directed against federal aid programs as a device for helping local communities, and the advertisements specifically mentioned highways and schools as types of aid programs that should not be used. Yet the company contends that none of its advertisements were directed toward specific legislation! Internal Revenue disagreed.

In these instances and others the Timken advertisements were rather clearly tied to legislative and political campaign purposes. Specific areas of federal aid were cited for disapproval; the inflation cry is a standard Republican argument; the "labor bosses" cry, by affecting the climate of opinion regarding labor unions, also affects the climate of opinion regarding the Democratic party, with which labor is informally though closely aligned.

But it remains to be seen how Internal Revenue will handle campaigns in which the connection is logically demonstrable yet in no way explicit. For example, on which side of the line will fall oil industry advertisements attacking government regulation of business in general while avoiding mention of any specific area of regulation? Or du Pont ads asserting the necessity of bigness for technological progress? Such advertisements are undoubtedly intended to forestall further antitrust action again du Pont, but they do not mention the antitrust laws.

The action taken by the Internal Revenue Service (begun, incidentally, during the Eisenhower Administration and hence not attributable to the purported anti-business orientation of a Democratic administration) may suggest that we no longer need concern ourselves with tax subsidy of the expression of the business viewpoint. But it is too early to jump to this conclusion.

For one thing, more subtle climate-of-opinion campaigns may continue to escape the net. Not all of them are as blatant as the Timken series. As an example, an advertisement by member firms of the New York Stock Exchange extols the history of self-regulation in the securities market. It does not say anything against government regulation, yet its clear purpose is to create a climate of opinion to support the notion that self-regulation is sufficient. By inference, then, it is a message against further legislative action. In addition, Internal Revenue is simply not equipped to monitor all advertising. Much of it escapes official notice.

But, most important, a counter-campaign mounted by the U.S. Chamber of Commerce and numerous firms and trade associations, with Congressman Hale Boggs of Louisiana as legislative leader and spokesman, has been successful in reversing the regulations cited above so far as direct lobbying is concerned. Expenditures for direct lobbying now are deductible on business tax returns. The Boggs forces tried for a broader deductibility, one which would have covered the expenses of propagandizing the voters as well as their elected representatives, but it was turned down in 1962. The financial advantages of business being what they already are, one can only hope that this attempt to create an even larger imbalance of financial power in the legislative process will be repulsed.

When business declares that opponents of such tax subsidies are trying to muzzle business's political expression, it may be well to remember that regulations against lobbying deductions leave business firms completely free to finance the expression of their views out of net profits rather than by subsidy. And, even if the firm's funds could not be so used, the individual businessman is as free to spend his own money on political activities as are wage-earners, farmers, independent professionals, or anyone else in the country. Free speech has nothing to do with the tax-deductibility cry raised by businessmen.

6 | Business Power and Influence: Impact

Reacting to the 1959 steel strike, the then Secretary of Labor James P. Mitchell expressed the thought that "the public is going to insist that its own interest be added to the others and that a chair be set for the public at the nation's bargaining tables." He recognized that when a "private" dispute between a firm and a union has widespread repercussions upon a sizable segment of the public outside of the two bargaining organizations, the dispute can no longer be considered a private matter. Indeed, such a situation is not confined to collective bargaining. It is quite often the case that seemingly private decisions of corporations affect both institutions and values far removed from the process of decision within the corporation. Powerful within its own jurisdictional confines as a private government, the corporation has an impact felt far outside those boundaries as well.

Our failure to recognize the public effect of corporate decisions is closely related to the custom, cited in the previous section, of considering only the business attitude toward matters that affect business *and* society. To suggest concretely the impact of private corporate decisions on the public economy, and the superior influence of business on the non-business institutions of American society, are the purposes of this chapter.

ECONOMIC IMPACT

Corporate decisions on wages, prices, dividends, and investment directly affect important public economic goals: economic growth, full employment, price stability. These decisions are made, however, on criteria of the firm's welfare rather than of the whole economy. And, it must be said, to some extent they must be so made as the system now stands, even if the individual firm wished to use broader criteria. The reasons are threefold: First, the price system is a better device for achieving an equilibrium for supply and demand of individual products than for achieving a national equilibrium of investment, savings, and consumption. Second, individual firms lack the knowledge of the whole system's needs that would be requisite to meshing their own decisions with those needs. And, third, the legal and customary obligations of management are not to the public but to stockholders.

It is at least a working hypothesis among economists that investment decisions bulk large among the determinants of national prosperity. When investment increases, all economic activity is stimulated; when investment declines, so do employment and the rate of production. Now suppose that a firm — say, the National Widget Company — has had a ten-year record of a 7 per cent annual increase in the sale of widgets, and that it has, accordingly, invested $6 million per year to increase its capacity to keep pace with rising demand. But suppose that this year, because of a decline in automobile sales, let us say, people have less money to spend and are only buying the same number of widgets as last year. The finance committee of National Widget's board of directors is advised by the president that further investment in increased capacity is not warranted at this time. The finance committee accepts his judgment, and the $6 million is not spent this year.

From the viewpoint of the National Widget management, this is a perfectly rational, responsible decision. Rational, because of the changed demand situation; responsible, because the stockholders' funds should not be spent unproductively. From the viewpoint of national stabilization, however, these virtues turn into corresponding vices. The rational requirement in a situation of generally declining investment and demand is to increase expenditures — to prime the pump. Nationally responsible action would consist in the finance committee saying that, while the firm did not need the investment, the economy did, and making the investment on that basis. But, to come full circle, this would be foolish from a supply-demand, profit-oriented, stockholder-responsibility viewpoint, which is the viewpoint embedded in our psychology and our institutions. The good of the national economy and the good of the firm are in short-run opposition. Only a very visible hand can bring the two together.

This situation is the typical one. It places management in a most unenviable dilemma. Collectively, business decisions of this kind have great impact on the economy, and businessmen are generally as anxious to operate in a full-profit situation as are wage-earners. Severally, the vast majority of firms cannot afford to invest when the return will not be immediate; and they cannot have sufficient impact individually for their decisions to matter very much. The businessman in this situation is more to be pitied than censured, unless he lobbies against effective action by those who are in a position to have a measurable, prosperity-inducing impact: the governmental authorities.

But the divided impotence of most businesses and their

collective impact upon stabilization and growth is only one part of the story. The other part, and perhaps the more crucial one from the standpoint of public policy, concerns the firms that are large enough to have individual effects on the economy. For we have today two economies: the traditional market economy in which price competition prevails and the individual producer has little power; and the oligopolistic economy of the giants, in which the scope of managerial discretion is wide and its impact on the public substantial.

In the 1954 recession, General Motors anounced that it was undertaking a one-billion-dollar expansion program. The public relations tone surrounding the announcement suggested that it was purposely timed and framed as a stimulus to the economy. Whether so intended or not, it was widely heralded as an act of economic statesmanship. The beneficial impact of such an announcement may have been considerable, particularly if it really is true that businessmen act positively to calls for "confidence," but in the case of General Motors there is no statistical evidence on how much other firms invested, or how many investments were saved from cancellation, by this particular announcement. If this was economic statesmanship, it was also evidence of something not so widely boasted of in the business and financial press: economic power. Consider the alternative possibility. What if General Motors had announced cancellation or postponement of a billion dollars of planned investment? Then the power implication would become a public issue, because the decision of one firm could be seen as a further depressant to a weak economy. When this power is exercised beneficially, no one calls it into question. If it can equally well have a harmful effect, and it can, should not the public be alarmed over its exercise by persons unaccountable to the affected public?

Presumably the auto maker's management saw that such

expansion was necessary to insure its future profits. But a company's planning for market conditions a decade hence is not automatically determined by the market. It is a matter of policy and choice made possible by the tremendous size and concentration of economic power in the hands of a single firm. In 1953, according to Morton S. Baratz's computations, 12 per cent of total private investment was accounted for by only twelve firms, the three largest in four basic industries: steel, autos, chemicals, and oil. This is a significant share of investment in the simple sense that its presence or absence could tip the scales toward inflation, recession, or "balanced growth." This fact immediately affects government's economic responsibilities, for, if these few firms substantially cut their investment, then the government might have to engage in countervailing pump-priming actions. These firms have great power without corresponding accountability.

Consider briefly the impact of one industry's price policy upon national price levels. Otto Eckstein has estimated that the wholesale price index would have risen by 52 per cent less than it did in the 1953–59 period if it were not for the "extraordinary" behavior of steel prices. Of course there was an equally extraordinary rise in wages, but the industry would not have been as willing to grant that increase if it were not for the strong market power of the steel companies. Thus the power of management in relation to the market is more basic than the pressure from the unions. It is also true that without unions the corporation would have less incentive or excuse to raise prices. The unions are not a negligible factor, even though they are a secondary factor, in power analysis. Even in time of slackening demand there is little pressure on firms in heavy industry to reduce prices — or at least not raise them — as a gesture toward economic stabilization. The reason is that such firms are now so situated that they can return a handsome profit while operating far below capacity. In the steel industry, for example, the break-even point — the point at which expenses are paid and profit begins — was calculated at 76 per cent of capacity in 1937–38. By 1950 the break-even point had been reduced to 50 per cent of capacity, and by 1958 to 41 per cent. Given these conditions, the classic force of change in demand as a determinant of price is greatly dissipated.

A second area of corporate decision-making which has significant impact on the public is that of income distribution. Except for diehard Spencerians, we long ago recognized that the community's notions of social justice are not automatically registered in the market distribution of rewards. Legal support for collective bargaining rests, for example, on recognition that unequal bargaining power between individual employees and the concentrated financial power exercised by the employer often resulted in a mockery of "freedom of contract." Minimum-wage laws are another effort to bring market results into line with the value placed by the community upon human dignity. Yet there remains an area of income-distributing power in which the values of management determine unilaterally the rewards going to themselves and to other participants in the productive process. Recently the most conspicuous example of this power has been provided by executive stock-option plans. If the stock rises in value, the executive exercises the option and sells the stock he has received from the company at the higher price; if it drops, he does nothing. He cannot lose; he can win tremendously. The corporation is deprived of the larger sum which could have been obtained by selling the shares publicly at the higher price. The rise in value will presumably be the consequence of improved corporate performance, which means that, of all employees, only the privileged few share in the reward.

When such other favored devices as delayed compensation, bonuses voted by the directors (often without relation to corporate performance), and the use of various company-provided facilities for transportation and recreation are added to stock options, it is clear that the ability of management to determine its own compensation becomes another significant impact of economic power. It is even possible that the amounts involved in a few corporations are large enough to have an inflationary impact. For example, Walter Reuther of the United Automobile Workers union claimed that executive bonuses at Ford Motor Company in 1960 totaled an amount that would have been considered excessive and inflation-inducing if it had been paid to the workers as a wage increase. And James Carey of the United Electrical Workers fears that the added inducement to raise profits so as to raise stock prices provided by stock options will mean additional management opposition to rank-and-file income increases.

The market power of large firms in concentrated industries affects income distribution in more subtle ways, too. The companies will insist that they pay reasonable prices to suppliers (and while the suppliers may disagree, they may be too dependent on their largest customers to say or do anything about it) and set reasonable prices on their products. But the comment of an economist, John B. Sheahan, on the 1961 price-fixing case is irrefutable:

> The difficulty is that justice on the other side of the fence is decidedly hard to evaluate from the seller's own position. Slightly higher prices than necessary on sales of equipment to electric utilities simply result in slightly higher schedules of electricity rates. It is probably a matter of a few dollars less left over for groceries in the case of most families, and a few hundred dollars a year added costs for other firms. It is simply a small tax, taken by the seller out of everyone else's incomes in order to

> support the concrete and worthy objectives of the selling firm. On sales of electrical equipment to government agencies, the point is even clearer. Government expenditures is a little higher than it otherwise would be, and everyone's taxes are raised a trifle. No wonder that General Electric finds it necessary to campaign actively for economy in government.

Dividend policy also illustrates managerial power over income distribution. The after-tax profits "belong" to the stockholders. On the average, they receive about 50 per cent of the pie, with the other 50 per cent going for internal financing of expansion. Maybe the stockholders would want to allocate their income to further investment, but the choice is not theirs to make; it is management's. If all of a corporation's net profit, or, say, 90 per cent of it, were given to stockholders, then they would really be free agents in the allocation of their income.

Another important area of impact consists of the patterns of consumption, both private and public. Economics starts with the pattern of consumer preferences and concerns itself with analyzing the process by which those preferences are expressed in demand for goods and in the production of the desired products in the desired quantities. But as our economy moves further away from "natural" commodities — food, basic clothing, basic shelter — into the era of invented commodities — TV sets, skiing equipment, power lawnmowers — consumer preferences themselves come to be an element in corporate calculations. The advertising industry, with expenditures amounting to twelve billion dollars per year and currently increasing at the rate of about one billion dollars annually, testifies to the effort made by business firms to mold consumer preferences, not just respond to them. The writings of Galbraith, Vance Packard, and Martin Mayer give details of the manipulative process and assess its significance. That there are limits to this malleability of the consumer's tastes no one would deny: the fate of Ford's Edsel car is a classic example of advertising failure. But that the limits are broad and permit considerable latitude is also undeniable: witness the Davy Crockett fad for coonskin hats, the rise of the tail fin on automobiles, and the impact of certain now defunct television quiz shows on the earnings of their sponsors. The larger the proportion of goods and services people were unaware of or did not know they wanted until advertising told them they did, the greater the manipulative power of the large corporations maintaining the most expansive research and development units. Conversely, many large firms with heavy investments in existing processes have not always been quick to introduce a new product or process that would hurt their existing investment, even though these innovations already existed on the drawing boards and could easily be put into production.

Our industrial economy is heavily dependent upon basic materials for the fabricating of finished products. The basic materials are in the hands of large, oligopolistic firms: in oil, chemicals, steel, copper, and aluminum, among other industries. Fabricators and processors are at the mercy of the allocations made by such firms when shortages occur. And there have been many shortages in the past few years. The power involved here is power to determine which goods are produced and which goods are not, by determining which manufacturers do and which do not receive the supplies. A recurring suspicion exists that independent fabricators get less than a prorata share of scarce materials, while fabricators subsidiary to basic commodity producers receive more.

By the kinds of decisions cited in the paragraphs above, corporate executives are not just setting "administered prices"; they are, as Edwin G. Nourse has said, administering the nation's resources. And their managerial discretion is not confined to the area of private consumption: their private decisions have considerable consequences for the public sector, too.

The most apparent influence occurs when developments in the private sector of the economy compel complementary expenditures in the public sector. This symbiotic relationship goes a considerable distance, in fact, toward explaining the growth of government in this century. The growth of the automobile industry is the classic example, in its requirements of roads, parking facilities, policemen, courts, traffic engineers, and so forth. There is no question that the public costs necessitated by this private invention have been worthwhile and productive for the economy, but there are some particular decisions made by the Big Three automobile companies in Detroit that one may not be so happy about. To quote Nourse, "Was it responsible administration from the standpoint of the economy to load nickel and chrome and other materials still in scarce supply and lavish labor on ever larger and more luxurious cars, of excessive power and gas consumption, which made obsolete our private garages and city parking meters, and required heavy municipal expense for street widening whilst extension of water and sewer lines lagged, slum clearance was deferred, and taxes soared?" Granting that the public did buy the outsized cars until Volkswagen and George Romney's Rambler reversed the trend, it is at least an open question whether the public would have done so if it had been aware of the costs cited by Nourse and if it had had a say in the matter once it was aware of the facts about the big-car development. But we were not aware of the costs, or that a choice existed. We were presented with a *fait accompli.*

This is just one instance of the social costs of private enterprise. Social costs are those burdens thrown on a community by one company's activity which are not paid for by that company or the purchasers of its product. A factory that creates a smoke nuisance and throws soot down on neighboring houses so that homeowners must paint more frequently is creating social costs in the private sector. A factory that pollutes a stream so that a community must install water-purifying devices is creating social costs in the public sector. In either case, the activity of one party is effectively influencing the allocation of resources employed by other parties.

More subtle than these types of allocation is the influence of advertising upon the balance between individual and community goods, meaning between those goods which are privately purchased and individually consumed and those which are purchased collectively for the use of all members of a community. Since this question of social balance is the theme of Galbraith's stimulating book, *The Affluent Society,* I will not dwell on it here. But Galbraith's thesis is pertinent: virtually all the weight of advertising — and twelve billion dollars a year amounts to a considerable weight — is devoted to pushing private sector products, while those public services which also contribute to the American standard of living, such as education, health services, and recreational facilities, go largely unadvertised. It is not possible to measure the impact of this imbalance in promotional endeavor upon the taxpayer-consumer as he weighs choices between what he can buy personally and what his tax dollar can buy for him (such as whether to buy an air-conditioner or vote for a bond issue for a new school), but the burden of proof must surely be on anyone who would deny that it gives an advantage to the private sector.

A touch of irony will complete the picture. Having made private decisions that cause a need for larger public outlays (such as wider cars requiring re-spacing of parking meters), some business firms then go on to spend the consumer's money in lobbying against the increase in governmental revenues that their actions have made necessary. Thus pulp and paper manufacturers, whose industrial processes are a prime source of stream pollution, lobbied vigorously against a national grant-in-aid program designed to help municipalities build sewage plants. What is the connection? Simply this: if human waste as a cause of water pollution is eliminated, the continued pollution will point the finger directly at another primary source: pulp and paper firms. Then they might themselves have to absorb some of this cost of production that they now throw onto the community and downstream property owners.

IMPACT ON SOCIETY

Among the more subtle types of business influence is the role business firms and businessmen play in shaping the directions taken by non-business institutions. Schools and colleges, churches, and charitable, cultural, and civic organizations are all expressions of various strands in the complex of values that gives our society its specific tone. In a free society, the independent existence of diverse value-forming institutions is an essential bulwark against totalitarianism, defined as unchallenged dominance over all areas of life by a single institution. And governments are not the only potential totalitarians. The situation in the U.S. is not totalitarian, yet one becomes concerned about the potential when one looks at the attempts of business to mold other institutions and general social values in its own image, and at the financial advantages supporting its incursions.

In education, for example, trustees of private colleges and universities are predominantly chosen from among men of wealth and high social status, business leaders and their attorneys prominent among them. Conscious of great financial need and desiring to avoid "federal control" through federal aid, trustees increasingly seek business support, as individual contributions are quite insufficient to pay a college's costs these days. At the least, there must exist an expectation that the size of corporate donations will vary with the college's reputation in the business community. How many deans, presidents, and trustees, then, will knowingly take on controversial faculty members? How many of them will as vigorously seek out community contacts with labor leaders or religious and social service leaders as with businessmen? Hard facts are very difficult to come by in this area, but the relative absence of extremes of opinion on our campuses today is apparent to any faculty member, and the heads of most of our institutions of higher learning were notably quiet on civil liberties during the McCarthy period. The problem is not eased when college presidents become members of corporation boards, as some do.

A more apparent business influence upon higher education is seen in the shaping of curricula to fit occupational criteria rather than the criteria of a liberal arts education. Take, for example, the great rise in the number of undergraduate majors in the field of business administration. While most Ivy League colleges and other well-endowed liberal arts colleges have avoided succumbing to the marketplace in their undergraduate curricula, the less affluent colleges have made their appeal for students fairly frankly in terms of offering them courses that promise an immediate occupational reward.

This kind of influence on curriculum is indirect. A direct impact on educational institutions is made by restricted donations, that is, money given only for a specific purpose. General Electric, for example, apparently knows what education needs: a couple of years ago it offered grants to small liberal arts colleges to encourage instruction in industrial accounting. Some aircraft producers offer scholarships and/or money to colleges to be spent only on engineering programs. Again, the strongest institutions may sometimes forego such aid, unless it fits in with plans they have made themselves. The weaker institutions will take what they can get, and the humanities that form the backbone of Western culture suffer in the process.

The type of business influence on education just cited at least has the merit of being fairly straightforward: the corporations say to the schools, you provide training in the skills we need and we will help finance you. But corporate funds are used in more devious attempts to stifle criticism of corporate power and practices which might normally be expected to come from institutions of learning. Thus the oil industry, which spends vast sums of money to influence the political atmosphere of the nation, has been able in a number of states to link severance taxes (those paid per barrel of oil extracted from the earth) to the financing of public education. Parents, teachers, and legislators thus come to have a specific, dramatic vested interest in the fortunes of the oil companies and understandably may become reluctant to "bite the hand that feeds them." A number of corporations have tried to influence their potential critics by inviting groups of teachers to visit their plants and attend lectures on the benefits the company is providing for the community. To inform teachers about the workings of industry is of course unobjectionable; but the line between informing and propagandizing is easily—and, one gathers, frequently—crossed in these programs. Business organizations, using tax-deductible corporate contributions, engage in widespread efforts to put their message across to teachers through special-audience publications. The NAM, for example, issues a publication called *Dateline* directed at teachers and church leaders. Seen simply as part of a free and equal competition in ideas, these efforts would be unobjectionable.

What is objectionable is the financial advantage that business possesses in this regard. The opinion-forming activities of business are financed by consumer and taxpayer, while the competing efforts of other groups are sharply limited by the size of the personal funds of their members.

In an effort to be the good neighbor in the communities where its operations are located, a company is often blatantly paternalistic in regard to the cultural, charitable, and civic activities of those communities. Whether a community needs a new boys' club, a hospital, or a higher tax rate to finance its school building program is a matter concerning all residents of the community, for the character and values of community life are involved. When a corporation (often a national firm whose home offices are elsewhere) gives the community a boys' club, it is exercising power over the community and establishing a base for influence on other occasions. The firm is imposing the values of its decision-makers upon the community — values that may or may not accord with the consensus of the community. And it is purchasing prestige and gratitude which it may well use to oppose the needed tax increase, even though the tax-increase issue bears no relationship to the act of generosity. Thus a contribution may have seemingly irrelevant but lasting secondary effects.

"We want people to like us and the free economy of which we are a part," says an oil company public relations manual. "Then the public will buy our products and take [our] side on controversial issues." In using its powers of persuasion, a company may often win people over to its side on an issue, not because its arguments are rationally convincing but because it has prestige purchased with other people's money.

In the previous chapter, we noted that public acceptance of business criteria and business definitions of public issues was a fundamental support for business influence. Closely related to this is the utilization of the communications media by business to help create this public acceptance.

The importance to democracy of the market place of ideas cannot be over-emphasized. A century ago, Abraham Lincoln saw the relationship of opinion formation to democratic government and expressed it as well as, or better than, any modern pollster:

> Public sentiment is everything. With public sentiment nothing can fail. Without it, nothing can succeed. Consequently, he who molds public sentiment goes deeper than he who enacts statutes or pronounces decisions. He makes statutes and decisions possible or impossible to be executed.

Three twentieth-century developments have increased the importance of public opinion: the extension of the electorate; the rise of national mass media; and the development of mass-persuasion techniques into quasi-scientific tools. Attempts to sway the public are not new, but in former times the scope of persuasion was limited by the slowness and limited circulation of the communications media employed. Today, the wire services, syndicated columnists, national magazines, and radio and television networks have all vastly increased the ease with which those who have access to these media can reach a substantial portion of the public.

Today no group which desires political action confines itself to direct lobbying in the old-fashioned sense; they all use the mass media. If access to the media is unequal, political influence is unequally distributed, even though there is still the fact of one man, one vote, at the polling booth. How, then, does business obtain access to the communications media? And how extensive is the business influence upon the ideas transmitted by these media?

Probably the least important part of the relationship is the ownership of media by firms that are not primarily engaged in communications. Avco Corporation, for example, owns a few television and radio stations since its acquisition of Crosley Corporation; Minnesota Mining and Manufacturing has a controlling interest, it has been reported, in the Mutual Network, and General Tire and Rubber purchased station WOR, New York, a few years ago. I am not aware of any direct exploitation of such ownership to affect the general substance of programming or the specific substance of political affairs broadcasting; yet I think it also reasonable to assume that no direct pressure would be needed to ensure that the managers of a radio station owned by General Tire would not devote much broadcast time to airing, say, details of an anti-trust indictment of the owning firm, or to general discussion of problems of business power. If there is any direct exploitation, it has not come to light; until and unless it does, we should assume that it does not exist.

Of considerably greater importance is the coincidence of viewpoint between media businessmen and non-media businessmen. One evidence of this is the pattern of political endorsements by newspapers; endorsements of Presidential candidates has run 65-85 per cent Republican over the past thirty years, or about the same proportion as that of business executives voting Republican. It is true that newspaper editorials are largely unread, and it is also true that Democratic candidates have not fared too badly at the polls, but still the political orientation of publishers is clearly the same as that of other businessmen. And the orientation may influence what is in the news columns as well as what is on the editorial page.

Perhaps the most striking evidence that the political preferences of publishers affect the news pages lies in the differential treatment of business and labor and business and government in newspapers and newsmagazines. Compare in almost any paper the attention given to investigations of labor racketeering with that given to the electrical equipment price-fixing case, for example, or to handling of strikes. Or the attention given a governmental error in comparison with that given to a business blunder of equivalent proportions, such as the Edsel fiasco. Or the economic and governmental content of articles in the *Reader's Digest.* Although it is only recently that the *Digest* has contained advertising, it has for many years serviced the business viewpoint. One recent example concerns the magazine's support of private utilities against public power. Addressing the Edison Electric Institute, the general manager of the *Reader's Digest* explained how several editors were going to write articles to explain "the advantages of private enterprise to our millions of readers," in the hope that the people will not "have to secure their electric service from any government."

Greatest of all the overt influences of business on the communications media, however, are those derived from direct use of corporate money for advertisements and to determine the program content of broadcasting. General Electric informs us on television that progress is its most important product. U. S. Steel "educates" us through television to an understanding of its justification for higher profits. Du Pont explains to us through television all the advantages of giantism in business. General Motors, licking its wounds after Senate hearings on dealer relationships, has published a series of full-page advertisements extolling the aid it gives to small business and then reprinted the ads in a booklet to mail to social science teachers across the country. Electric utilities extol the virtues of "investor-owned" power over public power in millions of dollars of advertising paid out of funds derived from consumer electric rates.

Much of this advertising — an increasing proportion in the

past few years — is directly political and indirectly partisan. That is, it expresses corporate views on legislative issues and, while it never mentions one political party or the other, the stand taken is almost invariably the one favored by the Republican party. Some of it is only indirectly political: it seeks to build a framework of opinion that would support the corporation if certain matters which are not yet legislative issues were to become so.

The impact of such advertising is impossible to assess accurately because it cannot be isolated from all the other factors in opinion formation. But one aspect is so plain as not to require precise measurement: the dominance of the corporate viewpoint in all advertising. Unions advertise on occasion — most frequently in connection with a strike, ongoing or imminent — but only on occasion, because the cost of advertising with the same frequency and breadth of coverage as business would very quickly exhaust their financial resources. Membership dues are harder to obtain than consumers' hidden taxes. Consumer organizations are invariably penurious; they do little or no advertising. Thus, while there does exist today a liberal-labor ideology, it has not the financial access to the media that the business creed enjoys. Business tells its side of the story and, naturally enough, avoids calling public attention to issues and criticisms that might prove embarrassing to it. Thus, the presentation of business and the related issues of bigness, of what constitutes progress, and of the social responsibility of corporations is almost entirely one-sided.

Covertly, corporate advertising may have other effects on the media. Dependent as they are on business advertising, newspapers, magazines, and broadcasting stations are notably reluctant to publish criticism of business. This is in good part, as noted above, because of the natural affinity of the owners of these media with business; the publications are businesses, too. But it is also in part due to fear of loss of patronage if they do otherwise — a fear that some advertisers are not bashful about exploiting explicitly.

The printed media have a tradition of separation of advertising from editorial content, a tradition honored at least by the stronger publications. But in broadcasting the dominant tradition has been to tie the two together under sponsor control. A magazine, say *Harper's,* would not dream of allowing an advertiser to buy pages 12 and 20, say, and as part of his purchase tell the editor what subject and viewpoint were to be placed on the pages between "his" pages. Yet this is exactly the way much television time has been handled: the sponsor buys the time, brings his package to the station or network, and the station or network only functions as a transmitting facility. Programs originated by the network, with some honorable exceptions in the public affairs category, are designed to attract sponsors, of course, and this means they are designed to please, not to offend, a potential sponsor.

Since about 1960, the three major networks — NBC, CBS, and ABC — have apparently put into force some degree of separation of sponsorship from editorial control in their handling of news and public affairs programs. And some sponsors, such as Bell & Howell, seem to be learning that such separation gives them a chance to garner public prestige by supporting "cultural" programs while avoiding responsibility for controversial subject matter which may offend some of their customers. These developments, plus a Federal Communications Commission that is at least temporarily revivified, provide some protection against the more obvious perversions of the means of public communication by business censorship. But not all sponsors show such self-restraint. A representative of the Prudential Insurance Company of America, testifying before the FCC in 1961, said that a program on the bank holiday of 1933 had once been proposed for the Twentieth Century series of television documentaries, but the company vetoed the subject because "it cast a little doubt on all financial institutions and all financial institutions these days are in pretty good shape." In the same hearings, du Pont's advertising director acknowledged that his firm exercised control over programs it sponsored so that the advertisements would have a good setting (i.e., "lighter, happier" programs make the audience more receptive to the commercials) and so that "offensive" viewpoints would be avoided.

Nor has the separation of sponsorship from content been rigorously applied to dramatic programs, even though some of these are in effect public affairs programs because they are concerned with social problems. There have been such ridiculous cases as the Chrysler Corporation's securing the deletion of Lincoln's name from a Civil War drama which it sponsored. More seriously, there is the problem of obtaining any sponsor support for controversial themes. Television playwrights have testified to the difficulties they face in finding sponsors for plays with "touchy" themes. The omission of socially significant themes is the most serious, though most subtle, consequence of business dominance over the media. It is not just a matter of the content of the restricted number of programs devoted to drama, but also a matter of the entire balance — or imbalance — of programming. Light entertainment is watched by more people than programs dealing with social inequities or problems of power in American society; thus, sponsors gravitate to such entertainment because it will presumably enhance their profits more than would socially conscious programs. Since the political objectives of business are more frequently negative than positive, which means maintaining the status quo, business's own cause is aided substantially by broadcasting's failure to handle social problems.

The corporations thus benefit doubly: their advertising creates sales, and the innocuous content of the programs they sponsor helps to forestall social criticism and governmental programs to deal with national problems.

It could be said that the fault here lies with the broadcasters, especially the networks, rather than with the sponsors. Legally, it is true, the responsibility for programming lies with the station owners. But the power of sponsors over networks, and of networks over individual stations, makes this a fiction. The fault of the broadcasting industry, then, lies in succumbing initially to the business pressures that debased this effective medium of communication. It need not have been so. When broadcasting began, it was assumed that financial support would be obtained through sale of sets. The first commercial stations were, accordingly, established by radio manufacturers. Program sponsorship and commercials were not used. But the pressure to transform a public medium into a private salesroom was too much for the broadcasters. Hence the present "vast wasteland." The criteria used to determine the content spread over the public airwaves is summarized in the bureaucratic prose of a 1960 F.C.C. report:

> All in all, the factors which go into the judgment of the advertisers and their agents as to the selection of a program, while they differ in emphasis and degree from advertiser to advertiser and agency to agency, are bottomed in the effort to attract an audience which will consist of potential customers for the product; to please that audience with the type of show that is appealing to it; to avoid "offending" any considerable segment of audience; and to continue the show on the network only so long as it retains its appeal and is, in fact, "doing the job" of selling the sponsor's product or service. A certain degree of diversity in programming results from the differences in objective and purpose of the advertisers, but that diversity remains

> within prescribed limits and will not include many program types and formats which are not of proven appeal to the audience. The reason for this is again tied to the "commercial considerations" of the advertiser.

It is for such reasons that, as these pages were being written, the press reported that Howard K. Smith's outstanding, prize-winning program of news analysis was to be dropped from the network schedule.

The problem of business dominance is thus greatest in the electronic media because sins of commission through private censorship are added to sins of omission, and the net effect is that virtually all opinion that might question the business view is absent from the airwaves.

7 | Corporate Conscience or Corporate Arrogance?

THE MORE THINGS CHANGE . . .

Such phrases as "the public be damned" and "let the buyer beware" may have characterized the prototype business enterprise of the turn of the century, but business's attitude has changed substantially in the intervening decades. Today the robber-baron approach, with its crudity of both attitude and behavior, is out of style. The prototype phrases are "corporate conscience," "social responsibility," and "corporate citizenship"; the goal of the great corporations is said by many of their spokesmen to be the achievement of the "balanced best interests" of all the groups affected by business decisions. Where, formerly, corporate managers emphasized their responsibility to make a profit for their stockholders, today managers put heavy stress on the corporation's responsibility for national well-being — economic, political, and cultural.

The claim of socially responsible behavior sounds good, and no one would argue today for a return to the robber-baron ethic. Yet a good many observers, including such free-enterprise economists as Milton Friedman and Friedrich A. Hayek, now question whether we have not moved too far. They are asking whether, by diverting business managers from their primary task of producing goods to the job of balancing community interests, we are not endangering the economic system and also making the managers liable to public supervision because of the essentially public functions in which they are engaged. Thus Hayek writes:

> So long as the management is supposed to serve the interest of the stockholders, it is reasonable to leave the control of its action to the stockholders. But if the management is supposed to serve wider public interests, it becomes merely a logical consequence of this conception that the appointed representatives of the public interest should control the management.

If the modern managerial creed stresses the discretion which permits managers to "do good" for employees, suppliers and distributors, local communities, and educational and cultural institutions, the implication is clear — though generally unrecognized by business leaders — that this constitutes a new kind of corporate power, an extension of managerial authority from its legitimate sphere of producing goods to an essentially illegitimate sphere of non-economic activities. The *reductio ad absurdum* has been expressed by one economist as "the danger of corporate totalitarianism." Writes Roswell G. Townsend in a symposium on American economic problems sponsored by the Committee for Economic Development:

> It is precisely the effectiveness of the modern corporation in meeting its social responsibilities that creates the totalitarian danger! Surely the American public would never accept any form of socialism or communism, nor any rightist totalitarianism, if business were obviously grasping for power or if any repression of personal freedom or any thought-control were apparent. The paradox is that the more the modern corporation accepts its own *public* importance, the more its managers succeed in living the

> good life in business affairs, the more effective its "human relations" with labor and unions, the more it improves the community through fine education and recreational facilities, the more it assists higher education and the more it insists upon exercising no control over it, the more it takes part in all kinds of charitable programs, the more it encourages its officers to do good through terms of government service, in a word, the more benevolent the corporation becomes, the more the citizens lose that self-reliance, that independence of thought, that initiative which have made America great.

Seen in this light, as a new feudalism with corporation presidents playing the role of lord of the manor, the doctrine of corporate trusteeship appears to bear a close resemblance to an arrogant assertion made sixty years ago when George Baer attributed the prerogatives of property owners to the infinite wisdom of the Creator. No executive today would be so lacking in a sense of public relations as to claim rule by divine right, and we are thus spared Baer's open arrogance. Yet the operational results for a pluralist society would not be notably different if the community permitted the corporation as presently structured to allocate resources and dictate the direction of development for non-business institutions to which the managers are not accountable no matter how "responsible" the latter may feel.

THE CLAIM OF TRUSTEESHIP

The claim of corporate trusteeship means generally that business managers are not bound to put stockholders' returns above all other considerations, but they are free to act as trustees or guardians for a variety of social-economic interests tied to the corporation, and they can direct the earnings of their firms toward managerially-defined cultural and welfare needs of society. Thus, this statement by Frank Abrams, emphasizing Standard Oil of New Jersey's "stewardship" function:

> We like to feel that it is a good place for people to work. We have equal responsibilities to other groups: stockholders, customers, and the public generally, including government. What is the proper balance for the claims of these different sections? What part of profits should go to the stockholders? What part to the employees' wages? What part to the customer in lower prices and improved quality? Keeping the proper balance in these things is one of the most important matters that corporate management has to consider.

Note that these phrases indirectly express a claim that managers will, in accordance with some unmentioned standard, determine the distribution of income between executives, workers, and stockholders, the appropriate price level, and the amount of internally-generated investment; and by means of all these other decisions they will largely shape the social-economic structure of the society.

Corporate power is not mentioned in this statement, yet power is but the prerequisite for responsibility: without the former there cannot be the latter. And once power is recognized, the question of its control must be considered. The most distinctive feature of the claim of corporate trusteeship, therefore, is its answer to the question of control — and that answer, very frankly stated by a Ford Motor Company vice-president, William T. Gossett, is the simple one of self-control:

> We find a new role and responsibility thrust upon management, the adjudication of the conflicting legitimate interests of the groups who are intimately involved with the corporation. *We find management learning to sit in judgment upon itself in those relationships where its power is preponderant and not subject to ready control or review by others* [italics mine].

Whatever else may be said of Gossett's claim of self-judgment, it has the virtue of bringing into the open the link between corporate conscience and corporate power, a link that most corporate spokesmen avoid. For the public to accept the corporate conscience makes that conscience an additional, and an important, source of corporate power. For to say that we will leave to the consciences of business managers the fate of all groups and interests touched by their decisions is to say that we will hand over to them power to affect all of our lives.

Let us turn now to the concrete manifestations of the doctrine of social responsibility.

ECONOMIC TRUSTEESHIP

The most obvious contrast between the claim of corporate conscience and the traditions of American business lies in the direct economic area: wage, price, and investment decisions. In the past, a business firm had to pay a wage sufficient to draw labor off the market and could not pay more because of the effect of wages on competitive prices; it had to set its prices at a level determined by competitive conditions — or, rather, prices were set for it by the market; and investment for growth was determined not by managers but by the independent decisions of individual investors acting through the specialized capital funds market, i.e., the stock and bond markets. In the typical administered-price situation of the prototype corporation today, the market forces may set outer limits, but they do not by any means determine any of these matters. For example, the firm does not simply respond to a market situation in pricing its products, but it determines the return it wants, setting a "target" of, say, 20 per cent on investment annually, estimates average production rates, and sets a price which will provide the desired return at the average production rate.

What does this have to do with the corporate conscience? First, the ability to plan one's profits makes possible a higher, steadier rate of return than in a more price-competitive framework and thus makes it possible to think in long-run terms, to resist temptations to unethical behavior in the search for profit, and to spend corporate funds in ways that have no immediate — and sometimes no discernible — connection with the balance sheet. For instance, a corporation may contribute to colleges or charitable institutions or to local community projects in order to buy public acceptance and improve the corporate image as an investment in the "environment." The small firm with its back to the wall is unlikely to devote much of its attention or its largesse to shaping the patterns of community social structure and welfare or aiding higher education. Nor will it proliferate fringe benefits to employees in pension funds, life and health insurance, or recreation facilities. It cannot extend itself so far from the central focus of producing goods for a profit.

Second, because the corporation can set prices and because it is aware of the power this entails, it is subject to demands that its pricing policies accord with the needs of the whole economy for price stability. The 1962 conflict between President Kennedy and the steel companies over their attempt to raise prices is a classic case in point. Put another way, the corporation, in acknowledging that it has discretion in pricing, acknowledges also that it has a responsibility for the health of the national economy — and, implicitly, asserts by the same token a degree of power over the national economy.

Third, by being able to anticipate the rate of return on their investment, the managers can plan the growth and strength of their firm. Their consciences must determine — much more directly than the "votes" of consumers' dollars can — the allocation of investment resources to their own product as compared with competing outlets for these same resources. Since the consumers of the company's product pay for this investment by means of a hidden tax above and beyond the current production cost of the item purchased, the company managers have a very considerable responsibility to these consumers, for it is their money which gives the company its increased power through expansion. The managers have an even wider public responsibility, too, for the large corporations have the ability to shape the growth of the national economy by using other people's money.

Perhaps the most striking manifestation of the claim of economic trusteeship is the approach in labor relations pioneered by General Electric and imitated by some other firms. In this approach, often called Boulwareism, after the General Electric vice president who fathered it a dozen or so years ago, the bargaining is taken out of collective bargaining, and, when contract negotiations take place, the company tells the workers and their union what is in their "balanced best interests."

The late Benjamin M. Selekman, a leading analyst of ethical problems in business, listed the following principles of Boulwareism:

1. Management knows best what should be done for its employees.
2. It should therefore make up its mind prior to any negotiations as to what should be its maximum offer to the union.
3. It should refuse to recede from or alter this offer in any substantial way.
4. It should take a strike, if necessary, and hold out until the union capitulates.

In 1960, G.E. had a high degree of success with its policy, routing the International Union of Electrical Workers in what *New York Times* reporter A. H. Raskin called "the worst setback any union has received in a nationwide strike since World War II." While other factors also contributed to the debacle, it seems reasonable to give some of the credit — or blame, depending on one's view — to G.E.'s hard sell for its trusteeship concept.

In 1962, the I.U.E.W. filed charges against G.E. before the National Labor Relations Board, contending that the application of Boulwareism to 1961 contract talks violated the requirement, written into national law in 1935, that both parties must bargain in good faith. In April 1963 an NLRB hearing examiner upheld the union. The company plans an appeal. Regardless of the outcome of the legal dispute, it seems indisputable that this approach to wage negotiations involves the unusual phenomenon of one party in interest asserting a trusteeship, on grounds that it can judge its own case, over the other party in interest — and over that party's vehement objections to the arrangement. If the Boulwareian concept were generally accepted — an unlikely occurrence — vast power over the distribution of income would accrue to the corporations. In fact, their power in this regard would be similar to that exercised in pre-union, pre-Wagner Act days, and the economic role of unions as an expression of independent worker sentiment would be seriously undermined.

Closely related to Boulewareism, and again in the realm of employer-employee relationships, is the view that employees should look to benevolent (and affluent) corporations, rather than to government, for such security measures as life and health insurance and pension funds. The widespread adoption of such programs — whether with the rhetoric of social conscience or with the more prosaic idea to reduce employee turnover — warrants notice because it poses a paradox in regard to business's general animus against "paternalism" and in favor of individual self-reliance. The paradox is apparently simply resolved: paternalism is a good thing when the corporation is trustee for employee welfare; it is a bad thing when the government is concerned with welfare, even though the government is comprised of the people's chosen representatives.

Where a union contract is not involved, and particularly when rights are not fully vested in the employees, fringe-benefit welfare programs in the private sector have the character of benevolent autocracy, for they exist on sufferance of management and may be discontinued without the employees having any recourse. They are then entirely matters of "corporate conscience" and not at all matters of individual right in an industrial society. Welfare capitalism seems to distribute such benefits unevenly. Different corporations appear to have different consciences in this regard. Or, perhaps more pertinently, different corporations have different competitive situations; for some of them it is relatively easy to assume the costs of such programs, while others, who may be very conscientious, yet find themselves unable to assume the heavy financial burden which is involved.

POLITICAL TRUSTEESHIP

In the conventional wisdom of laissez faire, the corporation had no political responsibilities, nor even a rationale for any interest in political affairs so long as governments did not "intervene" in private business. The firm operated as best it could within the legal framework of capitalism and the economic framework of competition. In the modern mixed economy, however, corporations are not only much concerned to protect their own immediate legislative interests, but are reaching out in an attempt to create a business-oriented political and social framework within which all public decision-making would be constrained. Instead of the society channeling business decisions within the bounds of public interest, the corporations seek to channel public-interest decisions within business-interest bounds.

The "better business climate" campaigns, for which General Electric Corporation and the Manufacturers Association of Syracuse can be given major credit, exemplify this tendency toward political trusteeship. The explicit goal of the campaigns is to shape community attitudes and public policies, as expressed in taxing and spending programs, in ways congenial to business interests. Low taxation becomes a civic obligation, regardless of what this means for the level of community services. Corporate executives are adjured to participate in community affairs as conscious representatives of their firms. Thus a G.E. spokesman has written that "the responsibility to step forward with his views on business-connected matters is a proper part of a manager's responsibility, and the stands he takes should be in the name of the corporation." And Richard Eells, in describing the "metrocorporation" (his word for the extreme concept of a multi-functional corporation), says:

> [Such a corporation] assumes a right — and a responsibility to its own constituencies — to *help shape the economic, social, and political environment to its own ends* [italics mine], as well as to what it considers to be society's ends. . . . It is actively concerned with the electorate at all levels of public government in order to insure representation that favors the multiple goals of a great enterprise.

G.E., Ford, American Can, Gulf Oil, and other firms have taken positions, as "corporate citizens," on such questions of public policy as medical care for the aged, foreign aid, and federal aid to education. Such subjects are "business-connected" only in the sense that their substantial financial dimension affects, directly and indirectly, the general level of taxation, including corporate taxes. Yet these corporations see it as their right — some of them call it an obligation — to intervene in political decisions affecting the "community climate."

The right to speak as corporations, as distinguished from the right of individual executives to express political opinions on their own, seems to rest on the legal fiction, stated classically by Justice John Marshall in the Dartmouth College case of 1819, that a corporation is a legal person, and on the Supreme Court's application, in the late nineteenth century, of the rights stated in the Fourteenth Amendment to the corporation because it was a "person." While this fiction seems essential for some purposes — e.g., collective ownership and defense of law suits — nothing in law or political theory or economics requires that it be given the same scope as natural personality. For example, the First Amendment's protection of religious belief is simply irrelevant to the corporate "person," though vital to real persons. Are we not also confusing fiction and reality when we speak of corporate free speech? The right to free speech of corporation executives and shareholders as real persons must be accorded exactly the same high constitutional position as the same right of all other individuals. But that is a quite different matter from giving this right to an inanimate collectivity that is a person only by legal courtesy.

Whether business executives can dissociate themselves politically from their corporate interests, as George Romney has suggested, or whether, as Leland Hazard believes, they will inevitably reflect their institutional interests in their political expressions, their corporations need not become their spokesmen. Free speech for executives and shareholders does not require free speech for corporations as autonomous persons.

Strictly speaking, the corporation, being an artificial person, can have no conscience or policy viewpoint of its own. When we speak of a corporate political position, we mean the political position of living men. The advocates of corporate political activity have failed to answer these questions. How are the positions taken by corporate officers or boards to be authorized? Who is being represented by these boards?

Corporate boards are formally elected to office, not by a majority of stockholders, but by a majority of shares of stock voted. A money-weighted suffrage may not have much public importance as it affects internal corporate affairs, but if this were used to legitimize political positions in the external world it would be in sharp conflict with the public ethic of a society that outlawed the property qualification for suffrage more than a century ago.

In any case, stockholders do not closely control corporate contributions for charitable and educational purposes, so there is little reason to expect them to assert themselves in the political activities of the firm either. But, if the corporation claims to act politically for a broader constituency of suppliers, employees, and distributors, does not the ethic of democracy require that those groups have a voice in determining their "representative's" political position?

If the corporate managers claim simply to be representing the corporation itself, then we are right back to the nonsensical situation of real men representing an artificial entity with no membership to instruct its representatives. And, if the resources of a billion dollar corporation can be thrown into the political balance by officers who are in effect accountable only to themselves, what happens to the principle of political equality?

Even if a basis for legitimacy were to be devised, the corporations' claim of conscientious trusteeship would still suffer from some notable gaps. Where large expenditures are involved, firms actively assert their conception of the common good — usually a conception in which the role of government is minimized. Where the public question does not basically involve expenditures, business interest is often minimal. The civil rights issue is the outstanding illustration. The president of the Chamber of Commerce in 1962, H. Ladd Plumley, told a *New York Times* reporter that business wanted more recognition from government of its community-mindedness. "Where a city or town is showing progress, they [the businessmen] are providing the civic leadership," said Plumley. Yet he also explained that the C. of C. considers civil rights to be "not part of the Chamber's business." Civil rights are thus adjudged not part of community progress!

This narrow view of community development, defining progress essentially in terms of business volume, may make more sense for the business firm than a more expansive approach, for the latter would create more conflict with the stockholder-profit orientation. But that is not the issue at the moment: we are simply noting that the claim to social and political trusteeship has some gaps in it.

THE NATURE OF THE CORPORATION

Paralleling, and in some ways underlying, the development of the concept of corporate behavior as socially responsible trusteeship is the development of a new concept of the corporate institution. The classical concept of the firm gives it a clearly defined group membership and a clearly defined goal: stockholders are the members and maximum financial return on their investment is the goal. In this model, responsibility is defined as running to stockholders only and as being exclusively financial. Public welfare is a public function or a job for eleemosynary institutions, but not one for business firms. Employee welfare — beyond payment of a going wage — is not a corporate responsibility, though at times it may be advantageous to the corporation's profit in the long run to provide fringe benefits as a stimulus to employee morale and a deterrent to turnover. Any contribution to the larger community's welfare, or to national economic stabilization, or to the health of the political system, is seen as an accidental byproduct of profit-seeking or as a matter for individual, not corporate, involvement. The business firm minds its own business and leaves the rest of the economy to the beneficent workings of the market.

A corollary to this classic concept of the corporate institution is that it would be logically contradictory for the corporation simultaneously to embrace the concept of the primacy of the stockholders and to claim to seek the balanced best interests of stockholders along with all other claimant or clientele groups. Yet it is also apparent that this concept does not entirely remove the corporation from welfare actions, to the extent that these may be seen as good business. As one executive has said, "good conscience is good business."

Quite different is the emerging concept of the corporation as a social institution with diversified member-groups and diffused and broadened responsibilities. A major element in this conception is the notion that the corporation acknowledges — nay, asserts — as close a relationship to employees (sometimes unguardedly called "members" of the corporation), suppliers and distributors, ultimate consumers, and the local and national community, as to stockholders. If the managers see their structural position as that of judges, or, less pretentiously, brokers, among all these clientele groups, rather than as representative agents of the stockholder group alone, then they have a plausible rationale for putting forth a claim to trusteeship and general social responsibility.

Further, this concept can point to foundations in the Berle-Means thesis of separation of ownership from control. How the managers envisaged their role could have little impact on their actual behavior if the shareowners were in fact in a position to demand single-minded devotion to their immediate interests. For example, Hayek has proposed that each stockholder's individual permission be required for re-investment retention of his share of each year's profits, instead of the directors determining this for him. Under such a system, it is dubious that the shareowners would permit managements to play the role of balancers of diverse interests to any appreciable extent. But the Hayek proposal appears to stand no chance whatsoever of being adopted, and it ignores the owner-control split.

Assured income and freedom from ownership pressures are thus two of the main prerequisites for a corporation which intends to exercise social responsibility. However, just as the older theory of the traditional corporation bounded by market forces and ownership interests does not entirely foreclose welfare expenditures, the new theory does not necessarily warrant that all interests affected by corporate actions will be equitably balanced: while it makes the claim of disinterested trusteeship plausible, it may nevertheless be defective and deficient. We turn now to analysis of the limitations and problems of the socially responsible metrocorporation.

CRITIQUE: IT CANNOT WORK

The thesis of social responsibility requires a lessening of emphasis on the profit motive. It assumes the reality of this de-emphasis because management is no longer compelled to bow to the stockholder. But, since the stockholder interest is not the only possible reason for an emphasis on profit, this assumption is not necessarily valid. And in fact we find good reason for denying its validity: profitability still overrides other considerations, though the "profit motive" needs some reformulation for modern applicability.

Profit still remains the life-blood for the corporate institution's survival and welfare; profit is not merely a return on investment for risk-taking stockholders. Also, the financially strong firms with substantial market power are more concerned with profitability sustained over the years than with maximum immediate profit. The modern rule appears to be to make immediate profit as high as possible without interfering with long-run profitability. The price-gouging and deceptive practices common to fly-by-night operators are avoided by brand-name producers because the boomerang effect would harm long-term profitability, if not survival. (Of course, other reasons operate, too: the large firm is not as tempted to operate unethically as was the individual producer of old who, because of competition, had only a small profit; and the ethical sense in these respects of many managers does appear to be better developed now than in earlier periods of business history, because community mores as a whole no longer embrace the dog-eat-dog philosophy.)

Many actions taken on behalf of long-run profitability have no provable effect on the balance sheet; much good-will publicity and expenditure are of this nature. Some observers have suggested that, because the connection cannot be proved, such actions constitute a shift away from the profit motive. This judgment seems unwarranted. The managers believe and hope that their good-will expenditures will enhance profits, and so long as they are operating on this premise, profit is still the motive.

There is even one recent development which re-creates the individual profit-making motive of old—not for shareholders otherwise unconnected with the enterprise, but for managers who receive part of their compensation in the form of stock options. The stock option, widely adopted in the past decade, directly interests the manager in maximizing profits — even short-run profits — and constitutes a structural feature quite contradictory to the concept of the disinterested trustee.

The profit motive does serve some crucial functions today. For one thing, it provides a measurable assessment of managerial performance. Perhaps it is not the only factor in making a man's career. Perhaps his civic participation, his ability to build employee morale, his success in general public relations count, too, so long as his operation shows a profit. But one doubts that any firm will long retain a division manager who excels at these ancillary parts of his job and turns in a recurrent deficit.

It is also not possible to contend that the business firm, at least within the existing system, can afford to ignore profitability or subordinate it to other considerations to such an extent that the firm operates at a loss and thus threatens its own survival as a goods-producing institution. Neither the firm nor the society would gain from such a mode of operation. The rate of profit will remain controversial. If corporations relied more on external financing of expansion they would not need as high a profit rate as they now insist on, as shown in Roger Blough's defense of the abortive 1962 steel price increase on the ground that only through higher profit could his firm expand. But that is not to say that the difference between profit and loss becomes a subordinate matter or one of indifference.

There is a sizable literature, written by sympathetic observers of the corporate scene and even by some participants, supporting the thesis that profit remains crucial to the managerial role. Indeed, some would go further and argue for a different model of the corporation, a model which sees the welfare of the institution, of the corporation itself, as the primary value, not the welfare of stockholders or surrounding satellite groups. Thus James C. Worthy writes of the need for a new theory of profit and the enterprise:

> The first responsibility of the enterprise is for economic performance. This is its social function and its *only social justification* [italics mine]. Under modern conditions economic performance requires organization, and organization requires stability and continuity. Thus in a realistic sense the modern corporation is run not for its "owners" but for the enterprise itself. . . . By adding a time dimension, the rise of the modern corporation has created a new situation. The standard is no longer the maximizing of profits but the continuity of the enterprise.
>
> . . . .
>
> A more realistic and more defensible doctrine of profits will have to be built around the survival needs of the enterprise as an instrumentality of social service.

Similarly, Peter Drucker asserts that the basis for a new theory of business lies in the question, what are the survival needs of the business? The firm's only purpose, he says, is to supply an economic good or service. Profitability is a survival need because of the risks attendant upon that purpose. This need, he asserts, is objective, existing regardless of motive. The appropriate question to be asked about profits, then, is simply: What is the *minimum* profit needed to face the risks?

Economist James S. Earley made a careful study of the statements and actions of large corporations and then summarized the role of profit in modern management theory:

> The major goals of modern large-scale business are high managerial incomes, good profits, a strong competitive position, and growth. Modern management does not view these goals as seriously inconsistent but rather, indeed, as necessary, one to the other. Competitive strength and even survival, management believes, require large innovative and substantial growth expenditures in the rapidly changing technical and market conditions of the present day. Since growth by merger is hazardous and frequently impossible, large and more or less continuous capital expenditures are necessary. For well-recognized reasons, management wishes to minimize outside financing, so the funds for most of these expenditures must be internally generated. This requires high and growing profits above dividend levels. So, too, do high managerial rewards. High and rising profits are hence an instrument as well as a direct goal of great importance.

Writing of the concept of balance of interest, Herrymon Maurer points to the overriding need for the executive to consider the welfare of his organization:

> The Radio Corporation of America has ten basic policies governing its activities; they relate to research and development of new products and services, high quality, low prices, reasonable salaries and wages, opportunity for advancement, reasonable dividends, contribution to culture, preservation of freedoms, cooperation with the government, and service. Were an R.C.A. executive to consider all these policies in arriving at a decision, he might easily find himself inextricably enmeshed in a variety of social problems to which there are no easy answers. But if he asks himself what sensible difference his decision will make to the continued good health of R.C.A., he is then in a position to give ready answers.

And a related viewpoint was expressed by Sylvia and Benjamin Selekman:

> It remains unreal and impractical to expect a corporation to operate with equal proficiency as a technical tool mobilizing economic and scientific power to produce goods and services *and* as a social institution with human beings depending upon it both inside and outside its gates. If power is a necessity to maintain and increase our standard of living, management's first response must always be to maintain the enterprise in good health; that is to say, its power must be kept at the highest level of efficiency. Certainly one must not risk bankruptcy. Thus, if, after careful and even painful consideration, transfer of a factory to a new location is the only way of survival, then move one must, regardless of the cost to the old community and its people. At best, only ameliorative measures may be applied, such as separation wages, help in finding other jobs, relief, and so on. Again, few if any enterprises have large enough resources to meet by themselves the impact of severe unemployment, or old age, or serious illness. To spend resources to meet total social needs might indeed imperil the corporation as a productive tool, so that it could no longer serve its main purpose of creating goods and services.

The problem of civil rights provides a concrete example of the conflict which sometimes occurs between corporate conscience and the profit criterion. In early 1958, chain variety stores in the South were caught between segregationists and integrationists when Negroes attempted to seat themselves at the lunch counters of the stores. According to the *Wall Street Journal,* the chains were "not anxious to say much" about the problem. A Woolworth executive said that the firm tries to be a "good neighbor" in the communities where it does business, by going along with what "our neighbors" want the firm to do. In days past the only neighbors who counted were the whites. Since Negroes have begun to assert their power as consumers, two opposing sets of neighbors exist. The stores are caught in the middle. Their response evidently is to consult not their consciences but their profit-and-loss statements in trying to assess the best policy. Fortunately for the cause of civil rights, the Negro market is growing larger and larger, so it is increasingly in the interest of corporations to see that the Negro is served in stores. Thus profit and welfare will gradually work together in this instance.

But what if one insisted that the corporation had a social responsibility to take a more conscientious position in such situations? Would any management voluntarily commit economic suicide?

In a related situation, a group of Greyhound Corporation stockholders tried to get the firm to cease segregation in Southern buses. Theodore Levitt, business consultant, tells the story and asks a question:

> It filtered up through the courts and finally was passed over to the SEC [Securities Exchange Commission], because they wanted it as a petition of the stockholders to vote on it. The SEC threw it out on the grounds that the Greyhound Corporation was in business for profit, not for social reforms. Now, everyone is arguing that the corporation should be involved in more of these welfare activities. If enough people continue arguing vigorously, one of these days the SEC is going to rule the other way. And that day will see the end of capitalism as we know it today. We will be motivated, not by gain, but by goodness; not by profit, but by service. Will this keep a business strong?

In another article, Levitt suggests that welfare capitalism "stops at the pocketbook," and indeed should do so. Consider General Electric Company's reasoning in a case where it was defending the dismissal of several employees who in a loyalty investigation had exercised their right to avoid self-incrimination contained in the Fifth Amendment. This company, which makes a greater public display than any other of its freedom from stockholder domination and its sense of social responsibility, nevertheless used the profit interest of the firm to justify these dismissals. It asserted that unless it dismissed the employees its institutional image might be harmed and customers lost.

In short, profit-making still counts; institutional survival is the overriding criterion. When welfare or cultural expenditures are seen as "paying off," they will be undertaken. When they conflict with profit, they will be passed by. In the cultural sphere, a good example is provided by Standard Oil of New Jersey's widely-heralded rescue of the "Play of the Week" on an independent New York area television channel a few years ago. The program had had a *succès d'estime*, but was a financial failure. Esso stepped in at the opportune moment to pick up the tab and keep the play on the boards. For this exercise of conscience, the company received the humble gratitude of television critics and audiences, including presumably a good many people who paid no attention at all to most of the company's normal advertising. A member of the firm's public relations staff later explained, however, that the instigation to act was a matter of timing: if Esso had not been prepared to move quickly when maximum exploitation of the sponsorship could be achieved, he suggested, it would not at all have been worthwhile to sponsor an independent, small-audience program of this type. That is to say, it was not a cultural conscience but a business calculation that led Esso into the venture. The corporate conscience is, then, a self-interested conscience and hardly a reliable vehicle for achieving the common good. It cannot work, at least not in the way asserted by proponents of social trusteeship.

CRITIQUE: IT DOES NOT WORK

Some have argued that, like the leaning tower of Pisa or the flight of the hummingbird, the corporate conscience does work even though in principle it cannot. To dispose of this argument we can recite briefly some corporate actions which demonstrate that conscience is an insufficient regulator of corporate power and an insufficient guide to public welfare.

Perhaps the most sensational example of the failure of conscience in recent years is the electrical equipment price-fixing case. Since it involved 29 firms, including the most self-conscious exponent of social responsibility, General Electric, it can hardly be contended that this instance of gross violation of the competitive ideal and of legally defined community standards was an isolated or individual failure. Some of the executives involved explicitly defended their behavior on the ground that it was good for the corporation. What was good for society was apparently not considered.

More broadly, what kind of business conscience do advertising patterns point to? Quite apart from fly-by-night distributors of patent medicine who do not claim to be conscientious, we have the example of major oil companies making wildly exaggerated claims for gasoline additives of, to say the least, dubious merit; of pharmaceutical manufacturers making slight changes in existing drugs and claiming major advances, and of the same firms rushing drugs to market without sufficient testing and without mentioning deleterious side-effects in their promotional literature to physicians; of detergent, shaving cream, and toothpaste advertising whose flagrant exaggerations and misrepresentations keep them under constant investigation by the Federal Trade Commission; and cigarette companies aiming much of the advertising of their carcinogenic product at teen-age youth in an effort to start them smoking. This last example is particularly instructive of the conflict between company interest and public interest: no one really expects tobacco companies to dissolve themselves voluntarily, or support educational campaigns to discourage smoking because of the probable connection with cancer. Yet the admission that we do not have any such expectation is also an admission that conscience is an insufficient regulator.

In another area, there is the widespread business attack on all job-protection efforts of unions as simple "featherbedding." Granting that featherbedding does exist, business's characterizing every union job-protection effort as such is distressing, because, in A. H. Raskin's words, it "blots out consideration of the human problems that must be solved as part of the shift to automated machines that eliminate men at the same time that they hold out the promise of a higher standard of living for mankind." Economic analysts have been saying for a decade that automation is not a self-solving problem, that imaginative approaches by business and labor and bold public policies will be needed to achieve equitable and efficient adjustments; yet some business spokesmen have insisted that there is no problem. Is it the conscience or the corporate pocketbook speaking?

Or take the American Jewish Committee's finding, a couple of years ago, that Jews comprise one-half of one per cent of executive personnel in a group of large corporations, yet account for 8 per cent of the college-educated population. The Committee's charge of discriminatory hiring and promotional policies seems warranted.

General Electric has a corporate policy of strict adherence to the antitrust laws, yet its top officials have confessed that they supervised their subordinate officials — even vice-presidents — so poorly that they were ignorant of illegal practices which had persisted over a period of years. The first responsibility of a firm is, surely, to treat its customers honestly. Yet G.E., Westinghouse, and more than 25 other electrical firms were apparently so busy proving themselves "good citizens" in other ways that they they neglected this basic duty. Would not both corporations and the public be better off if the former left community welfare to private and public agencies designed for the purpose and concentrated on producing the best product at the lowest, competitive price? Neither the corporate nor the individual conscience is served by patterns of business behavior that urge the executive to serve on the Boy Scout Council while he is breaking the nation's laws, conniving to raise costs for other firms by price-fixing agreements, misrepresenting the firm's product, or gouging a small distributor. In short, the doctrine of diffuse social responsibility has diverted management from its economic responsibilities and diverted the public's eyes from the many instances in which the result is economic irresponsibility.

The concept of social trusteeship thus belies the actual behavior of corporations, which remain profit- and institution-oriented. And, despite the owner-control split, the structure of the corporation remains equally unsuited to the larger role. In law, the structure remains one of accountability to stockholders, impaired as that may be in practice. While the law attempts, perhaps vainly, to maintain stockholder accountability through such devices as proxy rights and in some states cumulative voting, no mechanisms exist to give equivalent voice to other "clientele" groups. Collective bargaining gives, it is true, countervailing power to unions within a circumscribed scope of affairs and where unions exist. But few white-collar workers are covered by unions, and even a sizable proportion of blue-collar men remain uncovered. Furthermore, unionization can accomplish little when the concept discussed before, called Boulwareism, replaces bargaining in good faith.

Consumers remain almost totally unorganized; and, faced with massive advertising by business and having limited knowledge of what other alternatives are open to them, they do not possess, in their so-called "dollar-vote," an adequate substitute for organization. Distributors and suppliers are rarely able to achieve a power base to offset their dependence upon the giant manufacturers. And the community at large, both local and national, has no institutionalized voice at all in most business decisions, much as it may feel their impact.

Since the forces of the market place and the assumptions of the law both impel managements toward a balance-sheet view of their responsibilities, the absence or relative weakness of corresponding forces to make managements think equally of the interests and claims of other groups renders the business structure unsuited to the assumption of responsibilities for community welfare. As Abram Chayes has pointed out, the stockholder has probably the loosest connection with the corporation of any of the claimant groups, yet the only institutionalized accountability runs to him. A very considerable restructuring of the internal governing process of corporations would be necessary before it could be called fitted for the claims of social trusteeship.

In the area of employee and community welfare, for instance, the great weakness of corporate performance lies in the unevenness of welfare plans. It is not in accord with either equity or social necessity that the distribution of welfare benefits be determined by the relative market power, hence administered-pricing abilities, of different firms, rather than by the needs of individuals. Retail and service trade workers, and agricultural workers, are in greatest need of "fringe benefits," yet get the least of them, publicly as well as privately. Retail stores and textile manufacturing are low-wage industries.

Their employees need auxiliary welfare programs more than the high-wage employees protected by strong unions in the automobile or appliance industries. Yet they get less, for their industries are less profitable. Those who do get extensive fringe benefits are often getting them out of the pockets of those who do not, because they are financed through consumer purchases. Thus the inequities of distribution are compounded by the inequity of financing arrangements.

CRITIQUE: IT SHOULD NOT WORK

The fundamental argument against the more expansive version of the ethic of social responsibility is that, even if it could and did work, it should not. For it is anti-democratic to the core and and would tend toward a business-elite system in which corporate power would control society without any corresponding reciprocal control by society.

The opinion of Friedrich A. Hayek should be persuasive at this point for those who think this to be a "radical" or "anti-capitalist" view. Writes Hayek, with reference to such corporate activities as grants to higher education:

> If the large aggregations of capital which the corporations represent could, at the discretion of the management, be used for any purpose approved as morally or socially good, if the opinion of the management that a certain end was intellectually or esthetically, scientifically or artistically desirable, were to justify expenditure by the corporation for such purposes, this would turn corporations from institutions serving the expressed needs of individual men into *institutions determining which ends the efforts of individual men should serve* [italics mine]. To allow the management to be guided in the use of funds, entrusted to them for the purpose of putting them to the materially most productive use, by what they regard as

> their social responsibility, would create centers of uncontrollable power never intended by those who provided the capital. It seems to me, therefore, clearly not desirable that general higher education or research should be regarded as legitimate purposes of corporation expenditure because this would not only vest powers over cultural decisions in men selected for capacities in an entirely different field, but would also establish a principle which, if generally applied, would enormously enhance the actual powers of corporations.

One does not have to agree with Hayek's emphasis on stockholder rights as the major value to be served in order to agree with his analysis of the power implications of manager-determined social warfare activities.

If corporations, through their ability to administer prices, can tax consumers to obtain vast revenues and then determine unilaterally what use of these funds will most contribute to a good society, as the managers envisage the good society, their power is then extended from the economic realm — the production of wanted goods and services — to social, educational, cultural, and political areas, which would give them the ability to control other people's lives and the direction of social development. This is a task for the people themselves, operating through institutions formally and substantially accountable to the people, not for the self-perpetuating oligarchy of corporate directors.

Nor is it entirely a matter of employee and community welfare expenditures. It is also very much a matter of economic development beyond the confines of the company itself. That is, the size of firms and the interdependence of industries and regions mean that the impact of decisions of the corporate officers is not restricted to the internal structure of the corporation but may affect, directly and indirectly, ofter firms and their workers and communities. If corporate economic decisions are not controlled either by market forces or by stockholders, then, in the absence of new social inventions, they are essentially uncontrolled. From the viewpoint of society, control by the managers' sense of responsibility is no control at all.

In summary, then, we find that the concept of social responsibility and trusteeship or corporate conscience, however phrased, is to be rejected as unworkable in its extreme form. Since we have no desire to return to the dog-eat-dog days of robber-baron laissez faire, we are presented with an apparent dilemma. Is there a way out? I believe there is: we must adopt the concept of the corporation as a self-oriented institution (not one oriented either to stockholders or to the general welfare as such) and accept the inevitability of economic power, that is, the impossibility of restoring market competition as regulator of corporate conduct, economic and otherwise. What role, then, can the corporate conscience legitimately play?

A ROLE FOR THE CORPORATE CONSCIENCE

While many businessmen laud the idea that a corporation should be socially responsible, others join with social critics in deploring the notion that business firms can be run for goodness rather than gain. Some escape the problem by adopting the line that what's good for business is good for the country. Still others contend that welfare capitalism — in the form of pensions, life and health insurance, employee social and athletic facilities, and charitable and educational donations — is not the result of conscience but of long-run profit calculation; in other words, that good conscience is in fact simply good business, because it reduces employee turnover and creates a favorable public image.

The business community itself is in a state of uncertainty and beset both by demands to seek goodness and by critics' doubts that it can be other than profit-seeking. Economists, on the whole, tend to reject the social-responsibility argument, partly on the non-economic grounds of their distaste for paternalism, partly because they realize that the trusteeship doctrine is not consistent with what has been the very basis of their academic discipline: the concept of a powerless firm reacting as a rational, profit-minded man would to market stimuli and competitive forces. The integrity of the market mechanism as an allocator of resources and incomes and impersonal determiner of economic development ranks high in the economist's scheme of professional values. The substitution of a system of consciously managed resources, employing criteria other than short-run profitability, is very offensive. Thus, for example, economist Ben Lewis, despite his doubts regarding the viability of the competitive model, writes: "Profit-seeking is not only acceptable to our way of life, it is indispensable. . . . the logic of our economy will not permit the drive of profit motivation to be blunted or its direction to be diffused by the social conscience of individuals." This passage was written, incidentally, as part of an argument against "economics by admonition," that is, the attempt by recent Presidents to bring the behavior of individual firms into accord with the needs of the whole economy by rhetorical appeals to act "responsibly." If the thinking of businessmen is confused on this matter, it is equally true that academic economists have reached the point of no return. Their dilemma is our focal point here.

Rejecting reliance on the uncontrolled conscience of corporations, and rejecting also, as most of them do, any "hard" governmental controls over prices, wages, or investment of the kind accepted in wartime, economists are in the position of advocating what they know to be an impossible program: the re-creation of a classically competitive economy by vigorous enforcement of the antitrust statutes to obtain dissolution and divestiture of the giants. Barring success in this, and it is barred politically as well as economically, they end up, by logic rather than intent, as *de facto* supporters of the existing situation.

A few economists, perhaps most notably the elder-statesman of the profession, John Maurice Clark, Gerhard Colm of the National Planning Association, and Edwin G. Nourse, would accept the fact of giantism in varying degrees and that some criterion of responsibility on the part of private centers of economic power is an essential corollary to that acceptance. Thus Nourse has argued that, in lieu of government control, we can attempt re-establishment of "conditions of price competition instead of power competition," but, apparently doubting that this will go far enough, he goes on to assert, in direct contrast to Ben Lewis's statement above:

> With growing economic sophistication and clearer sense of their responsibility on the part of executives of large industrial, commercial, and labor aggregations, we may hope to move closer toward the self-sustained balance which both President Truman and President Eisenhower have repeatedly stated should be the contribution of private business. They have, I believe, been soundly advised in taking this position.

And Clark has made the inescapability of power and responsibility on the part of private economic groups a central theme of several books in the postwar years, including *Economic Institutions and Human Welfare* and *Alternative to Serfdom*. In the first-mentioned, he cites a range of value-laden considerations not accommodated by the money-measuring system of the market, and hopefully asserts of the large corporations that "there is more and more recognition of responsibilities beyond those which the market automatically enforces."

To Nourse's and Clark's stress on the need for private responsibility, Colm adds the necessary ingredient of a corresponding need for community-sanctioned guidelines within which private responsibility is to be exercised:

> The existence of countervailing forces may lead to a countervailing stalemate unless there is a superior concept of economic performance which defines the scope but also the limits of the power of organized groups. Powerful organizations can play a productive role in a democratic society only if there is in the community some notion of the role they can and should play in the economic and social life as a whole and of the limits beyond which their power can be harmful.

All three of these men recognize that self-interest cannot suffice as the regulator of powerful groups, even though it may have been adequate to control individual behavior in the preindustrial era. Thus the question becomes less one of whether corporations should act responsibly than of the scope of their responsibilities and the kind of institutional accountability required to ensure that private conscience acts in accord with public needs and expectations.

The hypothesis I wish to put forth can best be stated as a series of interrelated propositions:

1. The more closely related a problem is to the production process, the greater the need, and justification, for a sense of responsibility for it on the part of industrial managers. Conversely, the further removed a problem is from production — education, community recreation, national social legislation, for example — the less reason or legitimacy exists for corporate involvement.

2. We should not demand or expect social conscience to

overrule the survival needs of the firm. That is, we should not expect, or ask, corporations to balance all social interests equally. To do so would be futile because of the overwhelming evidence that even firms which claim to be Solomon-like arbiters, in fact, place the good of the firm first. It would be an invitation to chaos, for it would mean abandonment of market cues and of the price system, without being able to replace them with any other publicly sanctioned system of guidelines.

3. We should distinguish between the minimum standards of community conduct for which corporations can be made responsible and those activities of conscience which they engage in only if they wish to do so.

4. To supplement a greater social responsibility on the part of corporations, a system of accountability to the public should be established for those instances where the failure of business to act responsibly would cause not just individual distress but also grave consequences for the whole national economy.

5. The best proof of the existence of a true social consciousness on the part of corporate managements would be for them to cease their efforts to block adequate public-sector welfare activities.

6. Wherever general consensus can be reached, legal measures should establish minimum standards of welfare, thus leaving business's social conscience free, to the extent market conditions permit, to supplement the minimum. For example, as the automation problem increases, the community may determine that each firm should bear some part of the social cost involved in worker dislocations caused by technological change. Whatever was thus decided would become a legal minimum — perhaps in the form of severance pay — which all firms would then take into account as a cost factor in their automation planning. Until and unless such a consensus is reached and embodied in law, such matters as severance pay,

retraining and a right to move with the job when a plant is relocated will remain matters appropriate to conscientious action.

7. Paternalism and cultural dictation by corporate money should be avoided.

What would and would not be appropriate action for the conscientious and socially responsible manager under these broad rules? Here are some further illustrations.

We have already criticized the strategy under which some managements have extended the scope of their activities into areas whose connection with production is peripheral at best, while not meeting their responsibilities, legal and moral, under the antitrust laws. These latter responsibilities are by no means the only ones closely related to production toward which managements might well turn their conscientious attention. The industrial workplace still lacks a suitable human environment, as a reading of Harvey Swados' *On the Line* so feelingly illustrates. Here is a real challenge to all our consciences, but one in which the business manager, in co-operation with union officials, is most strategically placed to bring about necessary improvements. As our earlier critique suggested, the whole field of product advertising invites action in the name of the managerial conscience. In industries such as the automobile industry that are characterized by strong seasonal fluctuations, a sense of social responsibility could lead to efforts at flattening out the peaks and valleys of employment, since these are dictated not by technological necessity but by humanly created and thus humanly changeable marketing patterns. Industrial firms whose operations now pollute the streams and the air could support research into uses of waste materials and purifying processes so that we could breathe clean air and have a greater proportion of our water resources for drinking and recreation to meet the demands of a rapidly expanding population.

All of these matters intimately affect, or are intimately affected by, the process of producing and distributing goods and services, the central function of the industrial corporation. Action in the directions indicated would improve the climate for people and provide an outlet for managers' consciences far more appropriate than present attempts at charitable, educational, and community welfare activities not so closely related to economic functions.

What about race integration and the corporate conscience? This illustrates the difference between responsibility and actions which go beyond economic responsibility. Take the case of Modern Community Developers, a housing firm specializing in interracial projects. Acting within the price system, this firm builds groups of houses to be sold on an open-occupancy basis, which is made known to all comers. When this works, as in Princeton, New Jersey, the firm presumably prospers. When it does not work, as in Deerfield, Illinois, where a scared suburban middle class has embroiled the firm in law suits and stopped its planned construction, the firm loses money. Modern Community Developers had no responsibility (prior to President Kennedy's anti-discrimination order) to take the much greater risks of open-occupancy policy; in doing so, its exercise of conscience is that of an owner-manager who is risking his own funds and those of associates who are consciously committed to the same goal. And his community-welfare approach to housing is subject to external test: no one has to buy his houses. Both of these factors distinguish this exercise of conscience from most activities of the publicly held giant corporations.

Illustrative of matters beyond the appropriate scope of the corporate conscience as envisaged by our rules are charitable and educational donations; political propaganda (by institutional advertising, employee publications, etc.) relating to public welfare programs, local-national government relations, foreign aid, the balance of public and private expenditures; and community paternalism. These matters are clearly not production-related in major function and are not matters in which business expertise bears much relevance to the making of appropriate judgments. Corporate action in these spheres involves an attempt to dictate to the external world, to autonomous institutions, as we have argued earlier. And because the business manager cannot generally be expected to transcend the criterion of what is good for the firm, success in his efforts would mean subordination of broad community standards to narrow corporate-survival standards.

The pattern suggested here leaves ample room for social consciousness to be devoted to internal economic affairs and the human problems arising directly out of these. Yet it also leaves non-business institutions free to pursue the common good in their own ways and by criteria better suited than are business standards to community welfare and cultural development.

III | Government: The Visible Hand

8 | The Expanding Economic Role of Government

THE MYTH OF LAISSEZ FAIRE

Perhaps the greatest American economic myth is the belief that private enterprise is self-sustaining, that the only political requirement for a healthy economy is a policy of laissez faire. It is small wonder, given this belief, that every increase in the scope of governmental economic activity is met with cries of alarm. Yet it is easily demonstrated that the freest economy imaginable would still require a considerable range of governmental actions and institutions, supporting as well as regulatory. As Wilbert E. Moore has written, "competition without rules is a contradiction in terms," and social controls are necessary "not only to maintain order in an economy which is only nominally self-regulating, but also to ensure the consistency of economic organization with such values as individual health and familial stability."

If government really left the economy alone, there would be no system of competition but Hobbes's war of each against all. Without governmental enforcement of contracts, business men would not dare to make them. If government did not protect property, each firm would have to hire its own police force — or even an army. Without a money system backed by government, we would be reduced to crude barter or constantly subjected to ruination by extreme fluctuations in the value of private money substitutes. Without governmental mechanisms for adjustment of disputes between employers and employees, our industrial relations would be patterned on the bloody model of the coal fields of 1900.

Government also provides organizational forms to fit business needs: proprietorships, partnerships, and the privilege of incorporation which vests the firm with immortality and the investor with limited liability. It develops procedures for bankruptcy and reorganizations, to minimize the economic and social losses of business failure. It rewards invention by giving it privileged economic status through the patent system. It collects and disseminates knowledge in support of business operations, as in research reports on technological developments and market opportunities, and it establishes standards essential to common exchange: weights and measures, grading, and labelling.

It is inconceivable that any economy could long endure in the absence of these governmentally provided supports. Certainly the modern, interdependent, complex industrialized economy could not. And businessmen recognize this, at least implicitly, for one does not hear them calling for repeal of the kinds of "intervention" mentioned to this point. What they object to is not intervention as such, but intervention which is regulatory rather than promotional. That is, it is not principle but self-interest which provides the rationale for their position.

The real question of government's role focuses on those activities which go beyond the provision of a legal framework. Undeniably, the extent of governmental involvement has vastly increased in this century. What are the causes of the more extensive role of government?

WHY GOVERNMENT'S ROLE HAS EXPANDED

The reasons for expanding governmental economic activity are a mixture of circumstantial development, increased knowledge of how an economy functions, and changing community values, each related to and reinforcing the others.

The rise of industrialization and its social corollary, urbanization, represent the circumstantial development. Perhaps the broadest effect of industrialization has been to substitute formal social controls for the informal ones of earlier society and to create new controls to handle problems that did not exist in the simpler and less interdependent technology of agricultural society.

As an example of new formal controls, we have the pure food and drug statutes and the Federal Trade Commission replacing the old attitude of *caveat emptor*. When consumer goods were largely limited to food and fiber products, "let the buyer beware" was not an impossible rule, for the consumer could easily be as knowledgeable as the seller regarding the desirable qualities in a vegetable or a pair of trousers made of natural fibers. But when industrialization and technological progress introduced a new and vastly extended range of products, complex in their mechanism and often artificial in their materials, common knowledge became a poor basis for purchase. The informal control by consumer information then required supplementation by formal protection. The Pure Food and Drug Act established an agency and a set of rules to guard the hopeful and gullible consumer from harmful remedies and contaminated foods. Today we are moving toward additional protection: to ensure against the great economic waste and personal financial distress caused by purchase of products which are ineffective though innocuous, by requiring that the producer prove his remedy has beneficial effect. The Kefauver hearings on the drug industry, whatever they prove about profits, have certainly demonstrated the necessity to safeguard the consumer against medically meaningless though commercially profitable innovations in prescription and proprietary drugs. President Kennedy's 1962 consumer protection message to Congress and his establishment of a Consumer Advisory Council exemplify the increasing activities on the part of government in areas where lack of consumer knowledge needs to be compensated for by formal social control.

Or consider antimonopoly legislation. When production was agricultural and producers were many and small, the consumer was protected by the market mechanism itself, which enabled the retail distributor to have a choice of suppliers. With the rise of national markets and industrial producers, the maintenance of competition became a matter for conscious policy as concentration of production in a few firms came to typify the situation. It was not a change from no regulation to government regulation, but from market regulation to government regulation.

To illustrate the need for new controls where no controls previously existed, we can cite the development of traffic rules, motorcycle policemen, and traffic courts and, in quite another sphere, blue-sky laws and the Securities Exchange Commission. Also zoning and land-use regulations are the by-product of industrial urbanization, which makes my neighbor's use of his property a matter of economic, esthetic, and hygienic concern to me.

In addition to supplying the supporting framework for business, government in industrial society is also necessarily called upon to provide a supporting framework for individuals and families. This is not the result of an alleged loss of "moral fiber" in the people, but of the living pattern of urban culture and the specialization and interdependence of industrial employment. In the pre-industrial society, people were literally more self-sufficient than it is possible for them to be today: the farm family grew its own food, made some of its own clothing and built its own house and outbuildings. Families were large, and children contributed economically by working in the fields or the house at an early age. Because there was a minimum of exchange and minimal use of cash, there was not the dependence upon cash income that there is today. The grandparents could be cared for within the home, and usually could continue to be useful members of the family, not a drain on their children's resources. When industrialism began to make some headway, and a son went off to the city to become a factory worker, it was still possible for him to return to the family farm if he lost his city job or became ill. Family responsibility for each member was then more feasible than it can be today.

Contrast with this picture the situation today, and the underlying causes for the expansion of economic welfare activities by government become quickly apparent. Production and consumption are divorced. The man does not work on his own farm but for an organization. He does not produce his own food, let alone clothing and housing, but performs a specialized task for a cash income, which he then exchanges for all of his family's needs. Loss of cash thus means loss of all sustenance. The family farm is no longer there to fall back on in rough times, nor would the urban-raised man know how to do farm work if it were available. Children in the city are economically unproductive; they cannot perform small tasks on their father's assembly line or in his office, as they could on the farm. Urban housing and the concentrated living patterns of the city do not easily accommodate three generations under one roof, so the grandparents require separate housing at separate expense. Furthermore, industrial employment is subject to fluctuations against which no individual can protect himself. Given the consequences of unemployment, and this inability to guard against it, income-support programs by government, such as unemployment compensation, disability compensation, health insurance, and old age pensions, can be seen as simply the modern equivalent of protections once, but no longer, provided by the socio-economic system itself.

While agricultural societies had good and bad seasons, and incredible human suffering might be the price of the latter, they could still not have the complete collapse of economy that happened in 1933, when one-fourth of the work force was unemployed. The business cycle did not originate with industrialization, but its consequences were so vastly magnified that the price paid for a self-adjusting economy became intolerable. Hence changed circumstances called forth another whole area of governmental function: the stabilization of employment, production, and prices.

Yet it was not just changed circumstance, for when we say that a situation becomes intolerable we are making a value judgment, not just describing a situation. Community value changes were just as essential a part of the expanding economic role of government as changes in the objective situation. When unemployment was thought of, in Spencerian terms, as the justly deserved punishment of the shiftless and lazy, no one thought to provide governmental protection. When "the devil take the hindmost" and *caveat emptor* were the slogans of the day, the social and economic costs of the crude early brand of capitalism were ignored with good conscience — at least by those whose opinions counted politically. In short, when doctrines of individualism held a monopoly on the operative ideals of the community, collective economic action was by definition anathema. There were critics who posed more humane values — like Disraeli and Dickens in England, Lincoln Steffens and Ida M. Tarbell in the United States — but their impact was felt only belatedly.

Concepts of social justice began to receive more articulate support, and wider public awareness and acceptance around the turn of the century. The almost Marxian criticism of capitalism embedded in Pope Leo XIII's encyclical, *Rerum Novarum;* the growth of an industrial working class for whom the individualist precepts of the Horatio Alger literature had a distinctly hollow ring; the development of the Brandeis brief to break down with factual recitations of suffering and inequity the Supreme Court's dogmatic assumption of economic harmony under laissez faire; and the beginnings of sociological analysis of power relationships — all these were forces undermining the Spencerian-Darwinian scheme of values.

Simultaneous change in conditions and in values provided the elemental forces necessary for development of new governmental roles; the catalytic agent was often a crisis or a catastrophe. The Triangle Shirt Waist Company fire in New York in 1911, in which 146 workers died, led to much factory legislation in 1912–14; ship losses led to radio requirements and legislation; and the depression of 1929–39 led to a whole range of programmatic and institutional innovations patterned on an industrially oriented scheme of values: the Securities and Exchange Commission, Home Owner's Loan Corporation, Old Age and Survivors Insurance, and the Council of Economic Advisers — just to list a few.

Nor is the conflict of values over yet. Roughly speaking, what Galbraith called the conventional wisdom and what Barry Goldwater and the NAM preach in the name of individualism represent vestiges of pre-industrial thinking, which are still quite lively, unfortunately. Such thinking contends for the power to shape public policy with what may be called the liberal-labor ideology, which accepts industrialization and recognizes its social imperatives — indeed, it overstresses them, say conservatives. The recent and continuing conflict over the means test versus the social-insurance approach to publicly provided medical care is a perfect case in point. The means-test philosophy dates back hundreds of years. Its view of man is that his dignity counts only when he is self-supporting; its view of the economy is that no one ever lacks adequate means of support except through his own shiftlessness or inadequacy. The social-insurance approach emphasizes the technical concept of risk-sharing, the ethical concept that dignity resides in all humans, not just the fortunate ones, and the economic concept that social costs and benefits are not synonymous with private costs and benefits as measured by the market. Pictures of the situation and systems of values are thus fused into total approaches to socio-economic problems, approaches with quite different implications for the range of public policy.

Two other developments were highly instrumental, and in some respects requisite, to expansion of government's economic role of social control. There was a recognition of social-economic institutions as man-made rather than divinely ordained, and, concurrently, the technical development of economic analysis as a social-scientific discipline. When social and economic systems were thought of as divinely ordained or as natural growths, it was popularly supposed that men neither could nor should make changes in the framework. If some men starved, it was regrettable; but nothing could be done in the face of "natural law." Although the early factory wage system reeked of injustice, one could not tamper with the "iron law of wages." Such crude doctrines of natural law, widely believed, for a long time effectively stopped social and economic reform measures, for "interference" with nature was immoral and, by definition, futile because "unnatural."

As the scientific spirit began to invade the sphere of moral philosophy and men began to doubt the finality of social institutions which showed great variation between cultures, it gradually came to be understood that social arrangements are what we make them, that within bounds set by resources and knowledge there are a great variety of ways in which goods production can be handled. And men began to demand that governments act as instigators of change to produce institutional patterns more in keeping with an enlightened humanist image of man. Although social science has become heavily self-conscious about its self-imposed role of analysis without prescription in recent years, its early growth came largely through men committed to engineering a better world. The draft of objectives circulated by Richard T. Ely in 1885 as a prospectus for an American Economics Association, for example, began with an explicit rejection of the laissez faire doctrine: "We regard the state as an educational and ethical agency whose positive aid is an indispensable condition of human progress. . . . We hold that the doctrine of laissez-faire is unsafe in politics and unsound in morals." Not all the economists of that time agreed with Ely, yet a milder version of this statement was incorporated into the original constitution of the Association. And some men would have made the Association's role even more activist. Simon Patten, for example, felt that the Association membership "should give in some specific form our attitude on all the leading questions where State intervention is needed."

Use of governmental power to achieve reform objectives was made socially feasible by the social scientists' demonstration that economic and other institutions were not the immutable creations of nature but the conscious and unconscious creations of man. What once had to be accepted, though regretted, could now be attacked: men could be blamed and held responsible; their behavior could be required to conform to standards other than those enshrined in the market mechanism; and institutions could be reformed to accord with humanistic aims.

The best will in the world will accomplish little, however, if objective analysis of the problem is faulty or techniques have not been developed for directing social forces toward the desired goal. Advances in economic theory and in techniques of measuring performance of the economy were therefore prerequisite to the translation of humane ideals into programs of public economic policy. Concretely, the Keynesian revolution provided an essential key to understanding the nature of the business cycle and the failure of conventional budget-balancing economics to pull the economy out of a slump once begun. President Roosevelt's initial attempts to cut government spending are a leading example of the perils of action on the basis of faulty analysis. The development of the national income model and its accompanying analysis of the flow of funds and the relationships among savings, investment, and consumption are the intellectual basis for policies aimed at growth and full employment. While our understanding of economic behavior still appears to lag far behind our understanding of the physical world, and our institutional arrangements for using economic knowledge are about as well adapted to our needs as the old wagon trail would be to a high-speed automobile, we do know enough now to avoid the grosser fluctuations of the business cycle. In fact, these and similar technical developments in economic science have probably been themselves a causative factor in the change in values from acceptance of adversity as God-given to community demands that the economy be controlled in the interests of the general public.

For all of these reasons then, the economic role of government has been enlarged many times over in our day. The ubiquity of this development in all economically advanced or advancing nations is sufficient proof against the unenlightened conservative's easy explanation that it is all the fault of "that man in the White House," whether Roosevelt, Truman, Eisenhower, or Kennedy. And the nature of the forces catalogued suggests that the limits of essential intervention have not yet been reached. This will become clearer as we turn now to brief description of the traditional, the more recent, and the just-emerging roles of government (particularly the national government) that arise from the necessity for social control of economic life.

TRADITIONAL ECONOMIC ROLES

The role of government which is least often acknowledged by businessmen, although it is the most hoary and traditional of all, is as promoter and, especially since the 1930's, customer of private enterprise. In the introductory section of this chapter we cited some of the ways in which government promotes business. These are but a small part of the story. Protective tariffs, land grants to railroads, and Alexander Hamilton's funding of the Revolutionary War debt, exemplify earlier American contributions of government to business growth, as does the Supreme Court's reading laissez faire into the Constitution in the period from 1880 to 1937.

In the twentieth century, business promotion has been the direct goal of many measures usually thought of as "regulatory." The Transportation Act of 1920, the subsidies of the

Civil Aeronautics Act, and the aid to railroads given in the 1958 legislation, for example, fall into this category, as do the "hot oil" compact, by which crude oil production is limited to a rate estimated as appropriate to expected demand, and sugar legislation which allocates markets among domestic producers, importers, and foreign producers. Each of these measures, while ostensibly protecting or enhancing the public's interests, has the effect of protecting and enhancing the financial interests of producers.

Outright subsidy, without a regulatory aim, is also a time-honored characteristic of the American political economy. A few of numerous examples are the Reconstruction Finance Corporation — began under President Hoover but only terminated under Eisenhower — which primed business for a generation; the Small Business Administration, which has supplemented private banking capital in more recent years; and the lead-zinc stabilization program of 1961, which will subsidize small producers at least through 1965.

Promotion through tax incentives has made "depletion allowance" and "rapid amortization" every-day terms. A whole generation of business firms owes its power as much to war-time rapid amortization as to competitive acumen.

The most important of all promotional developments have been by-products of governmental growth in providing collective services generally: roads, schools, and, in particular, defense. Since governments themselves engage in little direct goods-production, the vast rise in public budgets has meant a corresponding increase in public payments to private producers, as government "contracts out" its hardware and service programs.

As the technology has become more complex, governmental promotion of business has also added a new dimension: the stimulation of productivity through research and development expenditures. Herbert E. Striner comments on this as an aspect of America's "economic explosion":

> At the present time, the federal government accounts for about 60% of all the scientific research and development in the United States — either on its own, or through contracts.
>
> Through this research and development program, which we translate into technological innovation, the government has had a number of effects on the economy. It has made it possible for business to develop new products, reduce costs, improve production methods. It has accelerated the development of automation, which may have brought with it some technological overemployment because of a lack of good planning. But the list of results is too long to present here; suffice it to say that the impact has been considerable.
>
> One of the most interesting aspects of this particular welfare program is that the government took it on partly because of pressures brought to bear by industry. In many instances, industry cannot perform the kind of research and development that it needs because of excessively high costs. . . .
>
> For example, few people realize that the computer industry was developed on the basis of a wartime need, when the government decided that it needed a rapid means of computing firing and ballistic tables. The Ordnance people in the Army let a $300,000 contract to the Morse School of Engineering at the University of Pennsylvania, in 1942, which produced the first modern computer. . . .

Although most spokesmen for the Establishment, whether on the government or the industry side, deny vehemently that our economy requires tremendous defense expenditures to stay afloat, it is an indisputable fact that such expenditures are a sizable portion of total demand. And it is equally clear that the least diminution in the distribution of this largesse will be met with screams of anguish from governors and senators, labor union officials and local merchants, as well as corporate managers, in whatever areas defense contracts may be cut back. In the aerospace industry, leading manufacturers of airplanes in the 'forties and early 'fifties, and of missiles and rockets in the 'sixties, have been dependent on government orders for from 50 to 100 per cent of their gross business. And the conditions under which contracts have been let have added frosting to the cake. Negotiated, guaranteed-profit arrangements, not competitive bidding, have been the rule.

Robert Heilbroner suggests that all past records of deficit spending as a stabilizing device will pale by comparison with future needs, regardless of which type of expenditure is used to keep the machinery going. Pointing to the fact that each anti-recession bout seems to take a larger deficit to produce the same lift as before in production and employment, he argues that deficits of thirty to forty billion dollars are likely to become necessary in a few years' time.

The record of the economy in 1962, when unemployment failed to recover from the 1960–61 recession at the same rate as in earlier postwar recessions, falling only to 5.5 per cent before showing signs of stalling once again, illustrates the deepening problem of maintaining full employment in the face of automation. For the sorry employment picture came simultaneously with a quite healthy pick-up in business output, thanks to increased productivity of new machinery.

In combination, these factors presage even greater governmental efforts in the future, if the goals of the Employment Act are to be achieved. Not only will stabilization measures have to be intensified, but it will be necessary to introduce specific public adjustment programs to cope with automation's problems, which go far beyond the meager retraining provisions adopted in 1962.

With the passage of the Sherman Antitrust Act in 1890, the national government took on the role of protector of competition. While this has become a traditional task, it remains a highly controversial one, as illustrated by the furor over such antimonopoly cases as du Pont–General Motors and Brown Shoe, and the electrical equipment conviction that sent many high executives to jail in 1961. Logically, antimonopoly action should be welcomed by the business community, for it is one type of regulation that stems from and fits precisely the traditional competitive, free-enterprise creed. The more vigorously the antitrust statutes are applied, the more competitive the economy will remain. Although students of the antitrust movement concede that its failures have been substantial, it is clear when one examines the cartelization of industry in Great Britain and Western Europe that antitrust has at least retarded similar development here. And the more competitive the economy remains, the less is the need or justification for continuing supervision of business power by administrative agencies.

Verbally, business spokesmen accept this logic and pay formal obeisance to the Sherman and Clayton Acts. Operationally, however, their support often turns into opposition — always, if one's own business is the subject of antitrust litigation. Small businessmen argue with considerable plausibility that, because of their power imbalance in relation to giant enterprise — especially when the small firm is supplier to or distributor for the large one — they need to be protected from too much competition. Competition that hurts is always referred to in the trade journals as "ruinous competition" or "cutthroat competition," as distinguished from "fair competition." Big businessmen, too, have developed a rationale for asserting exemption from antimonopoly action. They speak in terms of the contributions that only the giants can make in research, innovation, and the handling of very large defense programs, and the aid which big business extends to smaller firms.

A politics of competition has thus developed in which almost all pay homage to the logic of antitrust in the abstract while seeking to avoid its concrete application. When a President has an Assistant Attorney General who pushes antitrust vigorously, as Bicks did under Eisenhower, his Administration is invariably charged with being "anti-business," for the business community rarely admits that the health of business generally may require action against specific business behavior.

Businessmen prefer to think of competition as self-sustaining, although economists know it is not. The stronger firm can usually drive out the weaker one. If this occurs because of a superior product at a better price, one can hardly object to the process; but the end result — a single firm or small group of firms dominating an industry — is likely to lead to higher prices and less product improvement in the long run. And the cause is rarely so pure in any case. Sheer financial advantage, diversity of product lines, differential discounts, hidden rebates, selling below cost, and a hundred other devices have been used to destroy competition regardless of the comparative merits of the products. Thus, antitrust action is essential to a private-enterprise economy, both to maintain competition and to ensure that the competitive process adheres to the rules of the game. Abandonment of the antitrust role would mean abandonment of free enterprise.

The question today is not whether antitrust laws are needed but whether they are a sufficient or suitable form of regulation in all cases. Because the proponents of vigorous antitrust laws have never obtained the kind of "hard" legislation required to keep one business from gaining a position of substantial power over the market, and because opponents of these laws have been rather successful in emasculating such legislation as we have through judicial interpretation, in many industries it is now too late for the present antitrust statutes to accomplish their goal. And, given the real advantages of size, it is unlikely that modern technology can be rationally utilized if firms are broken up to the extent necessary to eliminate market power. The administered-price problem, endemic to a broad range of American industries today, cannot be handled by antitrust laws. Consumer protection against price gouging, not to mention the even more important goal of price stabilization, may thus increasingly require administrative regulation as a substitute for antitrust prosecutions. The traditional public utilities — transportation, water, electricity, and gas — have always been subject to governmental regulation exactly because they could not be arranged competitively. The steel industry, for one, may now also sensibly be viewed as a public utility.

The importance of the competition-protecting role, politically and economically, cannot be assessed by budgetary or personnel measurements. The Antitrust Division of the Justice Department had an estimated appropriation of $5.9 million in fiscal 1963 and employed only 600 persons. Its significance is thus qualitative rather than quantitative. It shares this characteristic with the boards and commissions through which much of the third traditional economic role is carried on: specific regulation.

By specific regulation we mean regulation of a particular firm or a particular type of action engaged in by many firms, as distinguished from general regulation, which refers to policies regarding the performance of the economy as a whole. The Federal Trade Commission, Federal Communications Commission, Civil Aeronautics Board, Federal Power Commission, Interstate Commerce Commission, National Labor Relations Board, and Securities Exchange Commission could all be abolished tomorrow and one would see no difference in the size of the federal budget or the civil service. Yet these very small agencies loom large in the businessman's eye because one or several of them may intervene directly to change his decisions or the way in which he reaches them or implements them.

While some of these agencies affect directly only a particular industry or group of industries — e.g., the CAB, airlines; the FCC, broadcasting and interstate communications — others exercise surveillance over many firms in many industries: the FTC over advertising and trade practices, the NLRB over collective bargaining, and the SEC over the sale of public securities. They are in effect an additional managerial layer in the industries they affect, or the representatives of the public conscience on the board of directors. Charged by law with protecting the economic health of the airlines, the CAB must "second-guess" the judgment of airline managements regarding, for example, whether low promotional fares or charging what the traffic will bear will prove more profitable over time, or whether a particular route will support additional service. As every American knows through Newton Minow's activities, the FCC has a legal responsibility to ensure that broadcasting stations operate so as to serve the public interest, while the FTC scrutinizes the advertisements that accompany the programs being monitored by the FCC.

Although businessmen and editorialists in general rail against regulatory commissions as alphabetical monstrosities, the historical record demonstrates that each of these agencies came into being because of some specific demand, made as often by a disadvantaged business group as by the consuming public, and not as the result of a "socialistic" or other ideology. Indeed, although the ICC came into being in 1883, economist

George Stigler quite correctly pointed out that as of 1960 we still lacked a theory of regulation for the whole field of regulatory commissions.

One of the major consequences of the pragmatic, *ad hoc* development of regulatory bodies is a lack of coherence and integration among them, and between them and other organs of economic policy development. In a devastating critique, former CAB member Louis Hector illustrated this by pointing to the way in which the ICC had authorized abandonment of unprofitable rail passenger routes which the CAB then authorized a feeder airline to serve with a subsidy as inducement. The FTC and the Department of Justice, as another case, may either duplicate or nullify each other's efforts in the field of antitrust activity. The closest we have come to practical recognition of the increasing need for co-ordination among regulatory programs was with James Landis's 1960 proposals to President-elect Kennedy. Landis's suggestions included creation of co-ordinating staff offices in the Executive Office of the President. While this idea was not adopted at the time, some similar arrangement must be made eventually. When program integration is achieved through White House centralization, specific regulation will become both more effective and more useful in relationship to the broader economic goals of the government.

There is one area of regulation, however, in which proposals for less regulation may have more than an ideology of free enterprise to recommend them. The specific instance is railroad rate regulation. Originally necessary when the railroads had a monopoly as carriers and were abusing their resultant power, rate regulation could now be achieved, for most products, by competition among carriers because of the rise of motor freight and, increasingly, air freight as alternatives to shipping by rail. President Kennedy's 1962 transportation message made such a recommendation. Aside from this, the likelihood is for more rather than less regulation as the effectiveness of competition diminishes.

NEWER AND EMERGING ROLES

With the Great Depression, realization finally came to the United States that income protection programs were an inescapable responsibility of the national government. When one-fourth of the labor force was unemployed and state and local governments had exhausted their resources, the choice became federal action or starvation. Relief funds — the dole — were the immediate response, but the modern sense of values finds this approach repulsive, so Old Age and Survivors Insurance, minimum wage and maximum hour legislation, and unemployment compensation were adopted in the 'thirties as "automatic stabilizers." The first and last of these, as well as non-insurance programs of aid to the blind, the needy aged, and dependent children, involve what the economists call transfer payments: moneys drawn through taxes and then redistributed to the program beneficiaries. To the extent that the funds come from those with greater incomes and go to those with lesser incomes, such transfers effect a partial equalization of incomes; however, this extent is not as great as is commonly supposed. The federal personal income tax, made possible by the Sixteenth Amendment in 1913, for some years also redistributed incomes, though more from top to middle than from top to bottom; but now the effect seems to be negligible. Taxes have, of course, always had an impact on the distribution of income and thus on the social structure of a society. What is relatively new, however, is our consciousness of this and our ability (improved though not perfect) to measure the incidence of this impact.

Together, the automatic stabilizers, federal welfare payments, and income taxes constitute a substantial array of government economic programs. To these we may add the agricultural price-support programs, whose particular form may be all wrong, but whose essential justification is valid: that the farm economy cannot of itself protect the incomes of its participants because the farmer has to take the price that is given for his product, while he must pay the price that is demanded for his purchases from the industrial sector. The agricultural sector of the economy thus remains competitive in almost classical terms. Similarly, the Wagner Act's legal support for collective bargaining can be viewed as income protection for industrial labor, which requires collective effort to match the bargaining power of capital as represented in the modern corporation.

Income-protection programs and those designed to lessen the unequal distribution of income under unrestricted capitalism are important not only in themselves but, perhaps more, as contributions to government's role in maintaining a balance of power among social groups. This role is a historical one, yet it has received explicit attention only recently as theories of the pluralist requirements of democracy have been developed. In sociological terms, in fact, a democratic society can be defined as one in which no single occupational group, class, party, or other social segment holds substantial or long-sustained power over another or all others, either in intergroup relations or through the political process.

The general theme of pluralism is well developed in William Kornhauser's *The Politics of Mass Society*. Specific application to government's role is found in Galbraith's well-known concept of countervailing power, elaborated in *American Capitalism*. It is Galbraith's contention that, although competition in the traditional sense has declined drastically, a substitute has been found in the form of large organizations which operate on the other side of the market from that where the power initially resided. Thus supermarket chains have countervailing power in relationship to food processors, automobile manufacturers in relation to steel producers, and Sears, Roebuck in relation to producers of mail-order items.

Critics have pointed out that the concept is not nearly so universal as Galbraith made it appear, and Galbraith himself has admitted that it has little effectiveness in time of inflation when both sides agree to pass on the higher cost to ultimate consumers. In part, however, Galbraith covered himself by suggesting that, when countervailing power did not arise spontaneously, it was the proper task of government to shore up the weaker side. The Wagner Act is one example. Another is the Robinson-Patman Act, which strengthens the independent retailer against the wholesaler and producer, who might otherwise arbitrarily give better discounts to chain stores. The Food and Drug Administration might also be viewed as countervailing power for the consumer. Strictly speaking, however, Galbraith's concept dealt only with relationships in the marketplace between economic groups. The power-balancing role of government is a good deal broader than this, for almost every piece of legislation will weaken some groups while strengthening others, will fit the demands of one group while rejecting those of a rival. In labor legislation this point is especially apparent. For example, the Taft-Hartley provision outlawing the closed shop and permitting states to outlaw the union shop represented a loss of union power and a gain for business power. But measures which are ostensibly directed only toward a programmatic goal also generally have effects upon the structure of social power. Federal Reserve decisions regarding the availability of credit illustrate this well. Their purpose is to stabilize the economy; one of their side effects is to aid or harm particular segments of the economy: a highly restrictive monetary policy may hurt home construction, agriculture, and retailing, and encourage unemployment. If the unemployment rate is high, labor's bargaining power is weakened. It is this impact on the power structure that creates much of the heat surrounding economic policy debates. Often the proponents and opponents are less concerned with the substance of the policy than with its anticipated effects upon their respective power positions.

The Employment Act has been on the books since 1946, but its full implications for governmental role and structure are only gradually emerging. In time, the Employment Act will be seen as the beginning rather than the culmination of an expanded regulatory role on the part of the national government.

The original impetus behind the Employment Act lay in the nearly universal fear that the discontinuance of war production would put the economy back where it was before World War II: in a state of severe depression. Thus maximum employment, production, and purchasing power were made the explicit goals of the act. While maximum purchasing power may be taken to imply a need for price stability, this was not explicit and certainly not considered of utmost importance by the principal proponents of the legislation. Similarly, economic growth was not of great concern when the problem seemed to be how to avoid shrinkage. If full employment could be attained, growth would follow naturally. Thus full employment dominated thought during the 1946 discussion.

The machinery and policies to be used to further the goal were thought to be fairly simple. The indirect controls of fiscal policy (taxes and expenditures) and monetary policy (availability and cost of credit) were assumed to be sufficient tools. An expert body, the Council of Economic Advisers, in the

Executive Office of the President and a Joint Committee on the Economic Report in the Congress were the institutional innovations called forth. The CEA would use national income analysis to predict what the economy was likely to do, whether this would be sufficient to create full employment, and what the President could recommend to make up the difference if private stimulation was expected to fall short of the full-employment need. Although the original bill, the Full Employment Act of 1945, had specified public investment as an additional device, the conservative opponents of the measure were able to kill this provision.

As things turned out, the assumptions of the Employment Act proved faulty on two counts. First, inflation became a larger problem than unemployment for a number of years, thus complicating the development of appropriate policies, because measures aimed at controlling inflation also tended to dampen production and employment. Second, as Robert Lekachman has pointed out in an article with the suggestive title, "Is Keynesian Economics Outdated?," the institutional structure of the American economy was not entirely responsive to measures which assumed for their effectiveness a more competitive structure than in fact existed. Thus in 1958 we had both inflation and unemployment simultaneously. Because the inflation came from market power (union organization plus administered-price industries, most notably steel) rather than from excess demand, it could not be handled by indirect means, except at too high a cost in general unemployment and reduced business activity.

Because market-power inflation arises from structural features of particular industries, effective public policy to deal with it must be specific rather than general; i.e., it must deal directly with the industries and firms involved, perhaps through a hearings and investigation procedure, with the investigating body making advisory recommendations, or perhaps through hard price control if half-way measures fail. Whatever action is taken to deal with this problem, it will constitute an extension of the range of governmental economic involvement under the goal requirements of the Employment Act, and will require administrative mechanisms beyond those currently existing.

Since the Soviet Union launched the first space satellite Sputnik I, in 1957, the nation's concern for economic growth has vied with its concern over price stability. The concern is intensified by our discovery, concurrently with increased recognition of a need for growth, that the "natural economic forces" seemed less and less capable of providing an acceptable rate of growth spontaneously. As fast as we came out of the 1958 recession we fell back into the 1960–61 recession. And by mid-1962 President Kennedy was considering a tax cut to prevent another recession.

Bankers and some others have feared (with some reason) that policies designed to quicken the growth rate may also quicken the inflationary pace, and have tried to denigrate the importance of growth or argue that it is not in any case the business of government to encourage growth, which occurs spontaneously in a free economy. It is notable, however, that there has developed, very rapidly in recent years, a broad public acceptance of the necessity of government action for the purpose of stimulating economic growth. This acceptance was no doubt aided by the fact that the Russian growth rate is higher than ours, and we must not lag behind, and by its espousal in a widely-noted report of the Rockefeller Brothers Fund, which insisted on the necessity of a 5 per cent growth rate for the welfare of our economy.

While economists know much less than they would like to know about what contributes to rapid growth, what is known is sufficient to warrant the assertion that government action seriously oriented toward a 5 per cent rate would mean a very considerable increase in the scope of government activity. Subsidies, research and development grants, expanded public works, and flexible tax incentives for investment may be called for, as well as measures to improve labor mobility, to upgrade skills on a mass scale, and to control the location of industry in relation to transportation and markets. In order to bring about this stimulation of growth, the structure and operation of government will have to be altered to provide for much tighter integration of all economic policies and programs so that they can all be directed toward growth. This will mean a degree of centralization of top policy direction far beyond what now exists.

Further complications flow from the growing separability of production rates and employment rates. Because of automation especially, and of technological advances generally, production can grow considerably without any increase in employment. The most startling example is agriculture, where production increased 28 per cent in a recently concluded ten-year period, while farm employment decreased by a like amount. This tendency itself would cause difficulty even if the working age population remained constant. Yet it will not: the greatly increased number of babies born in the immediate postwar period is just beginning to go out on the job market. As the tide swells, we may face extremely hard choices between more intensive automation to increase growth and controls on the pace of automation to protect jobs. So long as our economy continues to operate with less than full employment and less than full utilization of productive capacity, the gross national product can always be increased simply by stimulating consumer demand. But it seems likely that full utilization of capacity can now be achieved at less than a full employment level, and when that point is reached the problems will intensify. The government will face an increasing need to regulate the applications of technological developments or, more likely, to devise programs designed to cope with the economic and human dislocations which result from these technological developments.

The government will also have to assume the role of social balancer, in the sense in which Galbraith popularized the phrase: ensuring that private sector and individual economic activity are balanced by public collective actions, either to meet requirements called forth by private actions — e.g., air travel requires airports — or to supply services not supplied or inadequately supplied by private industry which yet contribute to the standard of living — e.g., schools, medical care, recreation facilities, and basic research.

When it comes to the matter of allocating the nation's resources to meet its social needs, there are two main approaches. One is the market mechanism, in which individual dollar "votes" are cast for one product or service as against another among those offered. Consumer sovereignty and producer freedom to offer any product the producer desires are the rubrics used by advocates. The other approach is collective or public allocation, in which the mechanism is representative government: voters choose representatives and political leaders who then, partly as followers of apparent constituency demands, partly as leaders independently assessing community needs, determine the scope of public services.

The issue of resource allocation goes to the heart of the current division of opinion over the role of government in the economy. Free enterprise ideologists contend that the market mechanism can satisfy all wants, except defense, education, and the maintenance of order. They believe that market allocation is the "democratic" way, and that every dollar taxed by government to pay for a collective service is a dollar less that the consumer is free to allocate as he wishes. Thus, in their minds, public allocation is "arbitrary" and "undemocratic," because the citizen pays the tax to supply a particular service, whether he wishes to or not.

In contrast, socialists and liberals though they differ on such matters as democratization of economic power and public ownership, believe that many public needs are better met by government than by private action and that public allocation does not involve a net loss of freedom or democracy so long as the political process is open, free, and democratic. Liberals tend more often to look upon government as a popular instrument to be employed freely to do what individual action cannot or does not adequately accomplish unaided, while conservatives — as least as defined in the American business community — tend to see government as something apart from the people and its decisions as unrelated to popular wants. They are, of course, quite inconsistent on this point, for they will speak of a new public service program as an arbitrary imposition by government upon the people and in the same breath speak slightingly of political pandering to public opinion.

Probably more nonsense is spoken about the relationship of public and private allocation to freedom and democracy than about any other question of political economy. Several points can be made on this subject. First, it is incorrect to assert that consumer freedom is invariably diminished in exact proportion to the level of taxation. This represents an overstatement of the valid point that every dollar taxed means a dollar less that can be freely spent on privately supplied goods. But if people desire better roads, better schools, more public housing, or increased foreign aid, then freedom of choice can only be exercised through public allocation, that is, through taxes. These wants cannot be purchased privately and individually.

Therefore people's freedom would be restricted, not enlarged, if public allocation were not available.

Second, even if a person disapproves of one or another of the public programs which his tax dollar goes to support, he is still subject to the doctrine of majority rule, which provides a legitimate political basis for compelling him to contribute. The only feasible alternative would be minority rule, which only a few extremists on the right and the left would prefer. Defenders of free enterprise are in a poor position to contest the argument of majority rule, it might be added, in as much as it is a rare corporation today that does not require the employee, as a condition of employment, to contribute to retirement, life insurance, and health insurance plans — without any vote at all.

Third, income inequalities mean unequal "votes" in the market place. The assumption of those who believe in the sovereignty of the consumer is that goods will be distributed according to composite social preferences if only each individual is free to buy the goods he wants. The validity of this rests on a further assumption, however, that each bidder for goods has the same number of dollars. And this assumption is manifestly not valid. The merest whims of a man who makes $20,000 per year may be gratified, while a man making only $2000 may not be able to provide for even his physical necessities. As long as extreme inequalities of personal wealth exist in this country, there will have to be public allocation of goods and services to mitigate the effects of this maldistribution.

While opponents of collective services continue to win occasional battles, like the one in 1962 over medical care for the aged, theirs is essentially a rearguard action which can cause frustrating delays in meeting public needs but cannot permanently stop such measures. The solidity of the social security system instituted in 1935 attests to this fact. As society in general becomes more affluent and the income of more and more of the population moves above the subsistence level, the demand for public services will increase, and this demand will be met out of a growing national income without cutting the private standard of living. Moreover, the growth of industrialism and urbanism continually increases the range of public services required.

Furthermore, as we become more aware of the inequities of a system of welfare programs through private collectives (corporations) which vary widely in coverage and adequacy, and as we come to see more clearly that proper public services are an important component of a high standard of living, the positive virtues of public as opposed to private programs will increase the political pressure for improved balance between the two sectors. The pace may be agonizingly slow, but the secular trend is surely toward increased public sector services.

As the self-sustaining, self-stimulating, and self-regulating forces of the private economy become more manifestly inadequate, the economic roles of government become more and more important. When opponents of government action charge that we are moving toward a planned or managed economy, they are quite right. Their error is in supposing that this is an arbitrary development rather than, a necessary response to modern economic structure, technological forces, and humanistic values. They are also wrong in assuming that the managerial role of the national government will produce a trend toward dictatorship or at least a less democratic system.

The fact is that only through public planning and management of the basic directions of the economy can we have any freedom and democratic control over economic development. For it is only over government that we have institutionalized popular control. Since there is no such mechanism for popular control of corporate decisions, and since the choice is not control or no control, but public or private control, we either have democratic public control or elitist, undemocratic private control. Thus we have to ask the following pertinent questions about the economic role of government:

First, does government intervene enough? Or does it leave to private, uncontrolled decision matters that we cannot afford to handle in that way, e.g., investment, price, and wage decisions having widespread public impact?

Second, how can the *ad hoc,* incomplete plans that have been developed for one problem after another over a period of many generations be fused into a mutually reinforcing, coherent, integrated set of goals and programs to ensure that first things come first and that one program does not undercut another?

9 | The Merger of Public and Private

While public attention has been largely directed to conflicts between government and business, a much more significant development has gone relatively unnoticed: the gradual erasure of long-standing distinctions between private and public economic activities, and, as a result, the increased amalgamation of the sectors. The most recent illustration of this trend is the communications satellite system and the peculiar corporate arrangement under which it is to operate—an arrangement which makes American Telephone and Telegraph, the National Aeronautics and Space Administration, and the Federal Communications Commission partners in the communications business. Special legislation created the corporation, which will have three board members appointed by the President and will operate within guide lines specified by Congress, in order to ensure operation in the public interest. Hence, it is not an ordinary private corporation. Yet it is not a public corporation in the sense that T.V.A. is, for half of its capital stock is available for sale to the public in the same manner as the stock of A.T.&T. itself, half to the communications carriers, and the investors rather than the public at large will receive the dividend share of any profits that may be produced.

GOVERNMENT BY CONTRACT

Experimental forms of collaboration between industry and government have also developed in the atomic energy program and in the field of missiles and rocketry, where defense agencies have not only placed orders for hardware, but have delegated to private, non-profit corporations the prior jobs of developing the weapons system and even the strategic concepts into which the systems are to be fitted. These programs — communications, missiles, atomic energy — are all notable for being dependent to a considerable extent on advanced scientific and technological research. Such research is becoming ever more prominent, but, since it is too expensive and risky for private industry to finance on its own, there is certain to be a continuation and expansion of government aid and participation in these programs. In 1962, the national government allocated 14.7 billion dollars for research and development, of which over 80 per cent goes for work contracted out to private industry.

The "contracting out" system of research and development under which a public agency contracts to have the work done by a non-governmental organization — which may be an ordinary business firm, a non-profit corporation, or an educational institution — is advantageous to the government because it provides greater flexibility and ease in shifting resources from one project to another than would be the case within a governmental establishment, and it bypasses the restrictive regulations on the number of employees and their salaries. Because salaries for top flight scientists, engineers, and other specialists in government laboratories and arsenals are so much lower than private pay for equivalent skills, the contracting system may be the only way that government can obtain the services it needs. By contract, public funds are used by the private contractor to pay specialists the higher salaries that government cannot pay them as civil servants under existing law. The government thus obtains needed services indirectly, yet sometimes loses those few men technically qualified to assess the quality of the contractors' work!

The problem of staffing the public service is not the crucial point, though; it is instead the confusion of public and private interest. When a research and development firm does government work on contract, and almost no work for private sector clients or customers, is that firm public or private? Are its employees public servants? In form, the firm and its employees remain private, yet the client is public, the task is public, the salaries are paid out of appropriations. Thus, the firm and its employees are public in crucial respects.

A number of questions have arisen in this area for which there are no ready answers. Since tax money is being used, should the government write into its contracts controls over executive compensation schemes? If government is indirectly exceeding its own salary limits, should the practice of competitive pay without legal limits be followed in the explicitly public sector, too, at least in certain agencies or for certain types of positions? (We have moved in this direction in a small way with special legislation setting higher salaries for selected categories and specified numbers of employees in certain defense and high technology programs.) When the firm is a profit-seeking producer, paid by government and often using government-owned plant facilities, should the contract include controls over dividends, advertising and promotion expenditures, patent rights, and collective bargaining agreements, since the taxpayers are often the largest investors?

So far, the questions concern how far the government should intervene in the "private" aspects of such firms. An even more important problem arises from the use of private firms as enforcement administrators for a variety of public policies. When a business firm enters into a contract with the government, the contract gives the government a handle for imposing requirements that would be beyond its authority in the absence of the contract. The quasi-public nature of the contracting firm is given implicit recognition by requirements that the firm conduct itself similarly to a government agency in abiding by policies that bind such an agency. The range of policies includes non-segregation in employment, adherence to prevailing wages in the area of the contractor's plants, determination of security risks among employees, and positive steps to promote maximum use of small businesses in sub-contracting of defense orders.

A kind of decentralization by contract ("federalism by contract" Don K. Price has called it) is involved here, with national policies carried to local areas through contracting firms rather than through subordinate layers of government. Each prime contractor, for example, has been required in recent years to maintain a subcontracting office whose public task is to seek out small business suppliers. This is done in order to counteract the main trend in defense contract awards, which concentrate prime contracts among a very small number of firms — for example, each year approximately two-thirds of such contracts go to 100 firms. Whether such a program can ever be very effective may be doubted, but that is irrelevant to the fact that private business firms are acting as *de facto* antitrust administrators under this system.

Although a non-discrimination clause is included in each government contract, producers, especially those with southern plants, have been slow to comply so long as the contracting agencies paid little attention to compliance. Under the present Administration, however, the President's Committee on Equal

Employment Opportunity has taken vigorous steps to ensure compliance. In at least two instances in the spring of 1962, firms were put on notice that because of their record of noncompliance they would receive no further government business unless and until they had shown compliance in good faith. Contracts thus become sticks as well as carrots, giving the government leverage over the internal policies of corporate managements wherever the contract relationship exists or is contemplated. As the size of the public sector and the purchasing role of the government increase, this leverage becomes more extensive. The relationship is not unilateral, however. By using firms as administrative arms, the government also becomes more dependent upon private managers for effectuating public policies.

Most dubious of the delegations of public functions to private managements is the industrial personnel security program, which has required contractors to make determinations of a strictly political nature regarding a man's political beliefs and associations. Managements have no competence in this area and are bound to play it safe at the expense of their employees, as in the General Electric instance cited in an earlier chapter.

DUAL ASSIGNMENTS

Another mode of public-private intermingling, not confined to defense, yet most highly developed there, is the fusion of public and private roles in the same persons. Because of the technical complexity of governmental programs today, government must have expert advice on whom to hire, what firms to ask to do certain jobs, and the feasibility of desired projects. To supply this knowledge, literally thousands of advisory committees have sprouted up all over the government. A Congressional committee report which just listed the members of each committee filled five substantial volumes in 1955. There is danger that public policy may be twisted or directed by such committees to the advantage of particular firms or industries. Sometimes a trade association may dominate a committee to the detriment of independent producers; sometimes the large firms may dominate to the detriment of the small ones not represented.

In the mid-'fifties, Representative Emanuel Celler of New York used his House Antitrust Subcommittee for extensive investigation of these and related problems, which have also greatly interested the Justice Department's Antitrust Division. The latter, partly in response to Celler's hearings, has set up guide lines for industry advisory committees which are designed to guard against the use of public policy for private purposes. Among the requirements it has established are breadth of representation from all segments of an industry and the chairing of meetings and setting of agenda by a government representative. But, most important, it has required that the advice of such committees be reviewed independently by the government agency receiving it. Without such checks on the committees' recommendations, the advisers from the private sector become in effect the public decision-makers, and public policy becomes controlled by private policy. Scandals in stockpiling programs and in the award of rapid amortization certificates during the Korean War exemplify what can result from carelessly entrusting public business to private persons.

A more direct problem of the conflict of public and private interest revolves around the use of W.O.C.'s (without compensation employees), successors to the dollar-a-year men of World War II. The W.O.C. is a person on private salary who is employed full-time by the government. The rationale behind this system is that some men cannot afford to take the great loss of income involved in switching from private to public payroll, but the government cannot afford to do without their knowledge; hence they work for the government but draw their private salaries. In war-time production agencies — the War Production Board in World War II, the National Production Authority in the Korean War — this arrangement was accepted as a necessary evil, and it was hoped that patriotic motivation would be sufficiently strong to cause the W.O.C.'s to work only for the public interest and not for the advantage of the industries from which they came.

Although the Eisenhower Administration espoused the idea of separating business from government, it actually took a further step in bringing them closer together by replacing the National Production Authority at the end of the Korean War with an agency which combined residual defense production controls and Department of Commerce services to business. The Business and Defense Services Administration until 1957 had W.O.C.'s in charge of most of its twenty-odd industry divisions. The aluminum division was headed by a W.O.C.; three assistant administrators of the agency were W.O.C.'s; and an industry advisory committee was used extensively. The result was a situation in which a committee of private representatives of aluminum firms chose a man to head the aluminum division, then gave advice to this "public" official who remained on his private payroll, and finally this advice and this man's decisions were reviewed by an assistant administrator of the agency who was also on private salary. Here a major component of a public agency had been effectively captured by private interests.

THE REGULATORY STRADDLE

Confusion of public and private purposes is notable also in the regulatory agencies, for it has been the standard observation in the past few years that the regulated tend to capture the regulators. The Interstate Commerce Commission, for example, was for many years more a protector and promoter of the railroads than their regulator. The same can be said, in lesser or greater degree at different times, of the commissions regulating power, communications, and air and motor transport. Partly this results from statutory requirements: the Civil Aeronautics Board has an impossible mandate from Congress, which directs it to promote the economic health of the airlines while at the same time regulating rates in the interests of maximum public use of air travel. In larger part it is a matter of political power. The regulated industries are well organized and in continuous contact with the regulators and with the nominally overseeing Congressional committees; the consuming public is not. And partly it is a matter of procedure: the regulatory agencies, encumbered in judicial procedures, have rarely had the time to draw up public policy guides to action. The policy vacuum has been filled by the initiative of the regulated firms and the accidents of case development. Motor carriers, for example, scored gains in recent years over the railroads, despite the ICC's apparent sympathy for the latter, by having a clear policy goal of their own and making it ICC policy through a series of initiatives in filing rate schedules.

To the extent that the commissions and boards are captured by the interests they are regulating, public policy becomes not an independent assessment of the consumer's needs but simply publicly sanctioned private policy. This phenomenon has led to some breast-beating among liberals, bemoaning their own failure to realize that the effective manning of a regulatory program depends on who the regulators are and which groups are exerting the most pressure on the agencies. Recent developments suggest, however, that there is a more hopeful view: if regulatory programs can become promotional, promotional programs can also provide a handle for regulation. To put it another way, what is designed as an aid to the private sector can be used to achieve public objectives.

Some examples of this phenomenon can be cited. The CAB promotes feeder airlines by direct subsidies where traffic is too light to pay its own way at approved rates. The subsidy can be used, as one report has hinted it will be used, to push mergers, desired by CAB, between strong and weak carriers even when the carriers involved are not eager to merge. Since the railroads are now living in part on government aid, they, too, may find that loan guarantees and other forms of aid can become levers for governmental intervention in managerial decisions.

When the Eisenhower Administration was encountering difficulties in persuading oil companies "voluntarily" to curb their imports of crude oil in 1958, a "buy American" order issued to federal agencies was used as a regulatory device as well, by requiring that sellers of oil to government agencies prove their compliance with the voluntary import curbs as a condition of participation in sales to the agencies. With the import curbs now on a compulsory basis (at the insistence of one part of the industry and against the wishes of the Eisenhower Administration), a stronger handle is available to the government. The national government lacks authority over oil and gasoline prices, but, if it considered a price boost to be unreasonable, it could threaten to enlarge the quotas for imports to force the price down by increasing supply.

Government involvement in housing holds a similar potential, as illustrated by the November, 1962, executive order forbidding racial discrimination in the sale of federally aided housing. Since almost all housing is federally aided in one way or another, the national government is thus able to implement a non-discrimination policy in a vital area through executive action linked to measures voted through Congress, with southern support, as promotion for the housing industry.

Quite apart from this bridging of the public-private distinction by turning promotional measures into regulatory instruments, the very nature of public utility regulation involves a fusion of public and private management as a half-way house between government ownership and private business. The moment government begins to regulate an industry, especially its prices and, therefore, its profits, it becomes a joint manager with the corporations regulated, responsible for their survival and concerned in all corporate decisions that affect survival. Outright government ownership would be less a violation of laissez faire expectations, for at least then an industry is clearly public; under the regulatory commission system, firms are neither private nor public but both.

AFFECTED WITH A PUBLIC INTEREST

Often public-private economic relationships are subordinated to the legal profession's understanding of the economic system. One example is the legal doctrine of a public utility, as reflected in Supreme Court decisions. For many years the Court drew a rigid distinction between private businesses and those which ancient English common law had defined as being "affected with a public interest." The latter category was a narrow one, including natural monopolies and businesses which by their nature opened their doors to all comers, e.g., a roadside inn. All else was private, and what was private was legally beyond the reach of regulation.

In time, however, even the law bends to the facts. In the midst of the Great Depression, a New York State milk-price control statute provided the occasion for Justice Owen D. Roberts to cast aside the received doctrine and proclaim the continuity of the public and private sectors. Said the justice, "There is no closed class or category of business affected with a public interest, and the function of the courts . . . is to determine in each case whether circumstances indicate the challenged regulation as a reasonable exertion of governmental authority or condemn it as arbitrary or discriminatory." Although there was some backing and filling in the next three years, the position Justice Roberts enunciated has established itself and thus accommodated the law to economic fact, at least in this respect. Now the questions concern the wisdom of the policy and the feasibility of achieving congressional backing where necessary, but not the constitutionality of the policy: the law no longer interposes a wall between government and the economy, between public and private.

The trend of our time is in quite another direction; it runs toward explicit recognition that what is private in form is often public in substance. The whole question of the constitutionalization of private governments is involved, and as Adolf Berle has observed, this is an area of inchoate law, but, nevertheless, of a clearly emerging pattern. An example Berle uses is the case of Marsh *v.* Alabama. It concerned a company town and the efforts of an evangelizing group to use the streets of that town to spread its message. Looking beyond the formal fact that the company owned the streets and sidewalks, the Supreme Court concentrated on the general public use made of the streets and found that, because a public function was being served, the constitutional protections of the people's rights that control governments applied to this company-owned community.

As this page was being written, sit-in cases were being heard before the Supreme Court. The question in these is whether a private restaurant is exempt from the equal protection clause because it is private, or is bound to nondiscrimination because it devotes itself to a public use. Whatever the outcome in these particular cases, the eventual constitutional position seems likely to be the latter one. Although courts are generally not considered the most innovative of social institutions, and although the Supreme Court once too rigidly separated the public and private spheres, the judiciary (at least the higher courts) seems today to realize better than Congress or the political parties the inadequacies of the conventional institutional labels.

POLITICAL COMPETITION

Now that business pays only lip service to the idea that government intervention should be avoided at all costs, individual businesses are increasingly using the political arena as an instrument in intrabusiness power struggles and are trying to influence public policies in particular industries to gain competitive advantages. Usually it is the weaker economic group which actively seeks to engage government as an ally, rather than government seeking out such groups. The groups holding original power are satisfied with the status quo and hence tend to use government less often; they can rely on direct economic power in their competition with other industrial segments.

The now classic instance of the use of political power by an economic group whose market power was low was the successful campaign of the National Association of Retail Druggists for fair trade laws in the 1930's, resulting in the Robinson-Patman Act. Independent druggists found themselves put at a disadvantage by cut-rate chain stores and by preferential discounts the chains received from producers and wholesalers, and they had no economic leverage with which to fight back. So they turned to politics. Being small businessmen, well distributed geographically across all Congressional districts, with homogeneity of interest and of semi-professional status (most drugstore proprietors are registered pharmacists), they had a good social-economic base for the exercise of legislative power. They used this base to good advantage, and the fair trade acts passed by Congress gave them price protection and a better market position in relation to the chains.

Since in most fields retailers are small and numerous, while manufacturers are large and few, market power most often lies with the latter. There are exceptions, as immediately after World War II, when automobile manufacturers were very dependent on the dealers, who were able to use the market situation to improve the terms of their franchises. But this is not to say that the development of this market power was autonomous and independent of politics, for it grew in a specific legal environment. In his description of attempts by the National Automobile Dealers Association (N.A.D.A.) to obtain legislative solutions to their grievances against manufacturers, Joseph C. Palamountain calls attention to the political and economic factors involved:

> Dealers' grievances existed because manufacturers were favored by the existing framework of law. Both the rise of large corporations and the interpretation of contracts resulted from a public policy primarily stated by the courts. Another general policy — disapproval of price fixing and other restraints of trade — limited dealers' attempts to end their grievances by joint economic actions. Thus even the initial economic problems were vitally affected — almost defined — by governmental actions made in pursuance of general policies. Yet the groups affected had virtually no part in the formation of these policies. . . .
>
> Thus far political aspects of our political economy seem to be more basic, since general governmental policies define dealers' economic conditions and confine their political reactions, but in just as many respects economic aspects appear to be more causative. When dealers did win aid from federal and state governments, it was not

> a simple and automatic use of political strength. Problems of organization constantly plagued the dealers. The N.A.D.A. never organized more than a small proportion of dealers, nor was it successful in producing programmatic agreement. This weakness in part reflects the economic power of the manufacturers, who prevented some dealers from joining associations, "persuaded" others not to seek certain political objectives, and placed wholesale distributors and manufacturer-controlled dealers in strategic offices in at least several state and local associations.
>
> A more important cause of weakness was diversity among dealers. . . . The economic environment not only provides the bases for political conflict, it also conditions the outcome.

Because congressmen and senators are often small businessmen or lawyers in middle-sized cities and have small businessmen as their major clients, Congressional committees are often willing to be used as sounding boards for retailer and small supplier grievances against the giant producers. Hearings by the Senate Antitrust Subcommittee in 1955, under the chairman at the time, Joseph C. O'Mahoney of Wyoming, are an outstanding example. Dealer after dealer went on the witness stand to give vent to his grievances against manufacturers who had given them impossible sales quotas, dumped unwanted accessories on them, told them what promotions to run and how to arrange their showrooms, and as sanction for these edicts forced upon the dealers one-way contracts in which the obligations fell on the dealer and the privileges—including cancellation without cause or means of appeal—on the producer. Although the legislative result of the hearings was meager, the publicity was sufficient to bring about some changes in the relationship. The producers gave longer-term franchises, and at least some of them established review boards for dealer grievances, although some of these were so structured as to make one wonder whether they would be effective.

Inevitably, as the government's purchasing role increases, so does competition among producers for relative shares of the procurement dollar. But the competition is of a different kind from that defined by the economists; it is political competition carried out through direct lobbying in Congress, through defense producers' hiring former admirals and generals to improve their access to Pentagon decision-makers, and through advertising campaigns used as indirect lobbying. In 1959, for instance, when there was a Congressional dispute over the relative merits of the Bomarc and Nike missiles, the respective manufacturers engaged in a battle of full-page advertisements. Some of these advertisements listed 8,000 subcontractors, showing the spread of these over many Congressional districts and implying that there would be a disastrous economic impact if the congressmen did not appropriate sufficient funds for continued procurement of the missile that kept all these suppliers in business. Douglas Aircraft has called its military advertising "a part of our partnership with Uncle Sam's Armed Forces," and the firm discusses its advertising program each year with the services for which it is producing hardware. Sometimes the initiative for these advertisements comes from the competing services, as when the Army asked Western Electric to extol the Nike-Zeus, to compete with the Air Force's Bomarc.

The financing of this form of competition also involves a mixing of public and private components, for the advertising costs are eventually charged to the government. The extent of lobbying for the aerospace industries as a whole — in their joint competition against other possible uses of public funds and to gain better contract terms for themselves—is indicated by the growth of the Aerospace Industries Association, with an annual budget of over one and a half million dollars. Defense contractors' contributions to this trade association are charged to the government in the contract as a cost of business and then deducted from income tax because the contribution is to a non-profit organization. Then the money is used to lobby for legislative measures favorable to the industry!

Sometimes the lobbying takes a form honored in private business but looked upon less favorably in the public sector: entertaining on a business expense account. Representative F. Edward Hebert, chairman of a House Armed Services Subcommittee, held a revealing discussion of public-private characteristics of the aircraft industry with the chairman of the Glen L. Martin Company. Hebert suggested that such wining and dining is inappropriate in public activity and the following exchange occurred:

> Bunker: Yes, but private industry, sir.
> Hebert: Totally a government product.
> Bunker:: Yes, but private industry, sir.
> Hebert: But totally government, totally subsidized by the government, if you will.
> Bunker: I don't like the use of the word subsidized.

A standard procedure of business is to claim defense-relatedness when this suits its purposes, even though the external observer may find the connection tenuous. Thus manufacturers of electric generators protested a TVA award of a contract for generators to an English firm (at a saving of $5 million) on the ground that the government should stop such foreign purchases for the sake of national security. They did not succeed in that particular case, but they, and other producers, have obtained a buy-American act which required that foreign bids had to be at least 6 per cent below the lowest American bid before a government agency could buy abroad. TVA had required 20 per cent, and still the British bid was lower.

As mentioned at the beginning of this section, economic use

of the political arena includes attempts to turn public policy directly to one's own benefit, as well as to improve one's position in relation to competitors. The tax laws and legislation for protection of workers are cases in point. The oil industry's successful defense of the depletion allowance has generated over one hundred depletion allowances of varying percentages for a great variety of extractive industries. The hour and wage laws, social security program, and unemployment compensation program are shot through with exceptions and exemptions that reflect the power of particular industries in Congress rather than any rationally defensible criteria for inclusion and exclusion. Farm workers being about the weakest bargaining group in the United States either politically or economically, farm owners and food processors have been particularly successful in obtaining exemptions from the requirements imposed on other employers to protect employees from exploitation.

A particularly good example of this political approach to competition is recounted in Cornelius P. Cotter's *Government and Private Enterprise:*

> An official of a regional trade association of exempt truckers went before the committee studying the problems of the railroads to "demand regulation." Regulation of what? Here lies the brilliance of the tactic: regulation of the exempt truckers. In other words, the truckers, who have built up their businesses under the protection of the exempt clause and on the basis of vigorous bargaining for rates, would not mind enactment of legislation which entitled each of the existing truckers to a certificate of convenience and necessity as a statutory right, and limited the access of newcomers to the field. Such legislation would "stabilize" competition in the trucking of agricultural products by restricting participation in the business and by eliminating rate competition — the ICC would set rates.

But it is in the area of collective-bargaining legislation that perhaps the most noticeable illustration of the political nature of the economic power struggles can be found. The old American Federation of Labor was just as adamantly opposed to "government intervention" in the bargaining process as was the National Association of Manufacturers, but, once the Wagner Act was passed, both sides abandoned laissez faire in favor of a more realistic strategy of influencing the direction of labor legislation. In fact, the NAM overcame its general opposition to "internal" interference to such an extent that it became the major proponent of measures to extend the degree of intervention far beyond that provided by the Wagner Act. That is, the Taft-Hartley Act's prohibition of the closed shop and its permission for states to outlaw the union shop also — both originated by the NAM — constitute intervention into the substance of the bargain, whereas the earlier law had affected only the procedure of bargaining.

A MARBLED MIXTURE

From these conceptual, legislative, judicial, and political mergings of the public and private spheres of the economy we can draw generalizations in three areas: the nature of competition, the meaning of private enterprise, and criteria for distinguishing between the private and public sectors.

The concept of competition in a politically directed economy should emphasize power rather than price. Market power on the one hand, political power on the other, and the interrelationships and reciprocal influences between these are the crucial factors in an economy where the private sector is characterized by administered prices and the decisions of the public sector vitally affect the environment of profit-seeking.

The skills of the political scientist and those of the economist must be fused if adequate analysis of the system and appropriate prescriptions for public policy are to be developed. As the multitudinous ramifications of public policy upon the fortunes of private economic groups become more evident, legislators and administrators will need to analyze more consciously and more systematically the consequences of existing and proposed programs, to ensure not only that public actions lead to desired economic performance but also that equity and a balance of power between groups are obtained. As we become more aware of the extent of political activity by economic groups, we will need also to examine more consciously its impact on the integrity of the democratic process. In short, we cannot afford to continue the outmoded, too comfortable pattern of separating the public and private spheres in our thinking about the role of government in a "free enterprise" system.

Secondly, we find that private competitive enterprise is no longer either private or competitive in the traditional meaning of these words. A realistic, if slightly cynical, definition of private enterprise as it now operates might be as follows: private enterprise is a politico-economic system in which each private group seeks to direct public policy to the improvement of its competitive position, share of national income, or bargaining power vis-à-vis other segments of the society. The private elements in the system lie in the insistence by business that, in return for public benefits, no limitations be placed upon resultant profits or managerial discretion, and that the public good is not to be planned for but is to arise as a by-product of private planning for private purposes.

Thirdly, what is public and what is private can no longer be defined abstractly or institutionally; the dividing lines are drawn rather from study of changing attitudes and situations.

Whatever is seen to affect the public interest *de facto* becomes proper matter for public action *de jure*. The price of steel, for instance, remains a private matter so long as it does not notably upset the stability of the economy or in some other way affect the larger public beyond the producer and the immediate industrial purchaser. But once it does have some publicly noticed effect, it becomes a matter for public action.

The definitions of private and public in the economy thus become relative, not absolute, concepts. An economic decision or situation or institution is private when, and only as long as, we think of it as private. It is public when another economic group, the general public, or a government agency thinks of it as affecting some publicly held value. The distinction between a public and a private matter now depends on the answer given to the question: How does it affect the public at this time?

Dealer franchises in the automobile industry, discussed above, exemplify this way of looking at public and private interest. Institutionally and ideologically private, these became public, at least temporarily, when a legislative committee became interested in their implications regarding the power position of small business, and the politically conscious community became disturbed over the problems of arbitrary control exercised by one group of men over another.

Often public programs develop as responses to inadequacies in the private sector which have public consequences of politically significant dimensions. As Gerhard Colm and Geiger have written, "Had there not been some misuse of economic power by private enterprise, there would have been no anti-trust laws. Had there not been some substandard wages, there would have been no Wage-Hour Act. Had there been no severe depression, there probably would have been no Employment Act." That is to say, when private handling of economic affairs went wrong, these affairs became public instead of private.

Once it is clear that the economy is a marbled mixture of private and public forces and institutions, and that the goal of obtaining the maximum in economic productivity with the maximum of democracy in processes and social structure requires constant, conscious deliberative action in both sectors, the leading question that emerges is the adequacy of existing institutional structure and public policies for dealing with a system far more complex than the Founding Fathers — or even most living legislators, public officials, and private managers — ever envisaged. The burden of the last part of this book, therefore, will be to show that the existing patterns are very inadequate and to put forth some propositions for reformation of the American political economy in the hope that they will be debated.

IV | The Political Economy of the Future

10 | The Crisis of Institutions

The literature of business management continually emphasizes the need to revise institutions to meet new situations. The firm that never changes its structure or processes to keep up with its challenges is the firm that goes under. Nor are the changes all merely incremental. The economic revolution of industrialization, for instance, contributed directly to a revolution in business forms from the individual entrepreneurship to the private collectivism of the publicly-held corporation.

The need for equivalent restructuring of governmental institutions and processes to meet modern challenges and respond to changed ideas is at least as great, yet it is rarely recognized—particularly by businessmen. In fact, it is one of the greater paradoxes of our society that men whose whole lives are bound up with innovation are the last to recognize or welcome innovation outside of the production process. Perhaps their yearning for stability in non-business institutions is explained by the fact that the world of business is in constant flux. Not that the proponents of the status quo in governmental institutions have had their way entirely. There has been, and is, change: the rise of Presidential leadership in this century is a constitutional change of considerable magnitude, for example. Yet the pace of change in the government has been much slower than the needs which have arisen. The framework established in 1789 will have to be substantially adjusted if American government is to be adequate to the tasks of 1989.

In a democratic polity the tests by which institutions are evaluated are dual: effectiveness is a goal, but it is effectiveness through a democratic process. The test of democracy asks whether institutions are compatible with democracy, whether they support democracy and freedom. And by these great words we mean to specify, at the minimum, a kind of openness with several components: universal suffrage and opportunity for political participation beyond the suffrage for all who wish it; the right to speak one's mind on public policy; the right to organize for more effective expression; and institutionalized processes whereby the people — or a majority of them — hold those who make public decisions accountable to them and exercise some continuing control over the directions of public policy.

The context in which we are applying these tests is, it should be noted, both broader and narrower than the usual one of political institutions alone. It is narrower because we are focusing only on the economic aspects of public policy; it is broader because we are concerned with popular control over economic decisions affecting the public whether these are made in the public sector or by the private "governments" of the corporations. Thus control over public decisions means control over decisions affecting the public, and public decisions so defined take us inexorably into consideration of the relationship of business management to the people, as well as the relationship of government and the people which is often discussed.

We should comment here on the absence of one component which is sometimes erroneously considered essential to the test of democracy: the scope of control exercised by government. Thanks to the laissez faire tradition, and to that perverted Jeffersonianism which identifies free government with minimal government, our national thinking about the problem of governmental power has been vastly oversimplified. Instead of one variable, that is, the range of power exercised by government, there are two, the range of power and the effectiveness of control mechanisms. The danger of tyranny relates more closely to the adequacy of control mechanisms than to the range of powers exercised by government. That is, we should be more fearful of a small number of powers which are uncontrolled, and arbitrarily exercised, than of a larger number of powers whose application is limited by procedural due process and popular control of the directions in which the powers are applied.

Suppose a government had only power to protect property as in the night-watchman state of the Spencerian ideal. And suppose that no "bill of rights" or independent judicial system existed. The police might then, if my neighbor accused me of theft, slap me in jail, refuse to let me have counsel or cross-examine the complainant, and sentence me without having to show cause before a judge. This would be tyranny even if government had no powers in any other sphere — unlikely as that would be. Conversely, a modern government operating a multitude of positive programs and regulating a broad spectrum of industry poses little danger of tyranny so long as the elements of control are vigorous and expression of grievances and of opposition is free. In the American regulatory system, for example, the Administrative Procedures Act makes regulatory commissions bend over backward to protect the rights of private parties, who are frequently able to maneuver the procedural protections so as to frustrate regulation entirely. Thus there is no simple equation of inverse proportion between freedom and governmental powers.

The test of effectiveness asks whether the political economy is capable of handling the society's economic agenda, whether it is able to govern the economy and to produce in accord with the people's needs and wants. The relations between the corporate-market system and the government, or the absence of such relations, are what interests us here. How well, for example, are we set up to achieve our objectives regarding growth, employment, price stability, and social balance? Is there anything lacking in our processes for planning economic development?

Let us now turn to evaluation of our institutions of political economy in terms of these tests — first considering the corporate-market system, then governmental institutions, then the mixture of the two — and draw up an inventory of the structural deficiencies that call for political-administrative innovation.

THE CORPORATE-MARKET SYSTEM

The democratic process has been severely affected by the loss of social control over private economic power, while at the same time that power has been increasing in scope and intensity. The sources of this loss are three: changes in the economy, changes in the internal structure of corporations, and the blinders of outworn theory that prevent us from seeing the need to introduce new controls to substitute for the traditional ones that have nearly collapsed.

The economy has changed, as we have noted, from a system of competition to one of administered resources and private planning, and as a consequence the market itself has lost the regulatory power it formerly had. The strongest argument made in behalf of the competitive system was that governmental regulation was unnecessary because the presence of competitors guaranteed the restraint of business power. Now that power exerted over the market is greater in many crucial ways than the power of the market, we can no longer rely upon this social control of the invisible hand.

Such power as business managers possessed in the traditional corporation was legitimated by the close link between ownership and control: either the owner was the manager, or else the manager had clearly identifiable owners who set the bounds of managerial decision-making through continuous review. Thus the owner was using his own property, in classic Lockean terms, and he was responsible for its use. The manager could not dispose of other people's property merely because he wished to do so, but he was bound by the wishes of the legitimate owner.

Now that people's capitalism has reached the point where some 17 million people are said to own shares in American industry, there is no clearly identifiable ownership interest to control the use of corporate property. Boards of directors are self-appointed and essentially uncontrolled. No outside, independent review of management decisions is institutionalized. Not even the stockholders, let alone the general public, who often feel the major impact of managerial decisions, are in a position to control the uses to which corporate resources are directed or to assess authoritatively whether the social gains are worth the social costs. Thus the second great traditional mode of controlling economic power has become ineffective.

Even if ownership control did still exist, or could be resurrected, we should have to add that it would be insufficient. It would presumably protect the owners' interests, but in an age when the impact of corporate power goes far beyond the internal corporate community to the general community as well it is not only the owners' interest that requires protection; indeed, that interest will often be in conflict with the interests of the community at large.

It is absurd to believe that these powerful systems of control can be replaced by a system under which management "learns to sit it judgment on itself." Would we be satisfied if President Kennedy's power were limited only by his own judgment? The burden of proof is on the business community to show that self-regulation is justifiable in the private sector of the economy while it is unjustifiable, in their own view, in the public sector. Yet we are so inured to the notion that business is private that we have not yet faced the fact that the only respectable, democratic solution to the problem of the loss of control is to build new external controls, with the government as the instrument of popular control, either directly through over-all public regulation of a continuing sort or indirectly through restructuring of business institutions. The basic problem, then, is to find ways to hold economic decision-makers to account for their actions and to ensure that their decisions are made in conformity with community values.

A variety of controls, rather than a single new control, is needed, for the types of power to be controlled are themselves varied in nature. Roughly, we can speak of internal and external exercises of power, or of economic and non-economic impacts. Internally, the authoritarian structure of private governments in large, hierarchic institutions, such as trade unions, universities, government agencies, and professional associations as well as business corporations, violates the democratic principle of participation in the process of decision-making by the rank-and-file members of the institution involved. (The trade union and collective bargaining process are of course a kind of rank-and-file participation.) Legislation aimed at ensuring "union democracy" is a way of recognizing this problem in one set of institutions, but why not an equivalent concern for participation in decision-making by the rank-and-file of business firms, too? It is even more important that employees, suppliers, and distributors, who are most directly subjected to the internal private governance of the corporation, be given proper constitutional guarantees.

The dealer franchise problems discussed earlier exemplify the arbitrariness of corporate government; the public sympathy for the dealers' problems engendered by the Senate hearings shows that the public expects that due process will extend to private organizations. Racial, religious, or political discrimination in hiring, firing, and promotion practices of business firms exemplifies the absence of a bill of rights, the subject rather than citizen status of corporate employees. In this regard, a young lawyer in Deerfield, Illinois, was told by his firm that he should either disengage himself from "controversy" occasioned by his involvement in the effort to locate an interracial housing project in his community or lose his employment. A similar denial of basic rights occurs when a white-collar, non-union employee at the middle-management level with, say, fifteen years employment is fired by a firm as part of a reduction in force without terminal leave or other compensation. Firms must recognize that non-union employees are entitled to the same recognition of job security that union employees have acquired forcibly through collective bargaining.

Unions, of course, pose equivalent problems. The International Machinists Union, for instance, expelled three West Coast members for giving public support to a right-to-work referendum. But unions have also led the way in voluntary constitutionalization: the United Auto Workers instituted several years ago an independent review board to hear certain types of appeals from internal disciplinary decisions.

On the other hand, it is a curious coincidence that the General Electric Company set an internal "statute of limitations" on antitrust violations at three years rather than the five that public law provides, and thereby salvaged its highest officials while sacrificing those at the next level down in the chain of command, when the price-fixing conspiracy case of 1961 exposed the wholesale involvement of company officials in the scandal.

I believe there is increasing public recognition of the problem of internal constitutionalization in corporations, which is helped along by books like Whyte's *Organization Man* and Harrington's *Life in a Crystal Palace* and given systematic underpinning by studies of conflicts between individual and organization in all kinds of large-scale institutions by such writers as Chris Argyris. At least in this area our tradition of individualism works in favor of needed protections. It will be much more difficult, however, for us to re-orient our thinking about the control of the external power of the corporation. For here the operative tradition is the rigid distinction between public and private spheres, a distinction which persists despite its manifest meaninglessness.

The corporation and the market system are simply ineffective mechanisms for satisfying the needs and achieving the goals of the modern economy. Business spokesmen themselves admit this, inadvertently, when they argue against proposals for governmental stimulation of the economic growth rate. They do not contend that business can do the job instead, but only that ups and downs in the growth rate are "natural" and that, consequently, no one can create a steadily higher rate. If one does not accept this defeatist outlook — obviously motivated by desire to avoid government action — one has to acknowledge that, for a national economic goal like growth, market action alone is inadequate.

Yet corporate action is necessary, even though it is insufficient. Hence the problems of full employment, growth, and price stability clearly require co-operation between government and business in making decisions. At the least, we must ensure that private decisions do not negate public action. This is the real significance of the Kennedy-Blough dispute over steel pricing in 1962. More hopefully, we must build a system that encourages joint planning on investment and on wage and price decisions. At present, government has been left "holding the bag": it is in the position of trying to compensate through fiscal and monetary policy for the unfortunate consequences of private actions. It must take many vital factors as givens — for example, the total annual private investment — although economic analysis and political imagination could enable government to influence such factors more actively along desired lines, either through tax incentives and penalties keyed semiautomatically to economic indicators or through more direct participation in investment planning. For example, corporate taxes could be arranged to rise when the indicators pointed to inflationary pressures, thus dampening down investment expenditures, or to fall when expansionary activity was needed to ward off recessions. This is done in Sweden. Similarly, individual income tax rates could be varied, as President Kennedy has proposed, to stimulate or cut consumer demand.

Moreover, the market system simply does not meet many particular social needs. Take housing for illustration. The real estate page of any newspaper contains articles from time to time reporting a real estate board's estimate that a particular community is temporarily "saturated" with housing. But what is true from the standpoint of sales and demand is often in bitter contrast to the truth from the standpoint of human need. Families or individuals with incomes ranging from six to eight thousand dollars per year are generally unable to obtain appropriate housing. Their income is too large to qualify them for public housing, while most desirable private housing is priced beyond their means. Not having enough dollars to register their need as "demand" in the economist's sense (need plus funds), they do not appear in the realtors' statistics. Hence the anomaly of saturated markets and unmet needs existing simultaneously. Public housing is one answer, the only one at some income levels. Another, which should be used more extensively than it has been, is governmental research to aid the private industry in developing designs and materials to make decent housing available at lower cost, for the typical firm in the home construction industry is too small to finance its own research.

Or take the problem of automation. The market system's unaided solution is to take jobs from some men, while automated productivity increases the incomes of those who remain employed. Private action, particularly joint company-union action, can ameliorate the situation, but it cannot alone solve it. The basic criterion of corporate action remains profitability. This is too narrow a goal for society as a whole, and the gap has to be filled by government. Government itself needs extensive remodeling, however, if it is to be adequate to the ever more complex tasks thrust upon it. When it is called upon to do little, its capacity for rational, effective action is relatively unimportant. Today, the capacity to govern is all-important.

THE GOVERNMENTAL SYSTEM

The most pressing question on the private side, because it is the most neglected, is the democratic one. On the public side, the adequacy of the democratic mechanism is constantly being discussed, but the effectiveness of government to govern is almost totally neglected. Thus our attention now shifts to the latter question. Happily, the measures needed to enhance the capacity to govern will also enhance the quality of democratic controls. Contrary to the political dogmatism of business, confined authority does not ensure accountability. On the contrary, only governmental leaders who have the power to act can be held responsible for their actions. Any businessman recognizes this as regards the president of a business firm; it is a pity so few of them recognize the same truth when applied to the President of the United States, when he must manage national prosperity.

Although the shortcomings of government comprise a long list in total, they are reducible to two categories, each representing the vulgarization of sensible doctrines: Madisonianism and pragmatism.

Karl Marx is reported to have commented upon the perversions of his doctrines by some of his self-proclaimed disciples by saying, "I am glad I am not a Marxist." James Madison, father of the American Constitution, might well say the same in regard to Madisonians. Madison's basic prescription for government, contained in *The Federalist* No. 51, was this: "In framing a government which is to be administered by men over men, the great difficulty lies in this: you must first enable the government to control the governed; and in the next place oblige it to control itself." The fact is that we have ignored—even denied—the first part of his dictum and so extended his second as to make it absurd.

Because the Founding Fathers feared democracy, which to them meant a mobocracy of the propertyless, and because the people feared a strong central government, which reminded them of George III's government, a system was devised that ingeniously gave strong powers to the President and Congress but made it possible for each branch to frustrate the other. Madison and his colleagues were not averse to strength in government. After all, a major motivation for the new Constitution lay in the inadequate capacity to govern afforded by the Articles of Confederation. What they feared was popular government, so their intent in creating the system of checks and balances was not to weaken government so much as to prevent mob passions from controlling government. Thus only the House of Representatives provided for direct popular representation. The Senate was one degree removed and the Presidency twice removed from popular election. In this way it was assumed that government could be kept responsive to the consent of the governed but sufficiently free of direct popular control so that it could govern effectively.

What has happened since 1789, however, is that we have greatly democratized the system by direct election of senators and, in effect, the President, development of a party system to mobilize popular opinion and link it to government, the removal of property qualifications for voting, the Presidential press conference, and, underlying all other changes, the emergence of the idea that government as a whole, not just one part of it, is seen as responsive to the people. But, inconsistently, we have also added to the Madisonian checks a host of extra-constitutional ones and so created a situation in which the checks are so effective that they weaken the governmment's capacity to govern and thus nullify much of the development of the democratic process.

Madison divided the legislature into two branches and staggered the terms between them and within the Senate, so that quite apart from the separation of powers between President and Congress there were a number of checks internal to the legislature. Not content with this, we have developed a system that includes the following additional checks:

1. the filibuster.
2. control over the legislative agenda transferred from the parties, which are linked to popular control, to the Congressional committee, which usually means control by the committee chairman who is not accountable to the nation as a whole but only to his own Congressional district.
3. the seniority system for selection of committee chairmen, which, together with item 2, almost ensures disproportionate weight to those sections of the country where thought is the most reactionary and there is least awareness of the major currents of the time in the economy, the society, and the world. Most such chairmen come from so-called safe districts, which re-elect them time and again without any really effective opposition.
4. separation, since the 1920's, of appropriation from authorization, with the consequence that each piece of legislation that requires expenditures — and few do not — faces four, often five or six, hurdles before it can reach the President. First, it must be authorized by the appropriate committee in each house —e.g., Foreign Affairs and Foreign Relations, or Agriculture, or Banking and Currency — and then it must again be justified by the appropriations committee in each house. If there is any difference between the House and Senate versions, a special joint conference committee tries to reconcile the two — and this can happen both to the authorization and the appropriations bills.

Between the President and Congress, Madison imposed the checks of the Presidential veto and the Congressional power to override the veto by a majority vote of two-thirds, plus the requirement of Senate confirmation of major nominations. Originally the threat of stalemate was warded off by the similarity of outlook between officials of both branches. As the Federalist monopoly on government quickly disappeared, the party system rose to provide a substitute link between the two branches. But we have recently, through a misguided notion of voter "independence," had a six-year period of divided control between a Republican President and a Democratic Congress, and some polls have shown a substantial minority of popular opinion approving such division as a useful check, though the Kennedy experience indicates that the impediments to swift action are quite sufficient even when the nominal unity of party control exists.

In the executive branch, too, vulgar Madisonianism has had its effects. From 1789 to 1883, when the Civil Service Commission was established, the President had at least formal authority over all executive agencies. Since 1883, a no-man's land has arisen of independent executive agencies: the ICC, FTC, FPC, SEC, NLRB, CAB, and FCC. Although Congressional ideology avers that these regulatory bodies are "arms" of Congress, the fact is that the main body cannot maintain effective control over them, and roadblocks have been thrown in the way of Presidential control despite the necessity for such control if the vital areas of economic policy covered by these agencies are to be integrated with the general economic policies of the Administration as required by the Employment Act.

These regulatory bodies are engaged in essentially executive functions: they make concrete applications of broadly defined legislative directives and carry out national policy in their respective spheres. The ICC, for instance, is charged with maintaining the economic health of the railroads, protecting the public from exorbitant charges, and furthering the most efficient pattern of traffic among trucks, railroads, and inland waterways. Commission decisions may affect the location of industry, the rate of economic growth, and the price level, and may overlap with programs of other agencies, such as the CAB and the Department of Commerce. Co-ordination of ICC programs with those of the CAB (also an independent regulatory commission) and with agencies under direct Presidential jurisdiction is thus essential if the left hand is not to undo the work of the right hand.

Yet no one, not even the President, is in a position to direct co-ordination and policy. The President appoints the members of regulatory bodies with the consent of the Senate, but the appointments have fixed, overlapping terms and, except for the Federal Reserve Board, are subject to the provision that not more than a bare majority be of one party. In the case of the FRB the term is fourteen years, with seven members. So, while cabinet members and sub-cabinet political executives serve at the pleasure of the President and may be dismissed because of policy differences with him, members of these important bodies are immune from Presidential removal except in case of gross malfeasance. If the President may not remove these men, he cannot ensure their compliance with general economic policy. No one expects the President to appoint a sizable minority of assistant secretaries of the regular departments from the opposite party, yet he must do the equivalent of this for the regulatory agencies, thus losing even the marginal assurance of policy compatibility that would be provided if he could make all appointments from his own party.

A series of reorganizations extending over more than a decade now have somewhat diminished other policy-making impediments in the agencies. Thus administrative direction has been centralized in the chairman of most commissions, and the President now selects the chairman of each regulatory board, except the ICC, which continues to follow an absurd pattern of annual rotation of the chairmanship among eleven members. Yet the changes made are minuscule in relation to the problems of rational policy development that arise out of this fragmentation of the executive function.

As the histories of the FBI, the Corps of Engineers, and the Extension Service have demonstrated, even when the President possesses authority over an agency, he may not have power over it because of the centrifugal force of clientele groups in American politics. That is, an agency may be so strongly bound by ties with congressmen and local interests that a President cannot budge it. Again, this political pluralism provides a more than adequate check against the possibility of executive tyranny and illustrates the superfluity of additional formal checks, which threaten the whole process of government with *immobilisme.*

Another great inadequacy of the executive branch — and of the combined functioning of Congress and the President — is the lack of institutions for adequate long-range central planning. Consideration of this problem leads us to the twin of vulgar Madisonianism: vulgar pragmatism.

The basic tenet of pragmatism as an approach to problem solving is that each situation must be considered in its concreteness and individuality. It is an antonym to doctrinairism, which assumes that one can apply *a priori* rules to any situation without taking into account its unique features. Between these two, no one would today dispute the superiority of the pragmatic approach. But pragmatism can degenerate into a mindless, planless chasing after events, so that one is controlled by situations instead of using thought to modify situations. And there are signs that the policy-making process in America is closer to vulgar pragmatism, which would not think about how to cross a bridge until one reaches it, than to legitimate pragmatism, which would think in advance about the kind of river to be crossed and plan a suitable bridge for a successful crossing. Among these signs are:

1. Congress's refusals to give the President stand-by authority to vary personal income tax rates to control economic fluctuations, to provide stand-by public works funds, to approve a Department of Urban Affairs, and to grant appropriations in a form sufficiently flexible to permit needed adjustments in the year-long period following the passage of an appropriations bill.

2. the absence of any central economic planning agency since the demise of the National Resources Planning Board in 1943.

3. the postwar history of foreign policy crises, in which the typical pattern has been for the United States to react to initiatives taken by Russia, China, France, Germany, South Korea, etc. The Marshall Plan constitutes one major exception.

4. our national reaction to the problem of automation. For a decade perceptive observers have warned us this problem would require public policy, but we did not even begin to devise a policy to meet it until the retraining legislation of 1961.

5. continued adherence to the annual budget in an age when almost every project undertaken by government requires several years for completion. Especially is this the case with aid to underdeveloped countries, which can serve its purposes only if planned on a long-range basis.

It is true that there are a few hopeful signs that the necessity for long-range planning is beginning to achieve some recognition. One is the ten-year federal budget projection issued on the last day of the Eisenhower Administration. Others include the present Administration's effort to establish a planning unit in each major department and agency, the Defense Department's fusion of planning and budgeting, in which each program is projected several years ahead as a basis for more realistic current appropriation requests, and the renewed adherence by the Council of Economic Advisers to the spirit of the Employment Act, which calls not only for analysis of what the economy is likely to achieve unaided, which is all the CEA did under Eisenhower, but also an analysis of what could be achieved with adequate stimuli and a program to bring about the goals thus established.

Vulgar Madisonianism reinforces vulgar pragmatism: so long as authority over economic policy and program development is fragmented both among executive agencies (Budget, Treasury, CEA) and between these and regulatory bodies — especially the Federal Reserve Board so far as general economic policy is concerned — a basis for effective planning does not exist. For coherent policy-planning requires that a single set of premises, a single image of the economy, a single set of goals, underlie the programs of the multitudinous agencies whose actions impinge on economic welfare.

In a recent magazine piece, Sidney Hyman wrote of the "expiring idea that the people are the source of all power over the government and are the ultimate judges of what the President and the Congress say or do." Some of the sources of difficulty for the democratic ideal are not amenable to solution by structural reform: such are foreign affairs, in which executive discretion must be at maximum and popular knowledge is likely to be at minimum, and problems of technological complexity with which government must deal. These are not like the simple, local problems which could be solved by New England grass-roots democracy or its equivalent.

But while we must struggle with such difficulties and in

some cases simply learn to live with them, there are others about which some action can be taken, if only we will. The keys to improved popular control of government lie in the party system and the use we make of the Presidency — the party system, as the essential link, for control and communication, between the electorate and the governors; the Presidency as the only political agency elected by the whole people.

The inadequacy of the present party system, both for effective governing and for democratic control, has never been more apparent than in the first two years of the Kennedy Administration. Tax revision, medical care for the aged, unemployment compensation, anti-recession legislation, an urban affairs department, foreign aid, public works, and aid to education, to name just a few of President Kennedy's legislative proposals, have all suffered emasculation if not outright rejection despite a nominal two-thirds Democratic majority in both houses of Congress. When party discipline is this lax, or even non-existent, the party system fails to perform the vital function of overcoming the separation of powers between executive and legislature. And it fails equally to link popular opinion and public policy. Public-opinion polls show a sizable majority of the public in favor of medical care through social security, for example, but Congress does not reflect this majority. The President does. Because the only effective focus on national issues comes in the Presidential election campaign, the results of that campaign are a better index to national opinion than the sum of Congressional races, the outcome of each of which depends so heavily on local factors irrelevant to national needs and national tides of opinion. Yet the burden of proof is on the President, the active, popular element; it should be on the inactive, less popular element, the Congress. He must build a majority; Congress need only stand pat to defeat the President.

Even worse than the general lack of party discipline and homogeneity in Congress is the parties' abdication of the agenda-setting and policy-setting function to committee chairmen not in any way accountable to the national public. Can anyone deny the undemocratic quality of a system in which the President of the United States must bend to the will of one member of the House of Representatives out of four hundred and thirty-five on a matter of crucial economic importance? Yet this was the case in the summer of 1962 when Wilbur Mills's opposition to a tax cut forced the President to back down. Who is Mills? A member of Congress from Arkansas, who has run unopposed for a decade. How many Americans voted for him? In 1956, 19,540. How did he achieve his position of power? The inexorable workings of the seniority system, which makes party regularity irrelevant in selection of chairmen, even though the label of the majority party is essential to securing a chairmanship. Mills had the power, while the President had the responsibility. Yet Mills was not accountable to the nation. Nor is this by any means a problem reserved for Democratic Presidents. Eisenhower, during the two years when his own party held a Congressional majority, had to contend with the Midwestern diehards of the Republican party as committee chairmen, men whose ideological affinities were with the late Senator Robert A. Taft.

Outside the Congress the party system remains largely a private preserve of the so-called professionals; yet the club movement and other reform groups in New York, Illinois, California, and other scattered spots demonstrate that participation in party policy development and choice of candidates does not have to be so narrowly concentrated. The great weakness remains, however, that there is little connection between local party groups and national party leadership. The national committees of the parties want the quadrennial support of all local groups, but they do little to help Congressional candidates and thus have little claim on their loyalty after election.

Reform of the party system, while necessary, is insufficient. The formal processes of government also require revision, especially the executive-legislative relationship and the executive machinery for the formulation and administration of economic policy. In the latter area, it is essentially a case of filling a gap, for at present we lack any institutionalized system for obtaining policy integration on common premises. In the former area, Presidential authority must be increased to match Presidential commitments and responsibilities, so that the President can give a clear direction to economic policy.

The need is indicated by Marquis Childs in a newspaper column on the 1962 tax cut problem. Hypothesizing that the President might seek a tax cut, Childs pointed out that he would have to stress the probable danger of a recession in justification. Then if Representative Mills and Senator Harry F. Byrd of Virginia, chairman of the Senate Finance Committee, resisted the request successfully until the adjournment of Congress, as might well happen, the President, in Childs's words, is left in the position of "having pressed the alarm signal, without any means to fight the rising tide of recession." And we can add that if the President had set off the alarm, without action being taken, the situation probably would have been made much worse, because there would be a bad psychological reaction in the nation at large.

But the tax crisis is only a symbol of the deepening institutional crisis.

11 | Restructuring the Corporate System

One of the greatest myths of what passes for conservatism in America is the belief that, if government would just stop rocking the boat, the status quo of economic institutions and the economic system would be self-sustaining. The truth, of course, is that all social institutions and processes undergo continuous change and that the one thing that cannot be done is to keep things as they are — with or without governmental action. The vast changes in the business system that are epitomized in the modern corporation have their origins in deep historical currents, not in the particular actions of governments. Given the advancing pace of technological innovation, the ferment of ideas about the nature and role of the industrial corporation, and the government's increasing involvement in the economy as underwriter of innovation, as industry's largest customer, and as the gyroscope of the national economy, the only thing certain about change is that it will occur — and probably at an increased pace.

What is not certain is the direction that change will take or the consequences for democratic society. We can make a few predictions with little fear that events will contradict us: that we will not return to an Adam Smith economy of many small, powerless business units; that tension between political equality and economic inequality will continue; and that neither the state nor the corporation will wither away and thereby solve our problems. But our certainties tell us only what will remain constant.

WINDS OF CHANGE

We can identify three possible lines of development for the modern corporation in terms of power and social accountability. The first may be that the corporations' scope of activity and power remain constant or increase, while the degree of social control lessens, partly by attrition and partly by popular and governmental accession to the demands of business to be freed from its "shackles." The resulting system would be analagous to fascism: rule by an industrial elite, exercising paternal control (benevolent or otherwise) over government and people, but lacking reciprocal controls.

The second possible line of development would involve a diminution in the scope of corporate power, a pulling back from the social and political roles that have been emerging for a generation, and a return to a more narrowly economic role, with a correspondingly lessened need for public controls — at least for new controls. This kind of development would be most in accord with the traditional model of the business firm, but most discordant to the actualities of present-day managerial practices and thought.

Thirdly, the corporation may continue its present trend of extending its activities and power to social and political realms and its involvement in over-all management of the economy, but with increased public controls imposed to produce an element now lacking: public accountability for those activities.

These are hypothetical developments, of course, and reality may combine their elements in varying degrees so that the actual development does not correspond to any one of these. For example, corporate power may increase without controls in one area — say, in charitable and educational grants — yet be restricted in another — say, public review of pricing practices. Despite the likelihood of some mixture, however, it is probable that one of these patterns of development will dominate. Of the three possibilities named, the third seems most probable, though I would personally prefer the second. Most businessmen would probably prefer the second also, but will be unwilling to pay its price and hence will inadvertently push us toward the third system, in which power is not reduced but put under explicit control.

The first, fascistic, line of development is by no means a fanciful possibility, as it has strong roots both in practice and in ideology. Notions of a "better business climate," of corporate trusteeship and the corporate conscience, of partnership between corporations and universities, of, in short, private enterprise as the end of social action rather than a means of supplying goods — these are all indications of the trend. There does exist in this country an anti-government attitude and a myth that only public governments exercise power, but private institutions never do. When these attitudes are combined with a governmental system that gives a vastly exaggerated weight to organized economic interests, one can see how the short-sighted demands of the business community — made for profit, not for a social ideal — might yet produce a kind of corporate totalitarianism. I am not accusing the business community of seeking fascism, but of failing to recognize that its demands for a privileged position for business and its unwillingness to accept public accountability would move us in that direction. But we need not move further in that direction, and there are countervailing factors: American ideology is, however inconsistently, egalitarian as well as respectful of money as a sign of success; it contains a strain of radicalism and a deep belief in the self-governing capacity of the citizen, as well as an orientation toward private enterpise. When privately held social power is seen to be abusive, we have not hesitated to use governmental power to control it; and our political process remains open to popular use.

What concrete steps can be taken to lessen the potential of business paternalism and increase the viability of economic democracy? By what means and to what degree can the economic power of business firms be reduced or made publicly accountable? How can we contain business's influence over other social institutions within the bounds of a healthy pluralism? That is, how can we regain social control over our economy? These are the questions that must concern us now.

The traditional answer to all problems of concentrated economic power is the antitrust answer: break up that power. If the character of modern technology permitted small enough units, if market concentration were the only source of business power, and if monopolistic pricing were the only consequence of business power, then antitrust action — under much strengthened statutes and with more vigorous administration than has yet been achieved — could begin to have the effectiveness that its more ardent and uncritical supporters presume it to have.

But these suppositions are contrary to fact, and antitrust action can only do a small part of the job of controlling business. It can protect us from single-firm monopoly, but not from oligopoly in greater or lesser degree. It can enforce a code of competitive conduct which eliminates the cruder kinds of collusion, but it cannot prevent follow-the-leader pricing practices. Its greatest value is probably as a deterrent to concentration, but it cannot recreate the conditions requisite to social control by the invisible hand. For what it can do, it is worth preserving and strengthening. Among the strengthening measures would be a requirement of advance notice to the Justice Department regarding mergers, adoption of *per se* rules to simplify the litigation process for the government (e.g., a rule that, whenever a firm captures more than 20 per cent of the relevant market, the burden of proof will be on the firm to demonstrate that it is not in restraint of trade and subject to dissolution), and a vastly increased and better paid legal staff for the Attorney-General.

No matter what degree of success antitrust action may have, a significant degree of bigness will remain, and so will the problems which arise from the anarchy of the market system as a device for governing an economy in the public interest and from the extension of business activities to non-business areas of life. No single form of social control can cover all types of economic power — certainly antitrust litigation cannot. A greater degree of social innovation is called for, with a variety of controls to match the variety of problems that have emerged in the modern corporate system. Broadly speaking, social control is required in the following areas: the external economic consequences of corporate decisions, the external social-political behavior of the corporation, and the internal system of governance by which corporate managers administer the affairs of stockholders, employees, suppliers, and distributors. An official inquiry into these politico-economic problems, like the Temporary National Economic Committee of the 'thirties, is needed. Meanwhile, because these problems have received so little serious attention from either politicians or intellectuals, all one can do is suggest some avenues that appear worthy of further exploration. These proposals are not utopian in the same sense as are proposals to re-create an early-nineteenth-century economy of multi-unit, small-scale free enterprise. For the proposals made here I claim consistency with the technological and political imperatives of our age. They are utopian in the sense that their immediate enactment into law or practice is not to be expected; but they are practical and pragmatic in the sense that they are directed toward the very real, if still largely unrecognized, problems that lie ahead in our continuing efforts to combine advanced industrialization with political and social democracy.

REGULATION BY CHARTER

The first of these, which the late Senator Joseph C. O'Mahoney advocated unsuccessfully in the years after the Temporary National Economic Committee investigations, is federal incorporation for the largest corporations — largest in assets, sales, or number of employees — about two hundred of them. Federal charters would provide an explicit base for regulation and would effectively symbolize the national character of these firms and the responsibility they have to the national interest — just as charters are already used as a basis for compulsory membership of national banks in the Federal Reserve System. And just as state-chartered banks need not join the Federal Reserve, smaller industrial firms with state charters would be exempted from some of the special requirements imposed on the largest two hundred.

Even though such regulation would be denounced as "socialism" or worse by the corporations affected, the use of charters as a regulatory instrument would not actually be a radical departure; it would be a conservative return to past history. State charters were used as regulatory instruments until the Civil War. Incorporation was a privilege, not a right. And the scope of activities permitted to corporations was limited by the terms of the charter. While no one would wish to limit the form of incorporation to firms in the traditional fields of public utilities, as was once the case, there is no reason why the charter need today grant unlimited scope to corporate activity any more than it did in the early nineteenth century.

What kinds of limitations might be written into the charters? First, because the conglomerate merger is so important a means of extending corporate power through financial means rather than through services to the consumer, a nationally chartered corporation might be restricted to market dominance in a single field. That is, a firm that already has 25 per cent of the market in widgets would not be permitted to acquire firms in the gidget line that would give it more than 20 per cent of that market. If it developed its own gidgets, without resort to merger, then, when its share of the market reached 20 per cent, it would have to divide into two corporations.

Each one of the two hundred corporations also might be required to establish a public review board modeled on the United Auto Workers' Public Review Board. In that arrangement, a varied group of distinguished citizens has been constituted as a judicial body to review certain categories of decisions made by the organization concerning individual members of the union. The board operates with funds irrevocably deposited by the union in a special bank account for the board. This ensures — as much as it can be ensured — the board's freedom from union pressures. As in the U.A.W. case also, the proposed charter for corporations could delineate the categories of decisions on which appeal can be taken to the board. This could be an important step toward the constitutionalization of corporate government, a way of protecting individuals in large organizations who do not have immediate resort to the public judicial system. The scope of the board's jurisdiction should include all direct employees, although the details would differ for union and non-union employees, since union employees usually have grievance procedures. Perhaps, too, the board should handle decisions affecting suppliers and dealers, in the manner of the dealer review boards established by the automobile manufacturers a few years ago. It might, however, be necessary to set up a separate board for the suppliers and dealers, one financed both by the large corporation and by the satellite firms.

Another possible way of organizing public review, one which would avoid the specter of hundreds, even thousands, of boards and the consequent problem of finding people to serve on them, would be to establish a national panel of industrial judges on the model of the American Arbitration Association. Perhaps even the functions of that organization could be extended to this emerging area, in which equity rather than specific contract provisions would be the basis of an arbitrator's judgments.

Concurrently with the development of public review boards, an effort should be made to write a "bill of rights" for the individual in economic organizations. The Bill of Rights in the United States Constitution prescribed certain prohibitions against the national government. Through judicial construction, some of these rights have been applied also against state governments, and against individuals acting under the color of law. But the Founding Fathers did not foresee the threats to individual liberty that would come from private governments in corporations; the gap thus left needs to be filled.

These propositions are meant to be suggestive, rather than exhaustive, of the ways in which provisions of national charters could be used to regulate corporate behavior. Other limitations might also be written into the charters; and one can also think of limitations which should be applied to all industrial organizations, not just to the largest two hundred. In such cases, general legislation should supplement the charters.

One example in this category would be a law which forbade industrial corporations from owning any of the communications media. Since these media must remain autonomous if they are to serve either as originators of, or vehicles for, public debate, they should not be subsidiary to institutions that may themselves be in need of criticism. As noted earlier, the number of industrial firms owning radio or television stations is not large; yet this is a case where even one is too many.

There is also a good case for the participation of public members and/or representatives of satellite groups on the boards of directors of the largest two hundred firms. The communications satellite corporation now in process of formation will have three public members, appointed by the President of the United States, on the fifteen-man board of directors. Presumably they will both symbolize the public interest in the affairs of this corporation and also provide effective representation of the public interest. Since the theme of this book has been that there is a public interest in all large corporations, perhaps a similar form of representation might be applied to these corporations.

There would obviously be some difficulty in finding enough qualified persons with a public-interest outlook to sit on the boards of the two hundred firms, and in ensuring that they act on common premises. Perhaps use of public members would have to be restricted to an even more select group of firms, say, the largest firm in each concentrated industry, such as General Motors, U. S. Steel, the Aluminum Company of America, and du Pont. This direct kind of public representation would have to be supplemented by the traditional kind of indirect public representation in economic decision-making: regulatory boards who would make certain that a public utility acts in the public interest. Both types of public representation would be useful.

Perhaps, too, employees, suppliers, and distributors should be represented on each board, although the West German experience with co-determination since World War II indicates that representation of this kind may easily degenerate into captivity of the represented groups. That is, a lone labor representative, isolated from his former associates and enclosed in the upper world of the directors, may soon cease to orient himself to his constituency. Similarly, consumer counsel in National Recovery Administration days was not notably successful because it lacked a power base. Yet further experimentation with these various forms of representation would be worth trying. If they could be made to work, they would lessen the need for more direct governmental intervention and would provide an internal balance of power now lacking in the corporate system.

The major difficulty in allowing each clientele group to have an explicit voice commensurate with its contribution to the productive process and the degree to which it is vitally affected by corporate decisions would be a tendency of the organized constituent groups — managers, stockholders, employees, suppliers, and distributors — to combine against the consumer, as unions and management have done in some instances. This is the reason why economic democracy cannot be constructed on the syndicalist premise of the autonomy of each industrial unit: the general public is left out, and the interdependence of each unit with all others goes uncared for. Conversely, however, economic democracy would be incomplete if we were to achieve popular control over the society-wide effects of corporate decisions while the internal government of each industrial unit remained autocratic.

What clientele representation may be able to accomplish is a shift of the internal system of business control from benevolent autocracy to constitutionalism and a limited consent of the governed. At the least, why should not employees have a vote in the election of the board of directors? The employees are much more a part of the corporation than are the stockholders: the latter invest only their money; the former their lives.

RESTRICTING NON-ECONOMIC ACTIVITIES

In the matter of social and political behavior of the corporation, two reforms seem absolutely necessary: repeal of the privileged tax position now enjoyed by corporations for lobbying and for cultural, educational, and charitable contributions; and new legislation preventing managers from spending corporate funds, with or without tax deductibility, on political activities — whether lobbying, electioneering, or propagandizing — until and unless stockholders and employees are given an opportunity to vote on the policy positions to be taken, and consumers are allowed to deduct from the price of a product that share used for political purposes by the corporation.

In the absence of these provisions, stockholders, employees, and customers are in the position of being compelled to contribute financially, or through work, to a political war chest. Taxation without representation is just as reprehensible in the corporate as in the governmental sphere. My proposal may be extreme, but it is proportionate to the danger a democratic society faces if one interest is accorded by public policy a favored financial position in the political process. Let businessmen and their allies among the general public remain as free as ever to voice political opinions, but let them do so at their own expense. The more a business firm engages in activities directed at shaping public policy, the more it becomes a public concern and the less claim it has to autonomy. Either corporations must pull back from political involvement, or they must expect the public to demand that their political activities be brought into accord with the democratic ethic.

SHARED MANAGEMENT OF THE ECONOMY

The corporate system also needs to be restructured so that decisions affecting the national economy are shared with governmental authorities representing the public interest. The public members of corporate boards suggested earlier may in some degree serve a liaison function, keeping managements informed of the public implications of pending decisions and apprising the government of industrial problems and needs. But this will not be enough. The investment, price, and wage decisions of the two hundred largest corporations have consequences which are too vital for us to rely solely upon this kind of liaison. Affecting the good of the society as broadly and crucially as they do, they must be made accountable to the public, and they must be made accountable in a milieu which stresses national needs rather than the needs of individual firms.

Roger Blough may feel that U. S. Steel needs higher profits, for example, but if a price increase would, in the judgment of responsible officials, endanger the whole economy, then there must exist a mechanism better than Presidential anger for ensuring that the lesser need does not override the greater. No such mechanism has yet emerged out of the 1962 steel-negotiation embroilment, nor even any sign of official analysis of the possibilities of such a mechanism. Continuance of such mindless avoidance of a demonstrated need can only result in a repetition of the same unrational, socially disturbing crisis sometime in the near future. That there will be another time when private behavior runs counter to the needs of public policy is beyond doubt.

Although I am not on the whole a partisan of Congress over the Presidency, in this matter it must be said that legislative committees have given more attention to these problems than has the executive branch, at least so far as published materials indicate. Senator Kefauver's Antitrust Subcommittee has held hearings at which prominent economists have been invited to offer suggestions for handling the public-policy problems arising from the system of administered prices. Among the suggestions was one by John Kenneth Galbraith for public hearings on major price decisions. And the Joint Economic Committee commissioned Professor Emmette S. Redford to make a detailed analysis of the administrative problems and possibilities for such a price review. Thus the matter has not gone unrecognized; rather — and this is worse — the thoughtful analyses that have been made were not drawn upon for institutional improvement, even though the crisis over steel pricing provided concrete evidence of the need.

The exact forms to be taken by new policy machinery designed to mesh private economic decisions with public policy requirements cannot be specified in detail without further analysis; yet the general outlines of what is needed can be delineated. First, we need public review of price and wage decisions in those instances where the impact may be important to the whole economy. This is a deliberately inexact statement, for public review may be either "hard" or "soft," consisting of binding directives or advisory conclusions whose only sanction is public opinion, and the selection of decisions to review is a matter for debate.

Initially, perhaps an attempt should be made to avoid hard price-wage control. The World War II experience with the Office of Price Administration is not one which the nation would like to repeat. Perhaps the holding of hearings, the drawing of explicit guidelines for corporate behavior by the

Council of Economic Advisers (carrying forward the effort begun in the 1962 report by the CEA), and the force of publicity would operate with sufficient effectiveness to obviate the need for more direct forms of control. Perhaps, too, further refinement of economic analysis will reveal ways to use the indirect inducements of monetary and fiscal policy to encourage appropriate behavior, though at this time the indirect tools can effectively forestall market-power inflation only at too high a price in unemployment and underutilization of plant capacity.

The appropriate scope of price-wage review will be in part a matter of trial and error. Yet economists can probably pick out a minimum of crucial types of decisions that call for public review because of their reverberating effects on the wider economy. "Big Steel" is the obvious example. Obviously also, we do not need public review of the pricing decisions made by hot dog and ice cream stands. The indicated approach is that of key-point analysis. Those particular industries (perhaps even particular firms within industries) whose place in the economy is strategic to other sectors should be identified through economic analysis. Some should be singled out for control, while others should be left uncontrolled so long as their decisions, even if contrary to public policy, would have only marginal impact. If hard price-wage control proves to be necessary, the administrative problems can be vastly simplified if such an approach is successful, as compared with the task of universal regulation. One small example of such a proposal, incidentally, has been made in the area of public utilities: in its price review of natural gas producers' sales to pipelines, the Federal Power Commission exempts several thousand small producers whose total production is not as important as that of a few hundred major producers.

The second type of politico-economic invention required is a government-industry investment council, whose efforts would be directed toward a stabilized high rate of growth. Such a council would not mean the intervention of government in an area it is not now concerned with, but simply an attempt to relate governmental responsibilities under the Employment Act more effectively to the patterns of activity in the private sector. Fiscal and monetary policy are now used to stimulate or dampen investment as the state of the economy requires; in 1962 the Kennedy Administration revised the Internal Revenue Service's depreciation schedules and persuaded Congress to pass, in a form considerably modified by Congress, an investment incentive tax bill; and the President's annual Economic Report is supposed to indicate the level of investment required for full employment. In short, involvement already exists, but it is incomplete.

Indirectly, we may be able to devise variable tax arrangements, as Sweden has done, to even out the investment cycle. This is an important problem since unevenness of investment is a major source of economic instability. More direct approaches are also needed. If we really mean to raise the economic growth rate, we will have to recognize that some types of investment are more useful to growth than others, both within the private sector and between the public and private sectors. Investment abroad has significant implications for the balance of payments and foreign policy, yet the decisions are currently made without any mechanism to ensure that public implications are adequately weighed. And, in general, there is insufficient communication between public and private decision-makers regarding investment plans, opportunities, and needs.

At the minimum, an investment council of an advisory character, perhaps modeled roughly on the President's Labor-Management Advisory Council, could be created to increase the flow of information and to improve the liaison between public need and private action. The council's action would be analogous to soft price review. A "harder" version would be a public investment council with authority to set in motion specific incentives and penalties to channel private investment into the most useful areas at the most appropriate rate, and perhaps even to veto certain types of investment at certain times. Such a council might also be the repository of operating responsibility for stand-by public works authority, for it is harder to stimulate private investment when business is slack than to dampen it in a boom. If it were organizationally subsidiary to the Council of Economic Advisers, maximum assurance of co-ordination with Presidential responsibilities and policies would be obtained.

The third type of politico-economic invention needed is an institutional locus for analysis of problems of manpower and industrial location. Investment decisions affect the pace of automation and, hence, the pattern of employment; they affect the location of firms and, hence, the growth or decline of cities. Public decisions by agencies such as the Department of Defense and the National Aeronautics and Space Administration also are vital factors in determining manpower and locational patterns. Again, the planning of future industrial development requires more exchange of information, more explicitly developed criteria for decision-making, and better co-ordination of decisions regarding manpower, materials, transportation, and urban growth.

The proposals made in this chapter by no means cover all the problems of power structure and public policy raised by the development of corporate power without the corresponding development of new social controls, nor will they necessarily solve all the problems covered. I hope, nevertheless, that they do suggest the far-reaching implications of the corporate system and the extent of institutional rebuilding required if we are to balance new forms of power in our society with new forms of accountability. A complete program of reforms to channel corporate power would cover, for example, a restructuring of the broadcast media to free them from corporate censorship via the advertising power. But to formulate such a program would call for a much more intensive investigation of all the possibilities. The effort here is primarily to analyze the problems and secondarily to suggest some possible lines of resolution. The remaining task in this book is to sketch the larger elements of government into which the new control functions suggested above should be fitted.

12 | Democratic Politics for the Age of Planning

The recommendations of the preceding chapter should not be thought of in isolation. They imply and presuppose a more general restructuring of the governmental and political system. They require a general strengthening of the federal government's capacity for policy planning, by which I mean the intelligent anticipation and analysis of problems, and the setting of priorities and drawing up of programs to achieve the chosen objectives. Without such planning by government, public policy tends to become the passive plaything of private planning, especially business planning. The major corporations plan their internal affairs and increasingly attempt to plan the control of the external environment, of which government is a major part. Governmental planning is thus an essential countervailing device, as well as an independent need. Too often, economic power groups are able to set one part of government against another or to make an agency's plans their plans. Central planning can help combat this.

A more active planning role by the government should not occasion ideological alarm, for it simply means the anticipation of problems before they reach crisis proportions. Planning need not, and in the American context certainly will not, mean a Soviet-style *Gosplan* established without popular consent and imposed by force on all areas of life. Rather, much of our planning, which goes on now in piecemeal, unintegrated fashion, must take the form of inducements rather than directives. Planning for economic growth, for example, consists of a tax incentive for extra investment by business firms, not an order that every firm must allocate extra funds to investment. Government is the only society-wide institution for which we have devised an explicit, formal, institutionalized system of popular accountability. If we maintain the substantive vitality of that system, we need have little hesitation about adding to the tasks assigned to government. In discussing how the policy-planning capability of the national government can be increased so that democratic mastery of the economy can be brought about, I will make recommendations in three, overlapping areas: the President and the executive branch, Congress, and Presidential-Congressional relationships.

THE PRESIDENCY AND THE PLANNING PROCESS

The State Department has had a policy-planning staff since the late 'forties, and the Bureau of the Budget is encouraging the development of equivalents in other departments. Yet the President himself has no such staff. He needs one.

The "program of the President" is arrived at now primarily by Budget Bureau review of proposals welling up from the agencies. This review covers the substantive merits of proposed programs, not just their costs, and competent observers give the Bureau high marks for co-ordination of on-going programs. But co-ordination of existing programs, difficult and important as it is, does not obviate the need for integrated policy initiation and development. This job is one the Budget Bureau may not be well suited for. Thus Arthur Maass and Lawrence Radway have written:

> Negative and piecemeal review of individual proposals flowing up from agencies to the chief executive cannot produce an integrated governmental program at the time it is required. It is becoming clear that top level executives require policy staff organs to formulate general programs which subordinate units cannot evolve because of limited terms of reference, inertia, organizational or professional bias, or inadequate factual information. Such a policy general staff, *by supplying common premises for action* [italics added], can help insure coordination "before the event," that is, by prior indoctrination.

While the Budget Bureau's jurisdiction covers all agencies, it does not cover all functions: its primary concern is with expenditure. Yet national economic policy also embraces monetary policy, taxation, loan policy, and debt management — all of which lie outside the Bureau's jurisdiction — and so it is less suitable than the Council of Economic Advisers for the task of integrating national economic policy.

Perhaps, then, the next step in supporting the President in his task of national goal setting and policy planning should be to create a Presidential policy-planning staff which could supply the common premises of which Maass and Radway wrote, develop alternative sets of goals in the matter of economic resources analysis so that the President can make a rational choice, and then ensure that programs in progress fit into the priorities the President has set.

Leon Keyserling illustrates the need for unified planning by telling how Napoleon was supposed to have preferred one bad general to two good ones. Our economic policy planning today may all be in the hands of "good generals," but there are far too many of them. The Treasury, Council of Economic

Advisers, Bureau of the Budget, Federal Reserve Board, and a number of lending agencies are all heavily involved in the determination of pieces of economic policy, but no one is in a position to insist that all these units operate on common premises. Not even the President can do so, because of the statutory "independence" of the Federal Reserve Board and of independent regulatory agencies whose functions importantly affect the nation's economic performance and structure. An interdepartmental co-ordinating device, the Advisory Board on Economic Growth and Stability, was created in 1953, but its record was less than impressive. The need now is to tighten up the hierarchic structure and strengthen the President's authority so as to reduce the fragmentation of policy-making among many agencies.

The following recommendations would provide a start to effective Presidential planning:

1. The three annual Presidential messages should be reoriented and reconstituted so that the State of the Union message becomes a statement of goals for an extended period of years and the Economic Report and Budget messages are combined into a single statement of national economic goals and requirements.

The State of the Union address should present the state of the union as the President envisages it five or more years ahead: it should present goals and assess prospects, as well as review the past year. It should be a candid message, setting forth the nation's problems as the President sees them, stating alternative policies with the expected consequences of each, and explaining the case for the specific goals to which the President is committing himself. Such a message, while avoiding the rigidity of a detailed "five-year plan," would force the President to think through long-range priorities and relationships among competing objectives. It would focus public attention on the basic value choices of future national development. And it would foster a shift in public attitude toward realization of the necessity for long-range, conscious anticipation of problems, if Americans are to continue to be masters, not puppets, of their fate. Congressional debate on this message, particularly the reaction of the party not in control of the Presidency, should serve further to quicken public engagement and aid in the development of a majority consensus on the broad outlines of policy. The public's reaction would then give the President guidance on what he can expect the public to support when his long-range goals are translated into short-run incremental legislation.

A Presidential National Economic and Budget message should go far toward forcing a close correlation of over-all considerations of economic development with particular programs, of long-term plans with short-term ones, and of governmental business with private business. The projection ahead for several years of the resource requirements stated in the message would serve as a powerful tool of public education. The long-range projection, plus a spelling out of the governmental policies designed to achieve the needed rate of production and the proper balance of resources and products to fulfill national goals, would form a basis for assumption of responsibility toward national economic needs by the decision-makers of business and labor in the private sector. The short-run budget section of the message would be placed in its proper perspective as the presentation of single-year steps toward objectives spread over a number of years.

2. The Council of Economic Advisers should become the nucleus of an Office of Policy Planning to provide the common premises upon which integrated planning must be based, to give the President an over-all planning staff, and to provide

a Presidentially oriented center for price-wage, investment, manpower, and industrial location decisions as these are added to the governmental agenda. The Office of Policy Planning would centralize primary responsibility for development of "the President's program" by taking over from the Bureau of the Budget the task of approving legislative proposals made by the departments, taking care of policy problems that fall between agencies, and emphasizing the development of new policies to meet problems that lie too far over the horizon for the operating departments to encompass in their concern with current programs.

The proposed office should have the following functions: it should devise alternative sets of policy goals for consideration by the President in the course of preparing his reoriented State of the Union message; it should provide the resources and requirements analysis to accompany the goals established in the State of the Union message; and it should prepare a National Economic Budget, covering both private and public sector activity under the clauses of the Employment Act which call for the President to specify the levels of employment and production needed to achieve the Act's goals and to offer a program for achieving those levels; and it should co-ordinate current programs with Presidential objectives and priorities.

3. The President should seek from Congress a degree of authority over the now independent regulatory bodies adequate to permit action, rather than mere exhortation, when it is necessary to bring their policies into line with national economic needs. The purpose of this recommendation is to strengthen the ability of the Presidential staff to counter the centrifugal tendencies of the departments, agencies, and independent commissions. Even within the regular hierarchy of the executive branch, co-ordination is difficult and often deficient. The existence of the CEA and the discipline of the

President's Economic Report have perhaps made each agency aware of the relationship of its own program to stabilization policy, yet the full potential of the CEA's authority to appraise agency programs and recommend to the President ways to improve their correspondence to general economic policy appears not to have been achieved.

Outside the Presidential hierarchy, as mentioned earlier, the President lacks the legal authority—let alone the political strength—to co-ordinate the policies of the different independent agencies, especially the Federal Reserve Board, with administration economic policy for purposes of stability. This situation contradicts the logic of the Employment Act and of national politics, which makes the President responsible for all areas of economic policy. At the minimum, the CEA should have a subsidiary unit to maintain Presidential liaison with the independent boards. In addition, a new President should be granted authority to name the chairman of each regulatory commission from among the hold-over members or by replacement with a new appointee, and he should be able to change the chairman when he wills (which he cannot now do in the case of the Federal Reserve Board and perhaps not the Federal Power Commission either). Abandonment of the bipartisan character of these boards would also enhance presidential authority and accountability. Better still, the Federal Reserve Board should be replaced by a single Governor whose status would be the same as that of a member of the President's cabinet.

CONGRESSIONAL POLICY MACHINERY

The twentieth century has witnessed a steady shift in legislative leadership toward the Presidency. The permanence of the shift was established during the Eisenhower years, when a President who had campaigned on the notion of limited Presidential power nevertheless carried on at least the mechanics of a Presidential program — special messages, draft legislation, etc. — established by his predecessors. Congress, in consequence, has been confused. No longer capable of independent policy-making, yet unwilling to accept a "rubber stamp" role, it has settled for an essentially critical role in recent years.

Academic critics of Congress have complained about the pettiness of Congressional policy-making — its emphasis on budget details and expenditure "scandals" — and have urged the legislators to concentrate instead on the task of formulating broad policy, leaving the Executive considerable discretion in execution. Thus, for example, Edward C. Banfield writes in a criticism of Congress from the viewpoint of a planner that the appropriate role for Congress is "to supply a pattern of key value judgments around which the budget is built."

Yet is this a reasonable expectation? Or should not Congress's task be to debate, criticize, and review the pattern of values submitted by the President in his economic and budget message? The United States is the only major country where the legislature makes its own budget rather than approving or rejecting the executive budget. There is a considerable difference between making its own budget on its own set of priorities and amending the President's budget. The latter I take to be a realistic legislative goal; the former, not.

It is not only in the area of the budget that Congress is unable to reach a consensus on goals. Congress resembles a committee with the problem of a party division among the members. And of committee planning George Kennan has said:

> Committees, operating on the basis of a negative veto, often come up with compromise recommendations weaker than any of the conflicting points of view originally put forward around the committee table. It would have been better, in many instances, to take the original view of any one of the participants than to attempt to work on the basis of the compromise language finally produced.

If coherence is a prime criterion for planning, Congressional participation in the goal-setting stage should be for the purpose of criticizing executive plans, proposing alternatives to stimulate public discussion and clarify party choices for the voters (this is of course the special task of the opposition), and limiting Presidential action when it exceeds the bounds of legislative acceptability. Such a role is not unimportant by any means. It would be more than rubber-stamping the President's proposals, although less than what Congress considered its proper function in the nineteenth century. There is still a need for Congress to take an over-all view, but it should be an over-all view of the President's program, not an interparty, multi-interest compromise.

There are three problems in having Congress as a partner of the executive branch in policy planning: the fragmentation of power and responsibility among committees, which is not adequately counterbalanced by party centralization; the excessive weighting of domestic over foreign policy demands, of local over national interests, of particular over general economic considerations; and, the obstructive power of minorities working through the interstices of the committee and party structures.

The most significant step Congress could take toward rational reconstruction of its own role in economic policy planning would be to delegate discretion and legislative power to the President. Proposals of this kind are contained in the next section of this chapter. Within Congress, the following changes should produce at least moderate amelioration of the three problems outlined in the preceding section.

1. Joint hearings of House and Senate committees should become the normal procedure for receiving testimony by Administration spokesmen on Administration-sponsored legislation. The memoirs of department heads are filled with regret (sometimes bitterness) over the time wasted in duplicate testimony necessitated by separate hearings. Joint hearings would save administrative executives more time for administering, and would also enable the senators and representatives to feel out each other's probable course of action at an earlier point in the process, thus making agreement more likely.

2. The jurisdiction of the Joint Economic Committee should be extended to include a review of the President's Budget message equivalent to that accorded his Economic Report. This would, of course, be inevitable if the two messages are consolidated as recommended above. Many commentators have noted the absence of any over-all look at the budget on the part of Congress. The devices of a legislative budget and an omnibus appropriations bill have both been tried and have failed, thus providing further evidence of Congressional unsuitability for integrated policy planning. There have been periodic suggestions for a Joint Committee on the Budget, which would be modeled partly on the Joint Economic Committee, but perhaps more on the staff facilities of the Joint Committee on Internal Revenue Taxation. Because the primary need, from a planning viewpoint, is that the national economic implications of the budget for stabilization and growth not be lost in the specialized, narrow foci of the appropriations subcommittees, it seems to me more logical to

consolidate review of both Presidential messages in the JEC than to establish a separate review group.

Such an over-all budget review by the Joint Economic Committee would also contribute to the economically impossible but absolutely necessary function of assessing the relative priorities and funds proposed for defense, welfare, agriculture, resources development, and other expenditures.

3. The report of the Joint Economic Committee should serve as the basis for a formal annual debate on economic and fiscal policy in each house of Congress. This debate should be controlled by the leader of the non-Presidential party in each house. The hearings and reports of the Joint Economic Committee now serve to make congressmen somewhat more aware of the need for integrated economic policy, and have even contributed, at least indirectly, to public education. By the device recommended, however Congress could make a greater contribution to the clarification of values and issues at stake in establishing national policy objectives. Greater general public awareness would be stimulated by the attention the nation's press would give to an annual, institutionalized legislative debate of this kind.

4. Elimination of the Senate filibuster, an increased majority-party majority in the House Rules Committee, re-invigoration of the party policy committees in the Senate, and the adoption of their equivalent in the House — these are needed to enhance majority action and increase majority-party responsibility in the legislative process.

The "packing" of the Rules Committee — by adding three new members — accomplished in January 1962 was a move in the right direction, but did not go far enough, as later events showed. Centralization of party leadership and a shift of the balance from minority to majority power also are indicated.

Obtaining a party consensus is difficult enough; obtaining an interparty consensus is often impossible. Hence, the majority party must be given greater power — and responsibility — if the legislative tendency toward inaction is to be overcome. And if the party policy committees could develop meaningful party consensus on the President's budget, for example, then a political centralization in Congressional handling of appropriations might be created, despite the formal decentralization of the appropriations subcommittees.

PRESIDENTIAL-CONGRESSIONAL RELATIONS

Because of the divergence of constituencies between the President and congressmen and the absence of such compensating factors as a disciplined party system, an inherent difference (often amounting to direct conflict) exists between the viewpoints of the executive and legislative branches. The President, because elected nationally, thinks of national problems; senators and representatives, elected locally, think locally. To the congressmen, the national interest is most frequently the sum of local interests. But the President's concern, in domestic as well as in foreign policy, must be on the interests common to the national community. These differences are reflected in the goal-setting process, for the goals of localities and partial interests will not entirely coincide with the goals the President seeks for the nation. In fact, the legislative view tends toward distrust of national objectives as such, toward faith that self-adjustment of divergent groups will obviate the need for any goal-setting. And when congressmen do see a need for national goals, the legislative process is such that goals set by Congress are likely to be internally inconsistent and bland. For example, the Full Employment Bill became the Employment Act, and that act's policy mandate covered both presidential planning and a reliance upon the market mechanism of private enterprise. Also, maximum employment and production may be in quite serious conflict with the third of the act's co-equal goals, maximum purchasing power, if the latter be defined as in recent years to mean price stability.

At present, partial and local interests — among which business institutions and business values are dominant — have the upper hand in Congress. The basic problem in the legislative-executive relationship may be expressed as the President's need to build a positive majority for his proposals by compromising with divergent interests each insistent on a different kind of action or no action. Can the burden of proof be shifted, while remaining with the present constitutional framework, so that the President's program goes through unless opposing forces are able to form a positive majority against it?

It is not merely a matter of whether coherence of policy can better be served by committee-style leadership (Congress) or through clearly focused leadership (President); it is also the question whether there will be any action at all. The legislative tendency is to avoid action, as it has done over the past decade on bills for aid to education. If we leave the setting of enunciated goals to the legislature, we will receive only those goals which have already been universally accepted.

Finally, a sizable obstacle to effective planning results from the excessive separation of power and responsibility which exists today. The President is responsible for achieving governmental objectives, while Congress has the power to deny him the necessary means. Presidential elections may be decided by the rate of economic activity, yet Congress may deny the President the measures he needs to build prosperity. Without denying Congress the ultimate power to thwart the executive, it should be possible to bring Presidential power somewhat more into line with Presidential responsibility.

The following recommendations seem desirable in this area:

1. By mutual agreement, the President and Congress should extend the logic of the legislative veto to the area of substantive policy making. The Reorganization Act, an example of the legislative veto, reverses the normal legislative procedure. Under it the President does not just propose a statutory change in administrative organization, but he declares that change, and his declaration becomes law without further legislative approval. Only if Congress — meaning, currently, a majority of either house of Congress — disapproves and "vetos" the President's action does it fail to become law. Thus the burden of proof is shifted: instead of the President having to form a positive majority for his proposal, it becomes law unless the opposition is able to form a majority against it. Granting that the opposition was able to do this in 1961 against Kennedy's initial reorganization plans for the independent regulatory commissions, this simply emphasizes that nothing can be done without building adequate political support. In the long run, Congress would be more hesitant to veto legislation of substantive importance than it is to throw out administrative changes that lack public appeal or understanding, so the chances for action on the President's proposals would be increased by this shift.

2. In order to make Presidential authority and responsibility more equal, and to make the plans more adaptable to changing circumstances, Congress should experiment with setting limits for the President's action, which would allow him to act within these limits without having constantly to refer back to Congress. The precedent and source of this idea lie in the reciprocal trade program statutes and their 1962 successor, the Trade Expansion Act, by which Congress delegates the tariff-making power to the President, within statutorily defined limits. The same principle could obviously be extended to

economic stabilization planning. If, for instance, the President had the power to raise or lower income taxes, as the Commission on Money and Credit recently proposed, he would have a strong weapon with which to combat the cyclical trend of the economy. Incentives and disincentives for investment require similar flexibility. Responsibility for the state of the economy falls largely upon the President's shoulders, yet there are often costly delays because he has to wait for Congressional action before he can move to stabilize the economy.

This proposal for increased executive flexibility might be combined with the first recommendation above or might even be substituted for it. These ideas might be made palatable for Congress despite its distaste for strengthening the executive, for, by giving the decisions to the President, Congress would also be transferring a greater share of the responsibility to the President.

Effective government, it might be said, requires that a closer liaison be made between the President and Congress, even though the Founding Fathers intentionally separated them. These recommendations would institutionalize the President's role as chief legislator and would thus be a major step toward the avoidance of a stalemate between these two branches of government.

PRESIDENTIAL PLANNING AND THE NATIONAL POLITICAL STYLE

Except during the wars of the twentieth century, our national social style has been one of looseness, of pursuing private goals in the faith that God would watch over the United States of America. Economic laissez faire was just one expression of this tendency, for we relied upon the invisible hand in other spheres, too. Our cities "just grew," and foresight was used only exceptionally, as in the preservation of Central Park in New York City or the creation of wide avenues in the District of Columbia. Natural resources were exploited with outrageous waste for a century before Theodore Roosevelt popularized the notion that we should plan their use and replenishment.

When not faced with an obvious crisis, our political process has reflected this loose national style to a high degree. Assuming that what was good for each person, interest group, or region was identical with the good of the nation, we have formulated public policies through the tug and haul of competing interests — what Robert Hutchins calls policy by bumps and grinds — and we have tended not to act at all until we had achieved near-unanimity of interest.

When our problems were largely domestic, when crisis was the exception, and when crises were visible to all, such an approach has worked. But now crisis has become the norm, survival is the central problem, and subtlety is the leading characteristic of the challenges that threaten us. The loss of our gold supply, for instance, is not a crisis of which we are immediately aware in our daily activities, but it is none the less serious. Urban-suburban housing and transportation problems have been desperate situations for a decade, yet even now they are not accorded full recognition. In short, as Richard Neustadt has aptly said, our situation is one of "emergencies in policy with politics as usual." This is not good enough. Instead of a system which, whenever an obvious crisis occurs, suspends the normal workings of centrifugal forces in favor of what Clinton Rossiter has termed a "constitutional dictatorship," we need a process that will provide sustained strength for effective government even when crises are not obvious.

A reorientation of our system in the direction of Presidential planning is the way to strengthen our capacity to govern, and it is to such a reorientation that most of the proposals made in this chapter have been directed. Informally, we have been moving in this direction for some time. But we have tried to do so without directly challenging the loose national political style inherited from the nineteenth century. It is time to make that challenge, time to institutionalize the logic of Presidential planning.

The Presidency is the symbol and effective focus of popular action in the American system. Strengthening the President's capacity to plan our economic development is the essential means by which mastery of our economic fate can be wrested from the private purposes and plans of the corporate elite. Democratic planning, under Presidential direction, is freedom's visible hand.

Bibliographic Notes

For each chapter, the notes below provide references to the books, articles, and other published materials cited, in the order in which they occur in the text, with occasional citation also of works closely related but not specifically mentioned in the text. No attempt is made to supply a full bibliography of the subject. The reader interested in going further into the topic will find that the items cited herein contain a good many leads to other pertinent writings. Many of the books mentioned, incidentally, are now happily available in paperbound editions.

CHAPTER I

Advertisements in magazines are a continuously fascinating source of illustrations of the myth of free enterprise. For a highly readable explanation of the differences between the myth and the reality, see John Kenneth Galbraith, *American Capitalism* (Boston: Houghton-Mifflin, 1952), especially Chapters 1–5. For an analysis of business ideology, see Francis X. Sutton, et al., *The American Business Creed* (Cambridge: Harvard U. P., 1956). For the electrical equipment industry's concept of free enterprise, see John G. Fuller, *The Gentlemen Conspirators* (New York: Grove, 1962).

Other references are: John Kenneth Galbraith, *Economics and the Art of Controversy* (New Brunswick, N.J.: Rutgers U. P., 1955); Nathan Robertson, "What Do You Mean, Free Enterprise?" *Harper's* (November, 1948); Joint Economic Committee, *Subsidy-*

like Programs of United States Government, 86th Congress, 2nd Session, 1960, Committee Print; Walter Millis, "How to Compete with the Russians," *New York Times Magazine* (February 2, 1958); Senate Subcommittee on Antitrust and Monopoly, Committee on the Judiciary, *Concentration in American Industry, Report,* 85th Congress, 1st Session, 1957; Senate Antitrust Subcommittee, *Hearings, Administered Prices,* Part 1, 85th Congress, 1st Session, 1957, and Parts 9 and 10, 86th Congress, 1st Session, 1959; W. Arthur Lewis, *Principles of Economic Planning* (Washington, D.C.: Public Affairs, 1950); Gardiner C. Means, "Collective Capitalism and Economic Theory," *Science* (August 16, 1957), also in his *The Corporate Revolution in America* (New York: Crowell-Collier, 1962); Richard Eells, *The Meaning of Modern Business* (New York: Columbia U. P., 1960); and see his new volume, *The Government of Corporations* (New York: Free Press, 1962); Sumner Slichter, "Are We Becoming a Laboristic State?" *New York Times Magazine* (May 16, 1948); Edwin G. Nourse, "Administered Prices and All That," in Senate Antitrust Subcommittee, *Hearings, Administered Prices,* Part 1, 85th Congress, 1st Session, 1957; Paul K. Crosser, *State Capitalism in the Economy of the U.S.* (New York: Twayne, 1960); Alvin H. Hansen, "Appeal for a Dual Economy," *New York Times Magazine,* (March 12, 1961); John Maurice Clark, *Economic Institutions and Human Welfare* (New York: Knopf, 1957); E. H. Carr, *The New Society* (Boston: Beacon, 1957).

CHAPTER II

Charles A. Beard's *The Economic Basis of Politics* (New York: Knopf, 3rd edition, 1945) reviews the classical doctrines and presents Beard's own position. Alpheus T. Mason's textbook in American political thought, *Free Government in the Making,* Chapter 10 (New York: Oxford U. P., 2nd edition, 1955) is the source of the quotations from the debates over extension of the franchise. It is also an excellent compendium of writings on the property-power relationship throughout American history.

Other sources include: Arthur Schlesinger, Jr., *The Age of Jackson* (Boston: Little, Brown, 1946); Goetz Briefs, *The Proletariat* (New York: McGraw-Hill, 1937); and Louis Hartz, *Economic Policy and Democratic Thought* (Cambridge: Harvard U. P., 1948).

CHAPTER III

The literature on income distribution and problems of poverty has had some useful recent additions: Gabriel Kolko, *Wealth and Power in America* (New York: Praeger, 1962); Michael Harrington, *The Other America* (New York: Macmillan, 1962); Conference on Economic Progress, *Poverty and Deprivation in the U.S.* (Washington, D.C.: The Conference, 1962); Robert J. Lampman, *Changes in the Share of Wealth Held by Top Wealth-Holders, 1922–1956* (New York: National Bureau of Economic Research, 1960); Robert J. Lampman, "How Progressive is Our Tax System?" *Commentary* (September, 1959); Herman P. Miller, "Is the Income Gap Closed? 'No!'" *New York Times Magazine* (November 11, 1962); and Dwight MacDonald, "Our Invisible Poor," *New Yorker* (January 19, 1963).

On the conflict between people's capitalism and corporate democracy, see Bayless Manning's review of Joseph A. Livingston, *The American Stockholder* (Philadelphia: Lippincott, 1958) in *Yale Law Journal* (July, 1958) and Victor Perlo, "'People's Capitalism' and Stock Ownership," *American Economic Review* (June, 1958).

Other references include: *Share Ownership in America, 1959* (New York Stock Exchange, 1959) and *The 17 Million: 1962 Census of Shareholders in America* (New York Stock Exchange, 1962); A. A. Berle, *Power Without Property* (New York: Harcourt, Brace, 1959); Paul P. Harbrecht, *Pension Funds and Economic Power* (New York: Twentieth Century Fund, 1959); a Berle-Harbrecht pamphlet, *The Paraproprietal Society* (New York: Twentieth Century Fund, 1959); Milovan Djilas, *The New Class* (New York: Praeger, 1957); David T. Bazelon, "Facts and Fictions of U.S. Capitalism," *Reporter* (September 17, 1959); E. E. Schattschneider, *The Semisovereign People,* Chaper 7 (New York: Holt, Rinehart & Winston, 1961); John Strachey, *Contemporary Capitalism,* Chapters 8 and 9 (New York: Random, 1956); Alpheus T. Mason, "Business Organized as Power: The New *Imperium in Imperio,*" *American Political Science Review* (June, 1950); Hans Kelsen, "Foundations of Democracy," *Ethics* (October, 1955); James Burnham, *The Managerial Revolution* (New York: John Day, 1941; rev. ed., Bloomington, Ind.: Indiana U. P., 1960); David

Spitz, *Patterns of Anti-Democratic Thought* (New York: Macmillan, 1949); Robert A. Brady, *Business as a System of Power* (New York: Columbia U. P., 1943); Robert S. and Helen M. Lynd, *Middletown* (New York: Harcourt, 1929) and *Middletown in Transition* (New York: Harcourt, 1937); Lynd's essay in William Kornhauser (ed.), *Problems of Power in American Democracy* (Detroit: Wayne U. P., 1957); C. Wright Mills, *The Power Elite,* Chapter 12 (New York: Oxford U. P., 1956); C. Wright Mills, *White Collar,* Chapters 1–3 (New York: Oxford U. P., 1951); Andrew Hacker, *Politics and the Corporation* (New York: Fund for the Republic, pamphlet, 1958), and see Hacker's essay, "Liberal Democracy and Social Control," *American Politicial Science Review* (December, 1957).

CHAPTER IV

See, for background, Wilbert E. Moore, "The Emergence of New Property Conceptions in America," *Journal of Legal and Political Sociology* (April, 1943). Other references in this chapter are Goetz Briefs, *The Proletariat;* C. Wright Mills, *White Collar;* Neil Chamberlain's essay in Edward S. Mason (ed.), *The Corporation in Modern Society* (Cambridge: Harvard U. P., 1959); William Gomberg, "The Job as Property," *The Nation* (November 26, 1960); Frank Marquart, "New Problems for the Unions," *Dissent* (Autumn, 1959); John Strachey, *Contemporary Capitalism;* Robert S. Lynd's essay in Kornhauser (ed.), *Problems of Power in American Democracy;* William Kornhauser, *The Politics of Mass Society* (Glencoe, Ill.: Free Press, 1959); Daniel Bell, "America's Un-Marxist Revolution," *Commentary* (March, 1949); John P. Lewis, "The Problem of Price Stabilization: A Progress Report," *American Economic Review, Papers and Proceedings* (May, 1959).

CHAPTER V

There have been a considerable number of empirical studies of community power structures in recent years, the take-off point for which seems to have been Floyd Hunter's *Community Power Structure* (Chapel Hill: U. of North Carolina Press, 1953). A substantial recent study is that by Robert A. Dahl, *Who Governs?* (New Haven: Yale U. P., 1962). One of the more suggestive pieces on political power is Herbert A. Simon, "Notes on the Observation and Measurement of Political Power," *Journal of Politics* (November, 1953). There have been very few attempts to define a national structure of power. Among the few are C. Wright Mills, *The Power Elite,* and Floyd Hunter, *Top Leadership, U.S.A.* (Chapel Hill: U. of North Carolina Press, 1959). See also Henry Kariel, *The Decline of American Pluralism* (Stanford, Cal.: Stanford U. P., 1961). The "veto group" concept is found in David Riesman, *The Lonely Crowd,* Chapter 11 (New Haven: Yale U. P., 1950). See also Earl Latham, *The Group Basis of Politics* (Ithaca, N.Y.: Cornell U. P., 1952) and David B. Truman, *The Governmental Process* (New York: Knopf, 1951).

Other references include James C. Worthy, *Big Business and Free Men* (New York: Harper, 1959); J. K. Galbraith, *American Capitalism;* Senate Subcommittee on Antitrust and Monopoly, Committee on the Judiciary, *A Study of the Antitrust Laws, Staff Report,* 84th Congress, 2nd Session, April 23, 1956, Committee Print; for the Roger Blough quotation, John G. Fuller, *The Gentlemen Conspirators;* for the Hartley-Case rumor, Daniel Bell (ed.), *The New American Right* (New York: Criterion, 1955); Morton S. Baratz, "Corporate Giants and the Power Structure," *Western Political Quarterly* (June, 1956); Corwin Edwards, "Conglomerate Bigness as a Source of Power," in National Bureau of Economic Research, *Business Concentration and Price Policy* (Princeton: Princeton U. P., 1955); Charles E. Lindblom's essay in W. N. Chambers and R. H. Salisbury (eds.), *Democracy in the Mid-Twentieth Century* (St. Louis: Washington U. P., 1960; reprinted as *Democracy Today: Problems and Prospects,* Collier, 1962); E. E. Schattschneider, *The Semisovereign People;* V. O. Key, *Parties, Politics and Pressure Groups* (New York: T. Y. Crowell, 4th edition, 1958); I. F. Stone, *Business as Usual* (New York: Vanguard, 1940); Cammarano *v.* U.S. and Strauss *v.* Commissioner of Internal Revenue, 358 U.S. 498 (1959); U.S. Chamber of Commerce, "Federal Tax Regulations Covering Expenditures for Efforts to Influence Legislation and Related Purposes," a statement issued by the Chamber, October 29, 1959; Robert A. Burns, "Should Businessmen Get into Politics?

Yes," *New Englander* (August, 1960); Leland Hazard, "It Takes Money To Get Elected," *Atlantic* (February, 1960); *Federal Register,* September 19, 1959 (24 *F.R.* 7584); *The Controversy about Advertising,* a brochure issued by Timken Roller Bearing Company, Canton, Ohio, April, 1959; Dana Latham, "The Internal Revenue Service: Recent Developments and Some Current Problems," a speech of September 30, 1959, printed in *The Tax Executive* (October, 1959).

CHAPTER VI

Morton S. Baratz, "Corporate Giants and the Power Structure"; Otto Eckstein and Gary Fromm, *Steel and the Postwar Inflation,* Study Paper No. 2, Joint Economic Committee, 86th Congress, 1st Session, November 6, 1959, Committee Print; Estes Kefauver, "The New Economic Crisis," *Progressive* (January, 1960); Joseph A. Livingston, *The American Stockholder;* Senate Committee on Finance, *Hearings, Stock Options,* 87th Congress, 1st Session, 1961; Ernest Dale, "Management Must Be Made Accountable," *Harvard Business Review* (March–April, 1960); John Sheahan, "Is the Corporate Conscience a Sufficient Safeguard for Society?" *The Berkshire Eagle* (Pittsfield, Mass.: February 18, 1961); J. K. Galbraith, *The Affluent Society* (Boston: Houghton-Mifflin, 1957); Vance Packard, *The Hidden Persuaders* (New York: McKay, 1957); Martin Mayer, *Madison Avenue, U.S.A.* (New York: Harper, 1958); Edwin Nourse, testimony in Senate Subcommittee on Antitrust and Monopoly, *Hearings, Administered Prices,* Part I, 85th Congress, 1st Session, 1957; Arnold M. Soloway, "Growth of Government over the Past Fifty Years," in Joint Economic Committee, *Federal Expenditure Policy for Economic Growth and Stability,* Papers Submitted by Panelists, 85th Congress, 1st Session, November 5, 1957, Committee Print; Karl W. Kapp, *The Social Costs of Private Enterprise* (Cambridge: Harvard U. P., 1950); oil quotation found in Robert Engler, *The Politics of Oil,* Chapter 15 (New York: Macmillan, 1961); W. H. Whyte, *Is Anybody Listening?* (New York: Simon & Schuster, 1952); Charles Siepmann, *Radio, Television and Society,* Chapter 1 (New York: Oxford U. P., 1950); Federal Communications Commission, Network Study Staff, *Interim Report of Network Study, Responsibility for Broadcast Matter* (Docket No. 12782), June 15, 1960.

CHAPTER VII

Milton Friedman and Friedrich Hayek, essays in Melvin Anshen and George L. Bach (eds.), *Management and Corporations, 1985* (New York: McGraw-Hill, 1962); Richard Townsend, essay in *Problems of United States Economic Development,* Vol. II (New York: Committee for Economic Development, 1958); Frank Abrams quotation in Herrymon Maurer, *Great Enterprise,* Chapter 5 (New York: Macmillan, 1955); William T. Gossett, *Corporate Citizenship* (Lexington, Va., Washington and Lee U., 1957); Sylvia K. Selekman and Benjamin M. Selekman, *Power and Morality in a Business Society* (New York: McGraw-Hill, 1956); J. J. Wuerthner, *Businessman's Guide to Practical Politics* (Chicago: Regnery, 1959). Robert A. Burns, "Should Businessmen Get into Politics? Yes"; Richard Eells, *The Meaning of Modern Business;* George Romney, "Citizenship vs. the Power Groups," in *Vital Speeches* (October 15, 1959); Leland Hazard, "It Takes Money To Get Elected,"; Michael D. Reagan, "The Seven Fallacies of Business in Politics," *Harvard Business Review* (March–April, 1960); Andrew Hacker, "The Corporation and Campaign Politics: Power and Legitimacy," a paper delivered at the annual meeting of the American Political Science Association, St. Louis, September, 1961. A. A. Berle and Gardiner C. Means, *The Modern Corporation and Private Property* (New York: Macmillan, 1932); Friedrich Hayek's essay in *Management and Corporations, 1985;* James C. Worthy, *Big Business and Free Men;* Peter F. Drucker, "Business Objectives and Survival Needs," *Journal of Business* (April 1958); James Early, in *American Economic Review, Papers and Proceedings* (May, 1957), quoted in Leo Huberman and Paul Sweezy, "The Giant Corporation," *Monthly Review* (July–August, 1962); Herrymon Maurer, *Great Enterprise,* Chapter 9; Sylvia Selekman and Benjamin Selekman, *Power and Morality in a Business Society;* Harry Ashmore, *Epitaph for Dixie* (New York: Norton, 1958); Theodore Levitt, essay in D. Fenn (ed.), *Managing America's Economic Explosion* (New York: McGraw-Hill, 1961); Theodore Levitt, "The Danger of Corporate Social Responsibility," *Harvard Business Review* (September–October, 1958); "Public Relations Today," *Business Week* (July 2, 1960); A. H. Raskin, "Deep Shadows

Over Our Factories," *New York Times Magazine* (November 29, 1959); Abram Chayes, essay in Edward S. Mason (ed.), *The Corporation in Modern Society* (Cambridge: Harvard U. P., 1959); Ben W. Lewis, "Economics by Admonition," *American Economic Review, Papers and Proceedings* (May, 1959); Edwin Nourse, essay in Joint Economic Committee, *The Relationship of Prices to Economic Stability and Growth*, 85th Congress, 2d Session, March 31, 1958, Committee Print; John M. Clark, *Economic Institutions and Human Welfare* (New York: Knopf, 1957) and *Alternative to Serfdom* (New York: Knopf, 1948); Gerhard Colm, essay in *Problems of United States Economic Development*, Vol. I (New York: Committee for Economic Development, 1958); Harvey Swados, *On the Line* (Boston: Little, Brown, 1957).

CHAPTER VIII

Wilbert C. Moore, *Industrial Relations and the Social Order* (New York: Macmillan, 2nd edition, 1951); Robin Williams, *American Society* (New York: Knopf, 1951); Paul Meadows, *The Culture of Industrial Man* (Lincoln, Neb.: U. of Nebraska Press, 1950); Henry S. Commager, *The American Mind* (New Haven: Yale U. P., 1950); John H. Bunzel, "The General Ideology of American Small Business,' *Political Science Quarterly* (March, 1955); J. K. Galbraith, *Economics and the Art of Controversy; Publications of the American Economic Association*, Vol. I (Baltimore, Md.: American Economic Association, 1887); Joseph Dorfman, *The Economic Mind in American Civilization, Vol. III: 1865–1918* (New York: Viking, 1949); Fred J. Cook, *The Warfare State* (New York: Macmillan, 1962); Herbert E. Striner, essay in D. Fenn (ed.), *Managing America's Economic Explosion; Economic Hazards of Arms Reduction*, a special issue of *The Nation* (March 28, 1959); Robert Heilbroner, *The Future as History* (New York: Harper, 1959); James M. Landis, *Report on Regulatory Agencies to the President-Elect*, Senate Committee on the Judiciary, 86th Congress, 2nd Session, 1960, Committee Print; Stephen K. Bailey, *Congress Makes a Law* (New York: Columbia U. P., 1950); Eugene V. Rostow, *Planning for Freedom* (New Haven: Yale U. P., 1959); Robert Lekachman, "Is Keynesian Economics Outdated?" *Commentary* (August, 1959); Richard Quant, *The New Inflation* (New York:

McGraw-Hill, 1959); Bruce R. Morris, *Problems of American Economic Growth* (New York: Oxford U. P., 1961); *Prospect for America: The Rockefeller Panel Reports* (New York: Doubleday, 1961); Klaus Knorr, et al., *What Price Economic Growth?* (New York: Prentice-Hall, 1961); Robert Dahl and Charles Lindblom, *Politics, Economics, and Welfare* (New York: Harper, 1953).

CHAPTER IX

Communications Satellite Act of 1962, 76 *Stat.* 419, P.L. 87–624; John G. Palfrey, "Atomic Energy: A New Experiment in Government-Industry Relations," *Columbia Law Review* (March, 1956); 1962 research figures in report published in *Syracuse Herald-American,* December 30, 1962; Interagency (Bell) Committee, *Report to the President on Government Contracting for Research and Development,* Office of the White House Press Secretary, April 30, 1962; Don K. Price, *Government and Science* (New York: New York U. P., 1954); House Government Operations Committee, *Replies from Executive Departments and Federal Agencies to Inquiry Regarding Use of Advisory Committees,* Part I–VII, 84th Congress, 2nd Session, 1956, Committee Prints; Samuel H. Beer, "Group Representation in Britain and the United States," in *Unofficial Government: Pressure Groups and Lobbies, Annals of the American Academy of Political and Social Science* (September, 1958); House Subcommittee on the Judiciary, *Hearings, WOC's and Government Advisory Groups,* 84th Congress, 1st Session, 1955; Michael D. Reagan, "The Business and Defense Services Administration, 1953–57," *Western Political Quarterly* (June, 1961); Michael D. Reagan, "Serving Two Masters: Problems in the Employment of Dollar-a-Year and Without Compensation Personnel," (Ph.D. dissertation, Princeton University, 1959); Marver H. Bernstein, *Regulating Business by Independent Commission* (Princeton: Princeton U. P., 1955); Joseph C. Palamountain, "The Administrator's Role: Issues and Hypotheses," a paper delivered at the annual meeting of the American Political Science Association, New York, September, 1960; Nebbia *v.* New York, 291 U.S. 502 (1934); NLRB *v.* Jones & Laughlin Steel Corporation, 301 U.S. 1 (1937); Marsh *v.* Alabama, 326 U.S. 501 (1945); Joseph C. Palamountain, *The Politics of Distribution* (Cambridge: Harvard U. P., 1955);

Al Toffler, "The Airpower Lobby: Salesmen in Uniform," *The Nation* (November 30, 1957) and "The Airpower Lobby: Who Will Make the Missiles?" *The Nation* (December 7, 1957); Cornelius P. Cotter, *Government and Private Enterprise* (New York: Holt, Rinehart & Winston, 1960); Gerhard Colm and Theodore Geiger, *The Economy of the American People* (Washington: National Planning Assn., 1958).

CHAPTER X

Robert L. Heilbroner, *The Future as History;* Arthur S. Miller, *Private Governments and the Constitution,* pamphlet (New York: Fund for the Republic, 1959); Grant McConnell, "The Spirit of Private Government," *American Political Science Review* (September, 1958); *First Annual Report of the Public Review Board to the Membership of the UAW, 1957–1958,* Detroit, Public Review Board, December 10, 1958; Jack Stieber, Walter E. Oberer, and Michael Harrington, *Democracy and Public Review,* pamphlet (Santa Barbara, Center for the Study of Democratic Institutions, 1960); John G. Fuller, *The Gentlemen Conspirators;* W. H. Whyte, *The Organization Man* (New York: Simon and Schuster, 1956); Alan Harrington, *Life in the Crystal Palace* (New York: Knopf, 1959); Chris Argyris, *Personality and Organization* (New York: Harper, 1957); Victor Thompson, *Modern Organization* (New York: Knopf, 1961); on natural growth, see *The Guaranty Survey* (March, 1959), quoted in W. H. Ferry, *The Corporation and the Economy,* pamphlet (Santa Barbara: Center for the Study of Democratic Institutions, 1959); see also W. H. Ferry, *The Economy Under the Law,* pamphlet (Santa Barbara: Center for the Study of Democratic Institutions, 1960); on government-business cooperation in planning, see Bertram M. Gross, "New Look for the Employment Act," *Challenge* (February, 1963); on American capacity to govern, see James M. Burns, *Deadlock of Democracy* (New York: Prentice-Hall, 1963); Robert A. Dahl, *A Preface to Democratic Theory* (Chicago: U. of Chicago Press, 1956); on transportation co-ordination, see Louis J. Hector, "Problems of the CAB and the Independent Regulatory Commissions," *Yale Law Journal* (May, 1960); on monetary-fiscal co-ordination, see Michael D. Reagan, "The Political Structure of the Federal Reserve System,"

American Political Science Review (March, 1961), and Commission on Money and Credit, *Money and Credit,* Chapter 10 (New York: Prentice-Hall, 1961); Sidney Hyman, "Presidential Popularity Is Not Enough," *New York Times Magazine* (August 12, 1962).

CHAPTER XI

Carl Kaysen and Donald Turner, *Antitrust Policy* (Cambridge: Harvard U.P., 1959); W. H. Ferry, *The Economy Under Law;* Arthur S. Miller, *Private Governments and the Constitution;* Bernard Nossiter, "The Hidden Affair Between Big Business and Big Labor," *Harper's* (July, 1959); Senate Subcommittee on Antitrust and Monopoly, *Hearings, Administered Prices,* Parts 9, 10; Emmette S. Redford, "Potential Public Policies To Deal with Inflation Caused by Market Power," Study Paper No. 10, Joint Economic Committee, 86th Congress, 1st Session, December 11, 1959, Committee Print; A. A. Berle, *Power Without Property,* Chapter 3; Eugene V. Rostow, *Planning for Freedom;* Bertram M. Gross, "New Look for the Employment Act."

CHAPTER XII

This chapter draws heavily upon an article of mine, "Toward Improving National Planning Policy," *Public Administration Review* (March, 1963) and I am indebted to that publication for permission to use the article in this form. Arthur Maass and Laurence Radway, "Gauging Administrative Responsibility," in Dwight Waldo (ed.), *Ideas and Issues in Public Administration* (New York: McGraw-Hill, 1953); Joseph I. Coffee and Vincent P. Rock, *The Presidential Staff* (Washington: National Planning Assn., 1961); Richard E. Neustadt, *Presidential Power* (New York: Wiley, 1960); Edward C. Banfield, "Congress and the Budget: A Planner's Criticism," *American Political Science Review* (December, 1949); George Kennan, testimony in Senate (Jackson) Subcommittee on National Policy Machinery, Committee on Government Operations, *Hearings, Organization for National Security,* Part VI, 86th Congress, 2d Session, 1960; Commission on Money and Credit, *Money and Credit;* James MacGregor Burns, *Roosevelt* (New York: Harcourt, Brace, 1956); W. W. Rostow, *The United States in the World Arena* (New York: Harper, 1960); Townsend Hoopes, "The Persistence of Illusion," *Yale Review* (Spring, 1960).

Index